Ethics and Professionalism in the Public Service

Ethics and Professionalism in the Public Service

Thomas D. Lynch and Cynthia E. Lynch

Melvin & Leigh, Publishers

IRVINE, CALIFORNIA

Ethics and Professionalism in the Public Service

Published by Melvin & Leigh, Publishers
6 Curie Court
Irvine, CA 92617

orders.melvinleigh@cox.net

www.melvinleigh.com

Cover design by Jesse Sanchez
Production by Stacey Victor

ISBN: 978-0-99923598-0

Printed in the United States of America on mixed recycle paper

Visit our home page at www.melvinleigh.com

Contents

Preface

AN OUTCOME-ORIENTED BOOK

We were firmly convinced that this book needed to be a text that was immediately relevant to the public service practitioner. In implementing that desire, two questions stood out: (1) What can the public administration professional do to be personally a more ethical individual? And (2) how can public service organizations actively address creating an ethical environment in their organization to better serve not only the organization's missions and at the same time serve the larger public good? The answers to these two questions became this book's chapter 11, which addresses the first question, and chapter 12, which addresses the second question. Our challenge, as authors, was to lay the ground work in the first ten chapters so that the reader could logically understand our answers in chapters 11 and 12. Those two chapters needed to be not only be reasonable but even rationally necessary to addressing the two questions. The following explains how we did that.

We start with the individual. Chapter 1 points out that individual self-identity heavily influences a person's awareness of the ethical context in which they exist. If a person is egocentric, their natural self-identity is tied to his or her physical self and their ethical awareness focuses on how a moral decision will impact them. If a person is altruistic, their self-identity is tied to something socially and environmentally larger than their physical self and their ethical awareness is tied to how his or her moral decisions will impact their social groups and the environment. Thus, egocentric and altruistic people normally make quite different ethical decisions based on their self-identity. In order to understand that phenomena, chapter 1 discusses the relationship of the brain to consciousness and the importance of Rene Descartes's famous statement—*Cogito ergo sum,* normally translated as "I think, therefore I am"—on the limitation of human awareness.

Chapter 2 moves the reader from the individual to the profession to comprehend ethics of public administration within our form of government as a critical contextual factor. For example, in the United States, public administrators must be relationally aware that they exist in a democracy. To appreciate why that is true, the chapter discusses (1) Machiavelli's argument that democracies will always eventually fail as a form of government because private interest groups' egocentric desires will eventually ensure its defeat, (2) Benjamin Franklin's observation that he and the other founders of the American republic realized that Machiavelli might be correct, and (3) James Madison—the primary author of the United States Constitution—spelled out the reasoning and tactic to prevent private interest groups from destroying the American democracy in his famous Federalist 10 article.

When Paul Appleby and Stephen K. Bailey—among the founders of American public administration as a profession—addressed our two questions in their writings, they were mindful of Machiavelli, Franklin, and Madison. Appleby and Bailey argued that public administrators and the profession of public administration must be an ethical counter weight to egocentric private interest groups by being the champion of the public good to maintain balance in our democracy. Clearly, not all public servants will care about the public good because their professional numbers tend to reflect the same mix of egocentric and altruistic people as the greater society. Appleby and Bailey gave our profession an explanation of how individual public servants and public organizations could assist in perpetuating the democracy that Madison and others envisioned. They did that by informing future public administrators with their writings how they should act ethically in the context of a democracy.

As a corollary to Appleby and Bailey discussion, chapter 2 also shows that individuals need not always be egocentric. They can learn to grow their concern for a larger good. Lawrence Kohlberg and others argued that humans can and do develop morally. By implication for public employees, training can help them move from being egocentric to at least accepting the concept of the public good. In addition, governments need not hire egocentric individuals as employees as personality and other attitudinal tests do exist.

Chapter 3 provides some international examples of what happens when ethics is missing in government. Without ethics, the "civil" of civil society disappears. This chapter makes the point that there is a world of corruption, including within the United States, but it varies in its negative impact on government. In the democracies, the corruption is much more sophisticated than in other non-democratic nations. For example, the United States has legalized many forms of corruption while ignoring the fears of Franklin and the words of Madison. This chapter points out that private interest groups have begun the process that eventually and sadly will prove Machiavelli's prediction to be correct.

Chapter 4 looks at how philosophers have viewed ethics over the centuries. It starts with the Greeks and Romans and ends with modern Western philosophers. Among others, it introduces Aristotle's virtue ethics, Immanuel Kant's rule-based ethics, and Jeremy Bentham's consequential ethics. It explains the impact of Nietzsche and the particular influence of modernist and post-modernist on ethics, which strive to reduce ethics to the status of nonsense. Modernism starts with René Descartes and progressed to philosophers (such as John Locke, G.E. Moore, Bertrand Russell, Alfred Jules Ayer, and Ludwig Wittgenstein) who maintained that the test for truth *must* be empirical. For them, ethical theory, such as virtue ethics, cannot pass that test. This essentially supplanted ethics with moral relativism.

Chapter 4 suggests a way out of the ethical *cul-de-sac* with some exceptions to moral relativism. For example, Wittgenstein cited one exception: if a social group (small or large, such as a profession or even a nation state) had a common set of ethical values then ethics, within that group, can logically be used in making moral decisions. In addition, this chapter notes that ethical theories like Kohlberg's descriptive Theory of Moral Development could also be considered valid because they use modernist empirical tests. However, except for those two exceptions, modernist and post-modernist maintained the normative theories (virtue ethics, rule-based ethics, and consequential ethics) are merely emotive and nonsense.

Chapter 5 is a critical look at deontological and consequential ethics as normative ethical theories that are applicable to making public administration ethical decisions. There are practical limitations to each of those ethical theories. For example, consequential ethics often requires the use of sophisticated numerical calculations that are beyond the expertise of many decision makers. Another example are codes of ethics, which are rule-based, because they lose their motivational influence if the persons using the codes are egocentric. In such situations, he or she will not follow a code of ethics unless there are sufficient rewards or penalties to induce them to adhere to the code. Rule-based ethics are often legalized and thus failing to abide by the rules can result in a criminal penalty. In order to demonstrate how this is done in practice, a State of Louisiana example is presented. Another limitation of consequential ethics is that its analytical test—the greatest good for the greatest number— has an inherent social bias problem against minorities. By definition, often those not part of the greatest number are various minorities and thus consequential ethics has an implicit hedonistic assumption that tends to favor large private interests over the public good.

Chapter 6 dives deeper into the discussion of virtue ethics by explaining the concept of *telos*—meaning end-purpose—as well as the notion of the "good life," as it relates to the essence of being human. Virtue ethics considers functionality important and thus cause-and-effect is central to that form of ethical theory. Aristotle assumed in his theory that the ideal essence of the human condition is altruistic and the human telos—meaning end-purpose—is living the good life. He fully realized hedonistic views existed but considered their existence the result of poor quality thinking. To reach the correct human essence, as put forth in his theory, people become virtuous and think rationally.

Chapter 6 notes that virtue ethics has come under particular attack by modernists and post-modernists. They argue the use of essence in virtue ethics is wrong because humans just *are* and there is no such thing as a human essence. Thus, they say this version of normative ethics is nonsense. To them, life is just individuals living in a social construct that varies across humanity. Because we just have social constructs, there is no such thing as a human essence that needs to be perfected. With their logic, beauty, love, and moral character exist only subjectively and not objectively. With no human *telos*, they argue that thinking that virtue should be internalized is foolishness and therefore virtue ethics is foolishness. The chapter ends on a positive note. It invokes the Wittgenstein exception presented in chapter 4 and builds on the arguments of Alasdair MacIntyre to maintain that ethics is applicable to the profession of public administration.

Chapters 7, 8, and 9 focus on the challenges of being ethical. Chapter 7 explains that an individual and a group must maintain self-control to act ethically and maintaining self-control requires specific knowledge. In addition, this chapter discusses the importance of emotional intelligence and will-power in controlling oneself with reason. The chapter then discusses common emotional fallacies that need to be avoided and how to confront faulty emotional thinking. Chapter 8 presents important tools for critical thinking that is so significant in reasoning ethically. This chapter builds on concepts introduced in chapter 1, such as the non-logic of egocentrism and the elements of ethical reasoning. Chapter 9 develops the relationship between ethics and organizational leadership. For example, if organizational ethics is to prevail, leaders must show wisdom and courage in carrying out their ethical decisions. This chapter argues against the practice of moral muteness, because it is particularly harmful to organizational ethics and ultimately the organizational culture.

Chapters 11 and 12 address our two major questions directly. We think of them as the *telos* or core purpose of the book. Chapter 11—Creating a Personal Ethics—speaks to the reality that all ethics are personal but nevertheless are contextual. All actions are undertaken by individual human beings and we all need to be aware of, and responsible for how we act and what we do. Consciously thinking about developing our personal ethics is not an easy task, to be sure. It often takes us out of our comfort zone but we argue such a process is an important one for those who have dedicated their lives to serving others.

Chapter 12—Creating an Organizational Ethics—confronts philosopher David Hume's *is/ought* dilemma, as explained in chapter 4—History of Ethics. The *IS* part of the dilemma is the descriptive analysis of what exists and the *OUGHT* part is the normative expression of what could be, with effort, the moral practice within an organization. This chapter explains that a public agency's or government's leadership can define the ethical values that it considers important to maintain organizationally. Ethicists can prepare and enact an implementation strategy to achieve the clearly articulated ethical values of the organization by its leadership and an empirical examination can determine if those values are accomplished over time. Thus, descriptive efforts, which see if ethical goals have or have not been achieved, can test normative efforts to achieve positive ethical goals overtime.

USING THIS BOOK

As authors, we are sensitive to students who are approaching ethics for the first time in studying public administration. We hope our quoted student comments and questions at the beginning and end of each chapter demonstrate that sensitivity. Ethics is a tough subject to grasp and eventually practice. However, it is particularly significant to not only the students but the future organizations in which students—now turned professionals—will help in elevating the moral compass within their organizations. Although this subject addresses philosophical matters, the book is meant to be practical. In using this book, students need to keep an open mind rather than fall into the trap of being an advocate of one or another normative ethical theory. Ethics exists in a relational context and their use of ethics must show an appreciation of that context. The moral relativists have a point, but so do the individuals who want an ethical workplace that pursues the public good. The task of the student becoming a professional is to find the wisdom and strength that will create that ethical workplace.

As authors, we are also sensitive to instructors, who will use this textbook in their classroom. Teaching ethics is not easy. It involves complex philosophical thought with the end purpose of helping students learn not only how to be ethical themselves, but how to be a force for the good in creating ethical workplaces. The format of the book presents key topics in chapters that (1) present the concepts, provide various exhibits, pictures, and case material to give more life to the material, (2) offers useful review questions that can be used for class discussions or essay tests, and (3) references for those who like to dig more deeply into the material. Collectively, these should help the instructor but the most important teaching to be done is opening the minds of students to how their knowledge of ethics can truly improve them personally but also make an important contribution to the organizations they will impact in their careers.

As we wrote this book, amazing new ethical stories and case material came up in the media every day, which directly related to the material of this textbook. Again as authors, we encourage instructors and especially students to make their ethics course more relevant and real by linking media stories directly to the text material. One of the constant challenges in teaching and learning ethics is to realize that ethics, as a subject, is vital to all of us and evidence of it working and not working is always occurring all around us. Making the linkage of the book's material to the world around us provides added understanding that our role as public administrators is to focus on the public good as we performance the public's service.

ACKNOWLEDGMENTS

The production of any book is a team effort and we believe that our team members need some well-deserved recognition. As authors, we like to think that the work we produce is perfect and cannot be improved. But in truth, we make many errors in a manuscript. Fortunately, our copy editor catches them to make us look good. Thanks to Molly Morrison for an amazing job of not only finding our errors but also challenging us to defend our logic in places for a clearer understanding and putting the manuscript into the proper format. Thanks also to Stacey Victor for the page proofs and producing very nice-looking book pages. Next, the painful task for creating an index occurs and thanks to Barbara Long for accomplishing that mind-numbing task.

For this book, one person needs a special recognition—Harry Briggs. He is an outstanding publisher and a dream to work with as a person. He has a hands-on style without micro managing, and is always friendly as he offers great suggestions in improving the product along the route to a finished book. We have written a number of books with various publishers and this is by far the best experience we have had. Thank you, Harry.

1 Consciousness and Ethics

Ethics education and training has long been thought of as a three-legged stool: (1) Kantian, or rule-based ethics, (2) Bentham, or consequential ethics, and (3) Aristotelian, or virtue ethics. Collectively, these three approaches were thought to represent a "unified process" for understanding public sector ethics (Geuras and Garofalo 2002). This book takes a broader view of what constitutes ethics, as it includes topics such as emotional intelligence, critical thinking, values, and, significantly, consciousness. This chapter explores the significant relationship between consciousness and ethics, which is fundamental to understanding the various theories of ethics and how ethical behavior results in viable, useful, and ethical public organizations.

Consciousness, according to the *Merriam-Webster Collegiate Dictionary*, is the state of being awake and aware of one's surroundings; the awareness or perception of something by a person; and the fact of awareness by the mind of itself and the world. If persons are *unaware* of a situation, action, or activity involving questionable moral or ethical implications, how can we expect them to be able to behave ethically or be able to make ethical decisions? Thus, awareness is not only important but critical for ethics to be influential in society.

Two determinants within a person's consciousness bring about how an individual comprehends ethical concepts. The first determinant, self-identity, is a person's self-identification of the boundary of what he or she considers to be his or her "self." That self-identity ranges from the physical being to one's place in the universe, as well as a combination of the two extremes. The second determinant, extrinsic/intrinsic satisfaction, is about extrinsic satisfaction (receiving pleasure and avoiding pain) and intrinsic satisfaction (achieving emotional gratification that comes from, for example, helping someone without receiving a reward). The second determinant can be either one or the other (extrinsic or intrinsic satisfaction), but most people experience a mixture of both. In other words, any informed expectation of ethical behavior is tied to a persons' level of understanding in regard to self-identify and the individual's foremost considered satisfactions. Few individuals critically consider these internal conscious fundamental assumptions because they exist implicitly in the mind.

Each of the two determinants exist as unities of opposites rather than as a continuum. A unity of opposites is not as familiar as a continuum, but it is equally or possibly more significant for perceiving complex interrelationships. Unity of opposites is most easily understood as two opposing concepts or realities such as the north and south poles of a magnet, male and female, or light and dark. Each opposite has meaning that is more fully comprehensible by appreciating its opposite and the relationship between the opposites. Sometimes, the opposites are diametrical but sometimes they exist in various combinations with the other. For example, in understanding a single human being one can say the person has a mix of female and male attributes but together they are part of the human psyche.

One of determinants can also be thought to exist on a continuum, whereas the other can only be thought of as two opposites that can exist separately in the same time and place, such as human sexual-induced attributes. A person's self-identity can range from only their own physical body to include their family, their ethnic group, their nation, and even the universe. Self-identity can be contemplated as a circle or cone that starts with the physical being and ends with an infinite universe. A person's extrinsic/ intrinsic satisfaction can be said to exist totally as one or the other means of obtaining satisfaction. However, what is also likely is that the means to obtain satisfaction exists in some mixture of satisfaction and gratification. For example, a person can experience superficial gratification from having material possessions, fame, and power, or and deeper gratification from feeling happy or good about a consequence or action that resulted from a selfless action. If someone's self-identity is only selfish and his or her satisfaction is only extrinsic, the person is egocentric. If someone's self-identity is only selfless and his or her satisfaction is only intrinsic, the person is altruistic. (See chapter 4 for details.)

Discussing consciousness as two unities of opposites and applying that thought to professional behavior can be done normatively or descriptively. A normative approach might be to say that being altruistic is the better way to exist in society. For example, Paul and Elder (2006) indicate that the terms "egocentric" and "altruistic" connote poor versus good, or ethical behavior. Additionally, much of the literature on the changing generational values in Millennials, Gen X and Y, and most recently Gen Z focuses on egocentric thinking associated with negative ethical behavior (Brooks 2015; Hsieh 2014). Descriptively, we might say that a particular person or group is egocentric or altruistic without saying one is better than the other. This book uses the terms "egocentric" (meaning selfish) and "altruistic" (meaning selfless) to represent the two discussed determinates of conscious awareness. That awareness or lack of it influences a person's understanding of ethics. Thus, the terminology in this book is sometimes used for descriptive purposes and sometimes for normative purposes (see the section on Moral Development in chapter 2).

WHY ETHICS IS IMPORTANT

What follows is an actual student question posed to the senior author of this book when he was presenting a code of ethics to a public administration class:

PROFESSOR: *We are now going to cover a professional code of ethics used in public administration. Yes, Leon, I see your hand. What is your question?*

LEON: *I think this ethics stuff is boring and useless in the real world. Isn't it just about doing it to others before they do it to you?*

Leon is only unusual in that he expressed his frank and actually profound questions about ethics in a classroom in a very direct but also jaw-dropping manner. As readers move through this book, they will notice that a brief dialogue between a professor and Leon at the start of each chapter. The above dialogue did happen, as did the story in Exhibit 1.1. The dialogues presented in other chapters did not occur, but nevertheless represent a "channeling" of what Leon might have said on the topics presented here. We hope readers will appreciate Leon's questions and personality, as they provide a profound insight into ethics.

The initial question to the professor reflected Leon's consciousness. The underlying but not announced truth in Leon's question is significant. He was correct in saying that he and others reading those codes of ethics do treat the codes as meaningless rules or aphorisms that are a waste of their time. Thus, they naturally ignore statements of ethics and sometimes—like Leon—even consider them to be subjects of humorous comment. Nevertheless, if those rules, or even aphorisms implicit in a code of ethics, have a known positive or negative consequence to the professional, such codes are not a waste of time. What is singularly important to grasp by Leon's question is that the awareness of a person does determine a person's views and likely actions that might flow out of ethical pronouncements. To help Leon get past his initial and limited awareness about ethics and to help the class understand that ethics is important, the professor addressed Leon and the class with the story presented in Exhibit 1.1.

When the story was finished, the class was remarkably quiet. Clearly the story had worked because the class, including Leon, realized a world without ethics does have negative consequences. The professor—the storyteller—turned to Leon and said, "Well, if you don't know anything else about ethics, I hope you will leave this class understanding that Karma does exist and the lack of ethics does cause negative Karma. Codes of ethics may be boring but they are also important."

Leon's question highlighted the importance of consciousness and its relationship to ethics. Consciousness varies significantly among people. That variation is not related to religion, sexual orientation, class, ethnicity, culture, or age. Individuals who make ethical decisions vary in their selfishness (egocentric) and selflessness (altruistic). Moral dilemmas largely exist within those who have a mixed egocentric and altruistic awareness. For example, a person's altruistic side says that I must act in defense of a larger good for society but I also wish to have loyalty to my spouse and the two are not always compatible and thus a moral dilemma exists. The existence of selfishness/selflessness influences how people comprehend and act upon ethics. Leon was egocentric, which meant that it was impossible for him to grasp the importance of ethics in and by itself. Ego-centered people cannot understand the importance of ethics but they can understand potentially being hurt and especially being killed. Thus, the professor's story showed him and others that there are real-world consequence for a lack of ethics.

MORE ON CONSCIOUSNESS

The subject of consciousness is not well understood. For a long time, it was assumed that there was a particular part of the brain that was the center for understanding everything, much like an on-off switch. As we learned more about the brain function, some considered consciousness to be about feelings. More recently, we have come to understand that it is about awareness. Although this distinction is useful, there is still a lot of misunderstanding about awareness related to the functions of the brain. Daniel C. Dennett (1991) addresses the mechanics of this complex subject. His thoughts on consciousness and their effects on human behavior influenced much of the material presented in this book.

Exhibit 1.1. Karma

This event occurred in Chicago during the Prohibition Era (1920–1933). Roli, a young man, was with Clarabelle, who was the daughter of an Irish saloon owner and Chicago ward boss for the Democratic political machine. She was quite an unusual lady for the 1920s. Not only had she earned two master's degrees from the University of Chicago—one in art and the other in education—she was also charming, attractive, and quick-witted. She taught art in the Chicago public school system, but she also liked fun and enjoyed the wild scene of her era.

Roli had taken Clarabelle to a baseball game at Wrigley Field. After the game, they stopped at a nearby speakeasy—an illegal bar—for a quick drink before going home. They sat at the bar and ordered their drinks. As Roli took a sip of his martini, he leaned over to Clarabelle and whispered," I taste almond!" She knew what that meant—the bartender had slipped a "Mickey Finn" into his drink. Roli would soon pass out from the drug and the barkeep, in this otherwise empty bar, would rob them and likely kill her and Roli. It was another way to make money on an otherwise slow day.

Roli put money for the drinks on the bar and said with a flourish, "Have to go. This will take care of the bill. We are a little late in meeting our friends." To the disappointment of the barkeep, they left quickly and were lucky to hail a cab as soon as they exited the front door. Even though the cab arrived within seconds, Roli started to collapse as the cab stopped. Clarabelle opened the back door of the cab, pushed the now unconscious Roli into the back seat, and got in next to him. Thinking Roli was merely drunk, the cab driver calmly asked, "Where to." She said, "The Majestic Hotel."

The Majestic was the headquarters of the Bugs Moran gang—a well-known criminal organization in that era. Roli worked for it as a pool player and expert on card games. Clarabelle knew that she could get help there from Roli's colleagues. When the taxi arrived and the driver was paid, Clarabelle got some assistance to get Roli into the hotel lobby and called the room where Roli's work associates maintained their office. Hearing the urgency in her voice, they came down quickly. They saw Roli, got him to the elevator, and eventually to their room with Clarabelle following. They knew what to do almost instinctively—they took off his outer clothes and put him into a shower with cold water. Next, the men ordered an urn of coffee from hotel room service. They needed to keep Roli awake until the drug wore off or he would die.

In time, the crisis was over, but Roli was not yet able to speak. His associates asked Clarabelle, "Where did this happen?" She told them and together they said, "Wow! That's one of our places!" They liked Roli as a comrade but they really appreciated Clarabelle for her remarkable character and the way she treated them with respect and thoughtfulness. In addition, killing customers was decidedly against the Moran gang policy, as it was very bad for their repeat business. Roli's colleagues knew what had to be done; and with rushed steps and fire in their eyes, they left at once.

Later, Roli and Clarabelle learned that the men found the barkeep at the speakeasy and he was retired, permanently. The irony of this story is the bartender intended to kill two people, but instead the actions he put in motion got him killed. In some parts of the world, that is called "instant Karma," but, in Chicago, it is called, "What goes around, comes around."

Source: Thomas and Cynthia Lynch.

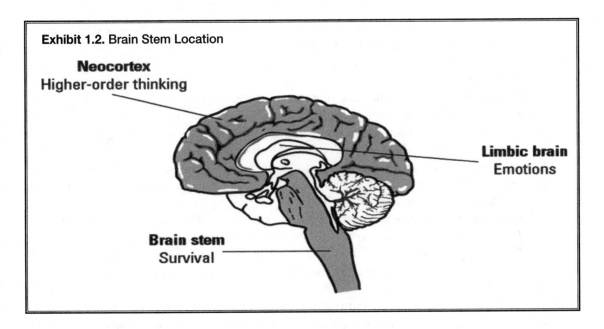

Exhibit 1.2. Brain Stem Location

Neocortex
Higher-order thinking

Limbic brain
Emotions

Brain stem
Survival

The egocentric (selfish) consciousness is the primordial hardwired part of the brain. It is likely found in the brain stem, which is the oldest part of the evolved human brain, and is responsible for our human survival instinct—often described as "fight or flight." It establishes the distinction between everything on the "inside" of a closed boundary and everything in the "external" world. This section of the brain is the product of the early evolution of animals and results largely from dumb-luck genetic selection over many millions of years (Dennett 1991, 174). The external/internal orientation of the brain stem easily becomes a dualistic concept—either you are with me or against me—which easily becomes "me (or my kind) versus them (or their kind)." This dualistic and very limited concept of self produces an awareness and consciousness called "egoism."

A much larger external world identification of "self" results in a conceptual unity referred to as "oneness" by many. If people are selfless, they are altruistic or oneness thinkers. The terms "selfless" and "altruistic" are misnomers because "selfless consciousness" is thinking of yourself but I the larger context of being in oneness with others. Thus, the self-identity called oneness includes minimal importance of the physical self. Altruistic (selfless) consciousness comes from the relatively recently evolved sections of the brain. The design of the complete brain, which is believed to house consciousness, is in the brain stem and the other sections of the brain. Those other sections are not hardwired and the content in them comes from features called plasticity and memes.

Plasticity has been around for millions of years and is well understood in the neuro-science community. It allows humans to learn in ways that connect multiple functions—for example, how to locate a target with one's eyes and communicating to coordinate arms and body muscles movement to shoot an arrow with a bow. Plasticity also allows speaking, which connects thoughts to the muscle function of the tongue and the vocal cords. In the brain, there are phenotypes that are not hardwired like the brain stem, but rather are variable thus allowing learning into various sections of the brain during a lifetime. Sometimes, a portion of a brain is destroyed or damaged, a person may lose memory or even the ability to speak. Plasticity permits another part of the brain over time to learn how to associate certain sounds with communications to the muscles that result in talking again.

The memetic evolution is the latest addition to the conceptual understanding of the brain. Memes replicate themselves with reliability and fecundity. Memes can be musical tunes, ideas, catch phrases, clothes fashions, icons, and so on. They propagate by leaping from brain to brain by a process of imitation (Dawkins 1976, 200). Memes take complex ideas and form them into distinct memorable units such as a wheel, an alphabet, calculus, and deconstruction. Unlike the other aspects of the brain, memes can induce learning within seconds and can spread around the world at the speed of light (Dawkins 1976, 205).

Humans can learn to be selfless due to plasticity and memes. Data and knowledge come from culture, religion, and formal education and training. If plasticity is involved, such learning takes time and it needs reinforcement. For example, military training is possible because plasticity allows cognizance to reshapes the brain of the trainees into a different person. The phrase—"Once a marine, always a marine"—captures that concept.

A less likely but possible way to learn selflessness is with memes. A person can read or hear about selflessness through memes and their consciousness can be altered. A recent example is the proliferation of the "mindfulness" meme. Originally used in teaching meditation and breathing exercises in yoga classes. Today, the term is so prolific that it is attached to everyday function activities and has become a billion-dollar industry associated with neoliberal modes of economics, social, and political life (see www.alternet.org). Such rapid change of consciousness does occur but it is also needs reinforcement to become a solid means to achieve continual change in behavior. Regardless, selfless consciousness comes about from sections of the brain other than the brain stem and thus it is in conflict with the brain stem's selfishness instinct. What dominates a person's ethical thinking depends on the perceived conditions and the strength of the person's selfless consciousness.

What do the selfish and selfless consciousness have to do with ethics? Consciousness is about awareness and that is how the human brain interprets the various senses delivered to the brain. Selfish (egocentric) and a selfless (altruistic) persons understand what they sense differently from each other. Thus, they approach ethics differently and often reach different decisions.

The inner self, which some call the soul, is an abstraction that is useful in considering consciousness and ethics. Although consciousness is awareness, the character and quality of that awareness varies from person to person. Almost all humans think with words and that is what permits communication and the transfer of knowledge between and among humans. Helen Keller became blind and deaf due to an early childhood illness and therefore learned words later in life from a remarkable teacher, said "Before my teacher came to me, I did not know that I am. I lived in a world that was no-word. I cannot hope to describe adequately that unconsciousness, yet conscious time of nothingness. . . . Since I had no power of thought, I did not compare one mental state with another" (1991, 227).

Rene Descartes's *Meditations* explored the famous mind-body problem: How can a person's thoughts and feelings fit into a place of nerve cells and molecules called the brain? How can a person have a dualistic reality consisting of something physical called a brain and a mind that has no substance? (cited in Dennett 1991, xi). To Daniel C. Dennett, the answers involve understanding consciousness.

Descartes is considered by some as the father of modernism, which emphasized the importance of empirical and careful observation to decide what is considered acceptable truth. Modernism, which is the basis of science, started with the phrase—*cogito ergo sum* ("I am aware [thinking], therefore I am"). Descartes's point is that anyone (including Helen Keller, because she could think even if she could not see or hear) can know for certain that they exist. Senses not related to words radically limit awareness. As Keller learned words in spite of her dual handicap, she achieved a greater awareness that significantly helped her identify herself in a radically more robust manner to the point she could fathom the deeper meaning of Descartes's famous words.

Before Helen Keller had a teacher, she knew she existed but beyond that her consciousness was to her own nothingness. Her awareness of self was from (1) her brain stem, (2) her limited but still operational other senses (for example, touch and smell), and (3) her brief younger period when she was not handicapped. After working with her teacher, her awareness grew radically with words and then language. Consciousness can and does grow and it is essentially a process of gaining knowledge that can be taught to expand a person's awareness. For those who wish to grow, as Keller did, they can. Of course the opposite is also true—those who do not care to grow will not increase their awareness. With growth comes greater awareness and thus an expanded consciousness that allows the person to "see" and "hear" more than before and maybe more than others. The more limited awareness from only the brain stem means that a person sees and hears less than those who have greater awareness from the rest of their brains. Brain stem thinkers are limited in their ability to think, interpret, and process what they see, hear, and feel. As their awareness grows from other portions of the brain, they can think more profound thoughts because their awareness is greater. In terms of ethics, awareness is largely dependent upon moving past the brain stem dualism of "internal and external." The philosopher Immanuel Kant famously moved past that dualism with his "categorical imperative" in his 1785 *Groundwork of the Metaphysics of Morals*. In brief, he maintained that an action to be ethical must be based on a maxim that should become a universal law. Thus, he rejected the internal/external dualism from the brain stem and accepted the external plus the internal (in other words, oneness) in creating his approach to ethics.

In summary, the human awareness that shapes ethical consciousness ideally must move past the external/internal dualism that naturally influences human thinking from the hardwired brain stem. This can only be possible through the plasticity and memes ability to learn. When that learning takes place (thus becoming more altruistic and less egocentric), someone can act ethically, meaning ethical concepts can and probably will guide their actions. If that is not done and individuals remain egocentric, cannot even understand ethics even if they appear to act ethically. For those who have awareness only from their brain stem, what pleases them or what hurts them determines what they do rather than any larger concept of right and wrong that comes from ethics. If professionals are to understand how to create an ethical climate within government, they must be aware of the egocentric/altruistic difference and its impact on ethical reasoning within the population.

HOW MANY OF US ARE EGOCENTRIC?

We do not have reliable statistics on how many people (American or otherwise) are egocentric or egocentric-leaning thinkers and how many are altruistic or altruistic-leaning. Egocentrism is hardwired into the human brain stem by evolution. However, despite that strong predisposition, many people are altruistic because those feelings and beliefs can also exist and even supersede the brain stem bias. Egocentrism is the lower bar of moral development but sadly, research indicates that American society has steadily become more egocentric over time (Hsieh 2014).

In her 2014 article, Esther Hsieh speculated that an overall rise in economic prosperity may play a role in increasing egoism, meaning the greater use of egocentric words such as "I, me, and mine." She notes that people who are young adults during hard times are less narcissistic than those who came of age during economic booms. Based on egotism word usage, Hsieh also argued America's presidential leadership was more altruistic prior to 1900 and after 1920 the leadership became much more egocentric. The article also quotes Sara Konrath saying, "This result (looking at cultural factors) tells me it's bigger than just a president."

Two experimental research studies give us a clue to the percentage of egocentric U.S. citizens since the last half of the twentieth century. In 1961 Stanley Milgram, a psychologist at Yale University, did experiments addressing the power of authority. Subjects were told to administer electric shocks from a low voltage to 450 volts to another student participant in the study. Of the forty subjects, only one subject refused to administer the mock shocks above the 300-volt level and about two out of three inflicted what they thought to be fatal voltage under orders from the experimenter. This study suggests that students at Yale or possibly all American college students and Americans in general are remarkably nonaltruistic ethical thinkers because they simple do not care about other human beings.

Another study, by Philip Zimbardo, a psychologist at Stanford University, addressed human brutality. He recruited twenty-one undergraduate students to pretend to act as guards and prisoners in a mock prison. All participants knew they were taking part in an experiment. The "guards" were given memes in the form of guard uniforms, mirrored sunglasses, and wooden batons. Those memes-inspired props served to identify their role in society. "Prisoners" were given ill-fitting smocks, stocking caps, chains, and numbers. Those props identified them as prisoners, especially by the "guards." From day one of the experiment, the "guards" clearly enjoyed their status over the "prisoners." By the end of the experiment, which was terminated early, one-third of them showed clear sadistic tendencies such as joyfully inflicting pain on the "prisoners." Zimbardo showed how easy it is for humans to slip into the grip of sadism. This suggests that in one-third of the Stanford undergraduates and possibly all American undergraduates or all Americans, the brain stem can easily dominate thinking and lead to a show of complete noncaring for another person.

These studies provide no clear conclusion about how many people in a country like the United States are egocentric, however, they are evocative. The populations in both studies came from students at elite universities. It could be that such students are more egocentric than the general population. Maybe the students chosen were not representative of even the larger student population in America. Clearly, the population sizes of the studies were too small to draw conclusive conclusions and larger generalizations. However, the studies do suggest that the great majority of people in America are dangerously egocentric or egocentric leaning under the right circumstances.

These college studies are small but do they reflect what could happen in an American governmental setting? The torture conducted by American soldiers at Abu Ghraib clearly indicates that the answer is yes. Exhibit 1.3 demonstrates that even in the highly controlled context of the U.S. Army, human ethical abuse can exist. Clearly, a lack of leadership and the absence of ethical training contributed to the ongoing torture at Abu Ghraib.

Exhibit 1.3. Abu Ghraib Torture

In the era of Saddam Hussein and the U.S. war with Iraq, the American military under the command of Brigadier General Janis Karpinski controlled the Abu Ghraib prison that occupied as many as 50,000 men and women. Some of those prisoners were suspected high-value leaders of the insurgency against the coalition forces. Karpinski's command included three large jails, eight battalions, and thirty-four army reservists, most of whom—like herself—had no training handling prisoners.

Kapinski was formally admonished and suspended for her lack of leadership due to torture that occur while she was in command An investigation into suspected torture at the prison found there were numerous instances of "sadistic, blatant, and wanton criminal abuses" at Abu Ghraib. The 372d Military Police Company and American intelligence officers carried out the acts. The evidence included photographs and videos of the abuses. Six American military persons at the enlistment level were prosecuted on charges that included conspiracy, dereliction of duty, cruelty toward prisoners, maltreatment, assault, and indecent acts.

The abuse of prisoners was almost routine and the soldiers did not hide what they did.

Source: Hersh, Seymour M. "Torture at Abu Ghraib." *The New Yorker.* May 10, 2004.

CONSCIOUSNESS IN PUBLIC SECTOR ORGANIZATIONS

Consciousness not only varies in terms of a person's assumptions about the world. It changes how a person sees what they consider to be reality. To an egocentric person, a code of ethics is pointless information from their perspective of how life really is. To more altruistic persons, studying a code of ethics may be dry and boring but it does make sense, because they can see a useful social application for it from their more universal perspective. A wider and deeper awareness of consciousness is important to discern that one type of ethics training will not fit everyone in an organization and using only one type of ethics for everyone in every situation is foolish. This is true for every profession, including public administration, because the learning limitations and advantages of both sets of people must fully understand when designing an ethical environment in an organization.

The field of public administration is dedicated to serving the public and therefore many who are attracted to it as a profession are altruistic, because they tend to be oneness oriented. However, some, who are more egocentric, may find the decent salaries and good pensions to be appealing reasons to choose the government as an employer. Other people, who have a mixed egocentric/altruistic nature, may find that both sides are satisfied by a career in public service. Government recruiting and hiring practices do not use consciousness as a selection criterion for public employment, so any public organization or work unit could have the many variations of consciousness represented within their unit. Thus, discerning how to operationalize ethics involves perception of how the impact of consciousness, within the confines of a particular organization, will influence the application of normative ethics.

Efforts to create an ethical climate in public sector organizations must reflect an awareness of the consciousness of the people performing the public function because their consciousness affects how they see and act in the world. For example, egocentric people need an enforced version of rules as they are heavily influenced by their desire to avoid punishment or gain material rewards such as status, material wealth, and pleasure. The military uses uniforms, medals, bonuses, and promotions as a means to influence their egocentric members to abide by their moral norms. The military also uses punishment, including dishonorable discharges, to help enforce its rules.

In contrast, altruistic people need to feel they are doing something worthwhile for society and thus aspirational ethics tends to be more motivational for them. The altruistic often find the rule-based approach to ethics too limiting in the performance of their work. They believe it is their ethical responsibility to do the right thing for the public good. Although they also prefer to avoid punishment, they are sometimes willing to take punishment if they feel compelled to do so by their ethics. They are more indifferent to status, wealth, and typical human pleasures.

Thus, the human context of public administration is a mix of people with varying types of consciousness and thus with varying influences on how they view and act upon ethics in the workplace. Leaders need to appreciate that this mix of consciousness exists and that one type of ethics will not fit all people in all situations, especially over long periods of time. For ethics to be influential in the workplace, it must dynamically evolve within its context. The organization needs to know the various ways that ethics can be structured and how to determine which setting requires what mix of ethical approaches.

CONCLUSION

Let us re-address the Roli and Clarabelle story based on what we have just read in this chapter. First, unless the individuals in an ethics class have moved beyond dualistic thinking, a voluntary code of ethics will mean nothing to them and will even seem unrealistic. Leon had not moved beyond that dualism and thus had an egocentric awareness. Second, the story provided a framing, and for some a reframing, of why ethics is important in society. Before sharing the story, the professor's assumption was that a voluntary code of ethics would inform the students on how an ethical person should act in public organizational situations. After Leon's question, the professor's assumption shifted to recognize that at least some of the students needed to understand ethics in terms that related to their possible personal safety because of their conscious awareness.

Why did this reorientation work? The stark fact that the barkeep died brought the students to link ethics to survival and this was something their brain stem could comprehend. Because of Leon's egoism, he could not grasp that ethics was meaningful because studying ethics, to him, was a useless endeavor. However, egocentric people can engage in ethical behavior even if they are not motivated by ethics. To achieve ethical results for them, training is necessary to get them either to think beyond their brain stem or somehow bypass their brain stem thinking. A viable approach is to frame their decision making not in terms of ethics but rather in terms of achieving pleasure or avoiding harm. The military uses this approach, which might explain why the military has been successful in minimizing racism within its ranks. However, it might also explain why they are sometimes ethically deficient because the military sometimes neglects to provide the necessary ethical training.

REVIEW QUESTIONS

1. How is storytelling useful in creating an ethical awareness?

2. The professional field of public administration is about public service. Why is that fact significant to ethics in government?

3. Many individuals join the public service out of a desire for a good salary with a good pension. Why is that fact significant to ethics in government?

4. Why is consciousness important to ethics? Why is the fact that consciousness varies significant to ethics?

5. What is the significance of having two determinants within a person's consciousness that bring about how individuals comprehend ethical concepts?

6. Why is the design of the brain important to ethics?

7. Why are the plasticity and memes important to ethics?

8. What insight is gained from the quote by Helen Keller that is important to ethics?

9. From the combination of the Keller quote, Kant's "categorical imperative," and Descartes's *cogito ergo sum* observation, what insight is gained that is important to ethics?

10. Why can't a purely egocentric person be guided by ethics?

11. What are the implications of having a public workforce that is highly egocentric? At the lower levels in government? At the higher levels in government?

REFERENCES

Brooks, David. 2015. *The Road to Character*. New York: Random House.

Descartes, René. 2002. *Meditations on First Philosophy in Which Are Demonstrated the Existence of God and the Distinction Between the Human Soul and the Body*. Edited by John Cottingham. Cambridge, UK: Cambridge University Press.

Dawkins, Richard (1976). *The Selfish Gene*. Oxford University Press, Oxford. Oxford, UK.

Dennett, Daniel C. 1991. *Consciousness Explained*. Boston: Back Bay Books.

Geuras, Dean, and Charles Garofalo. 2002. *Practical Ethics in Public Administration*. Vienna, VA: Management Concepts.

Hersh, Seymour M. 2004. "Torture at Abu Ghraib." *New Yorker*, May 10. http://www.newyorker.com/magazine/2004/05/10/torture-at-abu-ghraib.

Hsieh, Esther. 2014. "Kids These Days Really Are More Egocentric." *Scientific American*, November 1.

Kant, Emmanuel. 1996. *Groundwork of the Metaphysics of Morals*. Translated by Mary J. Gregor. Cambridge, UK: Cambridge University Press.

Keller, Helen. Quote in Dennett, Daniel C. 1991. *Consciousness Explained*. New York: Back Bay Books/Little, Brown and Co.

Milgram, Stanley. 1974. *Obedience to Authority: An Experimental View*. New York: HarperCollins.

Paul, Richard, and Linda Elder. 2006. *Critical Thinking: Tools for Taking Charge of Your Learning and Your Life*. Upper Saddle River, NJ: Pearson/Prentice Hall.

Zhan, Max. 2016. "Mindfulness Has Gone Corporate." *Religion Dispatches*, July 12. https://www.alternet.org/mindfullness-buddhism-capitalist-ends.

2 Ethics for Public Administrators

PROFESSOR: *Yes, you have a question?*

LEON: *I can see the law as something that is very real, but not ethics. People say it is real, but isn't ethics an illusion or a myth? For example, aren't those Codes of Ethics posters you see on office walls just words on a paper signifying nothing?*

DEFINING ETHICS

What is ethics? Leon evaluates ethics in terms of his egocentric consciousness. Egocentric individuals see only rewards or punishments as means to motivate the actions of people. Assuming everyone is egocentric and ethics are only words hung on wall without any means to enforce them, then such codes, at their best, are just a means to fool people that ethics both exist and are important. In other words, Leon would be correct if all people were egocentric. In addition, Leon's conclusion is similar to those of some important philosophers, such as Niccolo Machiavelli (1469–1527). Altruistic people, who define ethics in terms of their selfless consciousness, view aspirational ethics, such as a code of ethics, as useful guidance for how to act morally in the workplace. In other words, at a minimum, even a non-enforceable code of ethics is useful to a portion of the population. Going beyond such codes, ethics is a much more complex subject but it can be an effective positive motivator in society (see chapter 6 on virtue ethics).

Ethics concerns right and wrong behavior defined in terms of moral choice. However, some notable persons, such as the philosophers of ancient Greece, considered ethics to essentially be about living what they called "the good life," which to some meant living a life worthy of being lived and to others living a life that is satisfying. The first view is altruistic and the second is egocentric. In defining ethics, we commonly say it is the study of right conduct, however, a person's selfish or selfless consciousness defines "right conduct." Ethics is theorizing about right conduct and the good life; whereas morality is the actual practice of right conduct and the good life. Confusion about these two terms prevails because a person's understanding of ethics and morals depends of their level of consciousness and therefore a selfish person would see ethics and morals differently than a selfless person.

Other terms that are important to understanding ethics are moral, amoral, immoral, unethical, and non-moral. "Moral" has two meanings. One has to do with the ability of a person to understand morality as well as his or her capacity to make moral decisions. The second has to do with the actual performance of moral acts. "Amoral" refers to the inability to distinguish between right and wrong. "Immoral" actions transgress our understanding of proper morality. "Non-moral" and "unmoral" are commonly used interchangeably with "amoral." Again, selfish and selfless people apply the terms differently even though they agree on their definitions.

Another distinction, which is important in this book, is between personal ethics and social ethics. "Personal ethics" is applicable to the individual person and "social ethics" concerns itself with groups, such as the profession of public administration or a public organization. As a practical matter, social ethics concerns social and political philosophy; whereas personal ethics is psychological but also philosophic. Again, the selfish and selfless consciousness of persons using personal and social terms differ from person to person, and the result is that reasonable and thoughtful discussion becomes difficult. To achieve reasonable and thoughtful discussion, the parties must understand that their level of consciousness determines how they apply those terms in practical situations. If that understanding is not reached, the two parties will merely speak past each other without knowing why the other party cannot comprehend them.

DEMOCRATIC MORALITY[1]

THE CONTEXT OF DEMOCRACY

To understand democratic morality, the work of Machiavelli needs to be considered. Machiavelli noted that there were two kinds of government: monarchies (single person–ruled states) and free states (republics/democracies). He said that free states required virtuous citizens who cared more for the state than for themselves—that is, they must be altruistic. Realistically, however, he concluded that, in general, people were more concerned with their individual or group concerns—that they are egocentric. Thus, they would always corrupt the state to achieve their private interests at the expense of the state. Over time, he reasoned that any republic would have to fail because the collective consciousness of a state is that of an egocentric person.

Machiavelli's reasoning was that free states were not a feasible form of long-term governance. Instead, he reasoned that monarchies were the most feasible form of government because the monarch would simply define the government as the Prince's possession and with his clear and ultimate authority he would rule over everything and everyone. The Prince would be egocentric

---

[1]An earlier version of this discussion appeared in "Appleby, Democratic Morality, and a Worldwide Code of Ethics," in *Democracy, Governance and Globalization: Essays in Honour of Paul H. Appleby*, edited by P. L. Sanjeev Reddy, Jaideep Singh, and R. K. Tiwari, 93–116 (New Delhi: Indian Institute of Public Administration, 2004). A version of this chapter was also published as Thomas D. Lynch and Cynthia E. Lynch, "Democratic Morality: Back to the Future," in *Ethics and Integrity in Public Administration*, edited by Raymond W. Cox, 5–25 (Armonk, NY: M. E. Sharpe, 2009).

Ben Franklin

and his consciousness as the leader would sustain an enduring state.

However, he reasoned that for the Prince to maintain power, he would need to display dual characteristics—a thirst for power, like a lion, and deceit and cunning, like a fox—to achieve the acceptance of the people. The lion represents a strong selfish egocentric person. The fox is also an egocentric person that acts like a selfless person in order to gain the support and approval of his people. To Machiavelli, these two qualities complement each other and allow the Prince to effectively rule with his egocentric consciousness. The end justifies the means, even though the end is for the sole benefit of the tyrant.

At the end of the U.S. Continental Congress that drafted the U.S. Constitution, a lady asked Dr. Benjamin Franklin, one of the founders, "Well, Doctor, what have we got, a republic or a monarchy?". He replied, "A republic, if you can keep it" (McHenry 1906, 618). Apparently, Franklin believed that an American republic would consist of both selfish and selfless citizens and concluded that Machiavelli could be correct if the prevailing consciousness of the country was egocentric.

Paul Appleby (1891–1963) was one of the first presidents of the American Society for Public Administration. He had a remarkable influence on the emerging new profession. Appleby served in high-ranking federal and state government appointments and was dean of the Maxwell School at Syracuse University. He was professionally active during the Great Depression of the1930s, World War II, and the post-Cold War period. He authored five books. In spring 1951, Appleby delivered the Edward Douglas White lectures at Louisiana State University, which were later published as Morality and Administration in Democratic Government (1952).

Appleby looked at the issue of ethics with an altruistic consciousness while also reasoning that Franklin was correct. He saw democracy quite differently than Machiavelli, as he did not focus on general philosophy or suggest any particular kind of administrative ethics code. Rather, he instead examined the central moral issues of the public service in the context of democratic government or the free state. Appleby argued that if various private interests only think about maximizing their own good and refuse to consider the common good, then the state was likely to self-destruct. Therefore, the nation's leaders and the bureaucracy should act together to focus their public policy on the public interest rather than on interests of various private persons or entities.

Appleby felt that for a free state to remain free, the country needed virtuous public servants who shared the common social ethics of concern for the public interest. He felt that when citizens viewed their welfare as individuals and groups separate from the republic and more importantly from the welfare of the republic, then the society would become morally corrupt. To avoid that end, he argued that public servants must maintain what he called Democratic Morality. He believed that "ethical problems of public administration range from the very small, particular, and personal to those bearing in importance and highly complicated ways upon the nature of an unfolding democracy" (Appleby 1952, viii). Appleby concentrated his work on administrative ethics and the felicitous interaction of moral institutional arrangements and the morally ambiguous individual.

FUNDAMENTAL VALUES

Appleby was keenly aware of the fundamental values of his day, including (1) the commitment of the nation to continued economic and social progress, (2) the need for civic virtue, (3) the role of the state to curb the excesses and inadequacies of the market system, and (4) the importance of public trust in leading the nation. Arguably, these values are even more important today, especially considering worldwide globalization, corporate political influence, crime, environmental pollution, and terrorism. Appleby felt that matters of morality reflect values that operate in the context of the whole structure and process of public administration. In turn, he felt public administrators must view themselves as operating synergistically within general structures and processes of politics and society. Thus, the morality that he addressed was a matter of public organizations "having to do with complicated organizational conduct under public responsibility" (Appleby 1952, vii).

In Roscoe C. Martin's *Public Administration and Democracy* (1965), Appleby contributed a chapter titled "Public Administration and Democracy." In it, he summarized his views on this broader topic and stressed that often government action reflects a basic moral character. He felt that such a reflection can exist outside "the ideals or interests of single or factional citizens" (343). Appleby noted that basic moral character of government action manifests itself when:

- the action conforms to the processes and symbols developed for the general protection of political freedoms and is the agent of more general freedoms;

- it leaves open the way for modification or reversal by public determination;

- it is taken within a hierarchy of controls in which responsibility for the action may be readily identified by the public;

- it embodies as contributions of leadership the concrete structuring of response to popularly felt needs; and

- it is not merely responsive to the private or personal needs of leaders.

DEMOCRATIC MORALITY AS ETHICS

To Appleby, these five points defined Democratic Morality. In other words, he felt that public administrators should always perform their actions within the larger context of democracy. Democratic processes, such as elections and the rule of law, can and should serve as a means to guide public administrators. For example, a state judge might feel that his basic moral character requires him to place a religious symbol in a key public building. However, if a higher federal court rules otherwise, then the state judge or his associates must alter their decision and comply with the higher courts' ruling.

Another Appleby theme was the question of special political influence of private groups. He saw Democratic Morality as a refinement of that influence. He embraced a reduction of special privilege and "the opening of opportunity for the largest realization of the potentiality of citizens generally" (344). His vision called for:

- the elimination of paying for special influences, which inspires venal, wasteful, or discriminatory government action; and

- making the exercise of power both more responsive and more responsible.

Of three contemporary theoretical approaches to ethics (rule-based, consequential, and virtue), Appleby clearly advocated virtue ethics, or what David Brooks calls "eulogy ethics" (xi). Appleby said, "Moral performance begins in individual self-discipline on the part of officials, involving all that is meant by the word 'character'" (344). But character is not enough for his Democratic Morality. The administrative process must also support individual group judgment that reflects a whole public or oneness responsibility. The individual public administrator's honesty is necessary but not sufficient as there must also be "a devoted guardianship of the continuing reality of democracy" (Appleby 1965, 344).

CREATED EXPECTATIONS

To Appleby, Democratic Morality created expectations for the public official but it also created expectations for the citizen who should also show action based on character. For example, any citizen might wish for the public attention of being a candidate for governor of a state government. However, such a job requires many skills and talents. Not everyone who works in the private sector is competent or capable of performing well in a public leadership position. Therefore, they should voluntarily defer to others who are better equipped or are situated to provide such governance. Appleby (1965) thought citizen character meant that every citizen should constantly and consistently strive to relate their personal concerns to public concerns and "to help perfect arrangements supporting these citizen responsibilities" (344).

In this way citizen action would be for the larger community's needs rather than individual preferences. In one of former Congresswoman Barbara Jordan's last public appearances before she died, she described the responsibility of citizenship as follows:

A nation is formed by the willingness of each of us to share in the responsibility for upholding the common good. A government is invigorated when each of us is willing to participate in shaping the future of this nation.

Citizen is a noble word. It's an honorable position to be a citizen. It carries rights with it, and it carries responsibilities with it. But it is also a great delight. Citizen. The general welfare, the pleasure, the happiness of the citizen. That is what was at the bottom of the creation of the government. That is the raison d'etre of government. (1976, 105)

To Appleby, public interest was the ongoing search for the larger community's needs rather than any one or more individual or group private interests. It was not an end but rather a perpetual means of the present moment. The search itself was Appleby's Democratic Morality. Citizens and leaders must want to always seek higher standards for government. However, this desire must be in the context of the ultimate and absolute democratic value that permits disagreement over public policy. Certainly, loyalty to a nation is significant but more significant is the fact that democracy always includes the dissenting voices. Nevertheless, the advocates of differing opinions must voice their thoughts in a manner that does not seek violent overthrow of the democratic government or use speech that is likely to cause personal harm to others.

FEDERALIST 10

Appleby saw the American governmental system as a series of political and organizational devices for promoting ethical choices. In his time, the threat to a democratic society was not venality but rather the imperfection of institutional arrangements. In other words, for him corruption per se is not the problem for democracy. Instead, it is the mind-set with which our institutions of governance interact. To Appleby, politics and hierarchy were important to the basic morality of the government system.

To project Appleby into the twenty-first century, politics and a structured civil service are critical to the continuation of a democracy. For example, the privatization of a nation's military forces can lead to a breakdown in accountability and opens the door for massive venality by contracting private corporations. The active military are accountable first and foremost to the U.S. Constitution and secondarily to the president, through a chain of command. However, they are also accountable to the U.S. Congress, which appropriates their funds and to the people through an active free press. In contrast, private contractors perform their work for money and also actively engage in private interest lobbying to ensure they continue to get that work and more. Thus, the element of private interest lobbying changes and distorts the whole concept of public interest for the private contractors and cripples their accountability to the public. Essentially, private contractors can use legal ways to contribute to cooperating members of Congress and buy their special favors over the larger public interest of the nation.

Ideally, for Appleby, democracy should force private and special interests into a pluralistic mill that creates a majoritarian calculus that reflects the larger public interest. Eventually, the mill grinds and blends those private and special interests into one public interest. Hierarchy forces top officials to homogenize and moralize the private and special interests through the mill of organizational echelons. The role of the public servant is to sort through those various private and special interests and help transform them into a "public will." Thus, politics and hierarchy are causal agents to the public servant, who must creatively search for a "public will to be."

Any breakdown in public morality is directly related to a breakdown in politics and hierarchy. Regardless of bribery existing at low or high levels in government, corruption influences public policy and the eventual result is that government fails. Appleby was keenly aware of James Madison's argument in Federalist 10, which said the complexity of public decision making with its checks and

James Madison

balances would force unitary (individuals) claims into the mill of pluralistic (society's) considerations and eventually into an articulation of the "public will."

Appleby embraced Madison and argued that the milling of private and special interests could only occur if legislative and administrative devices, such as due process and proper administrative notice, existed together. They must ensure that the public policy decisions emerged out of the complexity rather than out of the simplicity of private and special interests. Appleby (1965) said, "Our poorest governmental performances, both technically and morally, are generally associated with conditions in which a few citizens have very disproportionate influence" (214).

PUBLIC SERVANT ETHICS

BUILT ON APPLEBY

Stephen K. Bailey (1965) summarized Appleby's vision of Democratic Morality and projected that vision to recommend a personal ethics for public servants. Bailey (1965) explained Appleby's grand design as follows: "Government is moral in so far as it induces public servants to relate the specific to the general, the private to the public, the precise interest to the inchoate moral judgment" (285). Appleby does not present a gestalt of personal ethics in government in his writings. Instead, he paints, a picture of Democratic Morality with broad brush strokes.

Bailey took up the challenge using fragments of Appleby's work to fashion and recommend a set of personal ethics for public servants. Building upon Appleby's virtue ethics, Bailey (1965) stressed the concepts of mental attitudes and moral qualities. He said, "Virtue without understanding can be quite as disastrous as understanding without virtue" (285). He identified three essential mental recognitions that a public administrator needed to come to terms with:

- the moral ambiguity of all humans and all public policies,

- the contextual forces that condition moral priorities in the public service, and

- the paradoxes of procedures.

For Bailey, creating a mental mind-set of an altruistic person is critical and requires effort upon the part of the moral public administrator to avoid being egocentric. Human ego makes exercising judgment, which recognizes moral ambiguity, especially in the person required to make those judgments, very difficult. The very processes of government require public administrators to take positions on public policies; and typically, the public administrator's human ego is present. Nevertheless, in spite of ego, public administrators must recognize the moral ambiguity in all public policies, including those favored by the public servants themselves. Bailey (1965) summarized this insightful selfless/selfish observation by quoting Reinhold Niebuhr: "Man's capacity for justice makes democracy possible, but man's inclination to injustice makes democracy necessary"

Essential Wisdom

Another challenge for the moral public administrator is to recognize that four essential wisdoms help us understand the context of public service. First, there is no way to avoid personal and private interest in the calculus of public decision making. Whether the motivation is survival or just greed, the human condition fosters personal and private interests. Second, as humans, we are often as much rationalizers as we are rational beings. The more educated and sophisticated we are, typically the better we are at rationalizing our actions, sometimes even to ourselves.

Third, more successful public discourse requires an effort to transcend, sublimate, and transform narrow vested interest (i.e., dialogical discourse) but this capacity is exercised imperfectly and intermittently. Dialogical discourse with others is difficult, time-consuming, and often overly emotional to the point that it is unsuccessful. Too often such discourse requires skills that are sometimes not present in public situations. Fourth, there is no public decision that is a total victory for one party and a total defeat for the other. In the milling to arrive at the "public will," all parties will ultimately feel that they either did not get all they wanted or that they did not lose everything.

Paradoxically, an awareness of these four insights can immobilize the sensitive public administrator like the deer caught in the headlights. Thus, like the deer, the administrator might very well suffer serious harm unless the four wisdoms are acted upon in daily work activities. Beyond the simple recognition of these four wisdoms, the public servant must have the character virtues of optimism, courage, humility, and a willingness to offer compromise.

Bailey (1965) tells us that "the higher a person goes on the rungs of power and authority, the more wobbly (sic) the ethical ladder" (290). He also says, "the heat in the ethical kitchen grows greater with each level of power, no public servant is immune from some heat" (291). Fear is the wasteland of ethical relativity because fear motivates a search for a moral rationale to avoid that which is feared. With moral relativity, there is no moral vice that thinking humans cannot turn into a "relative good" by redefining the context of the decision, by merely shifting the meaning of words, or by shifting values from those of others.

Moral ambiguity is rarely hidden and normally results in rising public frustration. In the rough game of politics, political and media personalities take on the role of the moral critic of others. With moral relativism, some critics believe there is no moral virtue and ethics is merely emotivism. Thus, critics of moral relativism merely cite the peculiar circumstance in order to appear morally superior and make his or her opponent look foolish. For example, the president might lie to the press to save the life of an American spy, as did President Eisenhower, but his political opponent would stress the lie to the media while downplaying or ignoring the circumstances of the larger issue, preserving a life.

PARADOX

Bailey spoke about "the paradox of procedures." He stressed that despite those who rebel against government regulations and procedures, the history of American freedom is the history of procedure. Policy makers, at their best, create rules, standards, and procedures (often called standard operating procedures) to promote fairness, openness, greater depth of thoughtful analysis prior to a public decision, and accountability. Thus, attacks on regulations and procedures are often against the rule of law, which earlier policy makers designed to promote the larger meaning of democracy.

Bailey's paradox of procedure is that those same procedures that are the friends of deliberation, order, and equity are also at times the enemy of progress and dispatch. For example, environmentalists see environment impact statements as appropriate deliberation. Others, such as builders, consider them to be the enemy of progress and the means to slow up the proper actions of getting the job done. However, Bailey also recognized that some procedures are simply inept despite the good intentions behind their creation. In other words, sometimes technique can triumph over purpose. Thus, the paradox is that procedures are essential but they can also be dysfunctional, especially with the passage of time and changing circumstances.

Competing philosophies of substantive purpose are related to government organizational structure and procedures. Thus, Bailey argues that a "public servant who cannot recognize the paradoxes of procedures will be trapped by them. For in the case of procedures, he who deviates frequently is subversive; he who never deviates at all is lost; and he who tinkers with procedures without an understanding of substantive consequence is foolish" (1965, 292). Paradoxes should not always be solved or overcome. Paradoxes are like a high-wire circus act. The opposing sides pull against each other creating tension and thus permitting the performer to walk along the wire. If someone were to eliminate either side, the tension would slack and the performer would fall. The wisdom that Bailey communicates is that the public administrator needs to feel comfortable with the tension, as it is functional and even important to accomplish the mission of the organization.

MORAL QUALITIES

Bailey also projected Appleby's virtue ethics into three essential moral qualities for the ethical public servant:

- optimism,
- courage, and
- fairness tempered by charity.

Bailey tells us that operating virtues must support the previous three mental recognitions or attitudes. The list of relevant virtues includes but is not limited to patience, honesty, loyalty, cheerfulness, courtesy, and humility. However, he limits his discussion to the previously cited three virtues, which he deems essential.

Language is our best tool for communication, but occasionally it fails us. To Bailey, the word "optimism" is one such word. He says that "optimism" connotes euphoria, which he sees as inappropriate in the context of what he already presented. Nevertheless, optimism is the best word he can find to capture being on the sunnier side of doubt. Public administrators must be able to face the ambiguity and the paradoxical nature of ethics without being immobilized by them. They must be purposive in their behavior rather than reactive and, most important, they must remain ever hopeful in their outlook.

Bailey said, "Government without the leavening of optimistic public servants quickly becomes a cynical game of manipulation, personal aggrandizement, and parasitic security. The ultimate corruption of free government comes not from the hopelessly venal but from the persistently cynical" (1965, 293). True optimism is the affirmation of the worth of taking risks. True optimism is also the capacity to see the possibilities for good in the uncertain, the ambiguous, and the inscrutable.

Courage is difficult for the public administrator because, as noted, public life is one of ambiguities and paradoxes. The uncertainty of the territory creates timidity and withdrawal. Thus, the public administrator must come to the workplace with an inner courage that overwhelms the organizational factors that promote timidity and withdrawal in persons with a weak inner-self. Certainly, cheerfulness, ambition, a sense of duty, and understanding are mitigating factors. Nevertheless, for the person with a weak inner-self, they are rarely sufficient to overcome the loneliness of authority.

To be successful, the public servant must have the courage to overcome self-arrogance and be impersonal in her or his organizational performance. Additionally, public administrators must have the courage to face down the expert opinion when it cannot be defended rigorously. Also, the public administrator should sometimes resist clamoring public opinion, powerful interest groups, and the media. Bailey tells us that possibly the most important act of courage for a public servant is ultimately the courage to decide. One of the most difficult things a public servant must do is to overcome their tendency toward inertia often as a means to protect themselves.

The third moral quality is "fairness tempered with charity." Courage can be dysfunctional unless it results in just and charitable actions and attitudes. The authoritative allocator in society is government and it must act with ineffable standards of justice directed to having a sound healthy state. That can only happen if its public servants have the correct moral quality of love toward all. People in society must feel that their public servants exercise their power with fairness and compassion for them. the public can eventually forgive almost anything if the ultimate motivation for the action was an attempt to be fair and to act with charity. It is those virtues that compensate for inadequate information and for the other mistakes in the making of judgments intended to be fair.

Contrary to what some might believe, charity is not being always best characterized as "soft." It can often require moral toughness. Charity requires teaching the inner-self to subjugate the personal recognition, power, and status demands of our egos. It is subjugating the ego-self to the true inner-self. This act of love defines the "good" in a society beyond a pattern of privilege.

OBSERVATIONS

Bailey ends with two observations. He first notes the importance of preserving and promoting the public as opposed to the private interest; and secondly, he stresses the central importance of

Appleby's notion of Democratic Morality. Clearly, public policies are significant and we justifiably focus on them in our decisions as public administrators. However, they pale in contrast to the importance of the Democratic Morality, which exists only if public servants create it with their mental attitudes and moral qualities. Public administrators are the ones who must nourish and establish those attitudes and qualities in our governments as they set the tone of public morality through their actions.

The "public interest" is the intertwining of the public servant's mental attitudes and moral qualities with our institutional arrangements that mill or grind the many private interests into the fine mixture of the "public good." Without a Democratic Morality, impersonal bureaucracy and cold technology drain the life blood of caring humanity from society. Certainly, both potentially give us order and prosperity, but they are insufficient.

Without some measure of Democratic Morality, society breaks down into endless cycles of political gamesmanship for personal gain without regard for the public interest, which ultimately results in the loss of democracy itself. Bailey (1965) tells us that "normative, procedural, institutional, attitudinal, and moral standards do exist" with Democratic Morality (298). They preserve and promote a "public interest" far more fundamental than any set of public policies. They are the heart that pumps the blood of humanity.

THE FRENCH VERSUS LADD DEBATE

Social Ethics

The social ethical concept of Democratic Morality developed by Paul Appleby assumes that government organizations can act as moral agents in terms of being protectors of the public's interest and democratic governance. American philosopher Peter French (1979) posits a theory "that allows organizations as members of the moral community, of equal standing with the traditionally acknowledged residents: biological human beings" (207). He says that organizations can be full-fledged moral persons and have the same privileges, rights, and duties that moral persons are accorded. French says the society can hold organizations morally responsible for their acts. This is possible because the legal system infers organizational intent from the organization's official mission and policies as well as the procedures that organizations use to enforce that mission's objective and official policies.

In contrast to French, John Ladd argues against an organization being considered a moral agent. He agrees that a mission's positions and central control imply organizational responsibility as it relates to moral responsibility. However, he argues that the separation of ownership and management in private organizations—by inference the separation of citizenship and elected officials in public organizations—radically changes the moral relationship between parties. Essentially, he says that holding citizens responsible for public organizations is senseless because they personally have no detailed control over the organization's operations or policies.

The French-Ladd debate helps us understand how we should think about the relationship between social and personal ethics. Most of their debate centered on private organizations, not public institutions. Should an organization be held responsible for its immoral actions? The debate informs us on the question: Is Appleby correct that we can create a social ethic in a public organization that would help reinforce democracy? Although the debate does not resolve this question, it does tell us that there is agreement that something called a "social ethic" can exist and can influence the behavior of public organizations. Unfortunately, the debate does not provide us with information about the specifics of the democratic social ethic and its impact on democratic decision making, but we have Appleby and Bailey to help us in that task.

CAN PUBLIC ORGANIZATIONS ACT AS MORAL PERSONS?

Patricia Werhane (1989) argues that public organizations cannot act as moral persons. She says that the moral responsibility commonly ascribed to organizations is at least partially redistributable to individuals. "We have not shielded individual wrong-doing behind the corporate veil but, rather, expanded the fig leaf" (Werhane 1989, 822). Manuel Velasquez (1983) also disagrees with French and argues that the organizations' acts do not originate in the organization but in the organization's individual members.

In this debate, there are two extreme positions: on one hand is the holistic and sometimes anthropomorphic perspective that views organizations as human moral agents; on the other hand are the reductionists who argue only actual people can act and therefore they alone should be held responsible for those actions. The holistic perspective leads us to say that organizations have brains with the ability to think and act. Meyers (1983) suggested a compromise position by saying an organization should be considered a moral agent if it is capable of second order intentionality and it exists in a responsible relationship with other moral agents. This would mean that high ranking organizational officials articulate intentionality with their policies and procedures, and lower officials act.

Much of this debate centers upon holding private organizations responsible for their actions, however, the concept also applies to public organizations. It also applies to creating a positive sense of moral responsibility within the organization. Managers, supervisors, division chiefs, and so on can assume the moral responsibility of Democratic Morality. They can say there is a public interest and demand that the public organization for which they work make its policy decisions using that assumption as defined by Appleby.

This debate can be better understood in terms of egocentric versus altruistic consciousness. As noted in chapter 1, egocentric thinkers see reality in terms of contesting individuals or groups. To them, applying human responsibility to organizations is logically foolish. Altruistic thinkers see reality holistically and thus organizations are merely a collective of social groups with a shared consciousness. Thus, holding a social group (for example, a government agency) responsible for a lapse of ethical judgment, such as not cleaning up an environmental hazard they created, is sensible to an altruistic but not to egocentric thinker. In most situations, the altruistic view is embodied in state and federal law.

MORAL DEVELOPMENT

In a social setting such as a public organization, shared social ethics do exist that originate from either a shared egocentric or altruistic consciousness. For example, social ethics, such as racism, flows out of an egocentric consciousness and racial equality social views flow out of an altruistic consciousness. Normally, the members of a social group are unaware of the con-

Abraham Maslow

sciousness that spawn their social ethics but with deeper consideration it becomes obvious. Regardless of their awareness, the descriptive theory of moral development is significant in understanding how an ethics understanding emerges in a person as their moral consciousness evolves.

Descriptive Theory

Two authors of importance in the cognitive development literature are Abraham Maslow (1908–1970) and Lawrence Kohlberg (1927–1987). Maslow argued that as humans we have a hierarchy of needs, including physiological needs, security needs, needs for esteem from others, need for self-esteem for a sense of competence, and finally a need for self-actualization. Maslow believed that needs fell into this specific continuum and that each level must be satisfied before the next could be attended. Thus, if faced with a moral choice, where the person is in their hierarchy of needs, will influence their decision.

Kohlberg is even more on point. He argued that there are six stages of motives for moral action, which also move step-wise incrementally on a continuum from one lower stage to the next higher stage. Thus, his descriptive theory is referred to as "moral development." The first three stages are egocentric focused and the latter three stages are more altruistic focused as they move to the final stage, principled conscienceness. Exhibit 2.1 presents a simple chart summarizing his typology.

Stages of Moral Development

Kohlberg argued that humans ethically mature along a scale of six moral stages of development within three distinct levels, but that most of us can and do get stuck in a stage along our potential moral evolution path and do not move on to the next higher stage. The first level is *preconventional thinking*, which includes stage one, heterogamous morality, and stage two, individualism, instrumental, purpose, and exchange. The second level is *conventional thinking* and includes stage three, being mutual interpersonal expectations, relationships, and interpersonal conformity, and stage four, social conscience with a focus on social systems. The third and final level is *postconventional thinking* and includes stage five, social contract, utility, and individual rights, and stage six, universal ethical principles.

Stage one—heterogamous morality—is clearly ego centered. For individuals with an egocentric consciousness, rules, which are enforced, are the effective means to define acceptable or nonaccept-

Lawrence Kohlberg

able behaviors. To others watching the changed behavior of the egocentric person, ethical rules appear to persuade them to be ethical. However, that is a misperception as they changed their behavior due to the likely enforcement of the rules rather than the rules themselves. To those persons, the ethical basis for the rules meant nothing but the rewards and possible penalties meant everything. The brain stem with its dualistic thinking controls these people. A social perspective is nonexistent at this moral stage as such persons do not consider or even appreciate and give value to the views of others.

Stage two is individualism, instrumental, and purposeful when there is an exchange that is centered on reciprocity. Rules do not define what is right but the reciprocity agreement does, as it is in the doers' best interest to adhere to the deal. Right is *what is thought to be fair* given the meeting of the minds by the stage two thinkers. In this case, right is defined when the persons in question acts to meet their own interests and allow others to do the same. What is different from stage one thinkers is that a limited social perspective exists, but nevertheless individualism and egoism dominate their consciousness.

Exhibit 2.1. Kohlberg's Stages of Moral Development

Level One Preconventional	Stage One. Heterogamous Morality and Ego Centered. Stage Two. Exchange and Reciprocity Centered
Level Two Conventional	Stage Three. Mutual Interpersonal Conformity Stage Four. Social Conscious with a Social System Orientation
Level Three Postconventional	Stage Five. Social Contract, Utility, and Individual Rights Stage Six. Universal Ethical Principles

Source: Thomas and Cynthia Lynch based on Kohlberg, L. 1976.

Stage three is mutual interpersonal expectations, relationships, and interpersonal conformity. In other words, this stage is centered on mutually conforming relationships in the minds of these individuals. Living up to the expectations of others such as such family, war comrades, or professional peers defines what is right for stage three persons. The reason for doing right is a desire to *be considered a good person* in the eyes of others who are considered important. Thus, in this stage, there is a much larger social perspective than in stages one and two, but the dualism within the brain stem still prevails in stage three thinkers. This is a further expansion away from being egotistical and toward being altruistic, but the brain stem dualistic thinking explained in chapter 1 still remains as the assumption that defines the self.

Stage four is an even stronger social conscious orientation because these thinkers have adopted a clear understanding and acceptance of a social system's ethics. For them, fulfilling a sense of duty defines what is right. In this stage, there is the beginning of altruistic reasoning, where ethical rules or virtues are meaningful and rewards and punishment are less important. This person follows rules and laws based on their understanding of ethics flowing out of the non–brain stem portions of the brain. To them, right is *contributing to the larger society*, group, or institution. The reason to do right is to keep the institution going as a whole and to avoid a system breakdown. Their social perspective is to differentiate societal points of view from interpersonal agreements or motives. Thus, such persons have a holistic viewpoint of the entire system.

Stage five is a further expansion of altruistic thinking to the larger social contract, utility, and individual rights. These people feel those higher values are central to what they consider to be function and utility oriented. For these person, some universal values such as life and liberty can and should override a group's relative values. The reason for doing right is out of *a sense of obligation* to the law and especially the higher law (such as the nation's constitution). To them those laws are considered an implicit social contract and are contractual commitments between the individual and the larger group such as the nation. In this stage, individuals use a utilitarian calculation in their decisions. Their social perspective is the society and their decisions tend to be highly rational.

Stage six is universal ethical principles or theory, which are often addressed as a paradigm of thought. This is the highest degree of altruistic thinking and few exist at this level of moral development. Following a *self-chosen and created ethical theory* defines what is right. If they discover that the laws violate their theories, then they abandon the law and follow the logic of their theory. The reason for doing right is an overwhelming belief that there is a valid universal set of ethical theories to which they are deeply committed. The social perspective is a moral point of view reflecting belief that any reasoned person can recognize the nature of morality as they understand it.

Each of these stages of moral development has its advocates in philosophy (discussed in greater detail in chapter 4). For example, Hobbes was a stage one ego-centered thinker. Adam Smith, as normally understood, was a stage two reciprocity–centered thinker. Max Weber aligned with stage three, mutually conforming relationship centered; Karl Marx with stage four, social systems centered; John Stuart Mill with stage five; and Aristotle with stage six, universal theory centered.

Empirical Research

There is extensive empirical research on Kohlberg's theory of moral development and it has stood the test of time. As White (1999) describes, "it has endured and become a rare psychological and philosophic paradigm" (121). In 1971, James Rest and other researchers, following in Kohlberg's steps, designed the Defining Issues Test, which is an objective multiple choice instrument that enables researchers to use a quantifiable, standardized assessment to determine and predict moral judgment. Essentially, their research made moral maturity a continuous variable rather than a series of discrete stages. Rest supported Kohlberg's general theory that individuals mature morally through cognitive sequential moral development stages. The moral judgment scores are only structural in that they measure how people think. They do not and are not used to judge *what* people think (Rest, et al.1999).

If Kohlberg, Rest, and others are correct that people ethically develop and stop their development at various stages along the scale of six, what does that tell us about ethics in the context of public administration? In any public organization, we can anticipate that various individuals in the organization will fall at various points along the Kohlberg scale. Richard White (1999) tells us that various occupational groups tend to group together at different stages with public administration in the middle stages. We also know that because moral development is cognitive, individuals can increase their moral development scores overtime. In fact, training can increase moral development scores.

EMOTIONAL INTELLIGENCE

Daniel Goleman (1995) notes that grade point averages, intelligence quotient (IQ), and scholastic Aptitude Test (SAT) scores are not always good indicators of success in life largely because the brightest among us can "founder on the shoals of unbridled passions and unruly impulses" (34). For Goleman, emotional intelligence (EI) needs to be appreciated and used. EI is defined as the ability "to motivate oneself and persist in the face of frustrations; to control impulse and delay gratification; to regulate one's moods and keep distress from swamping the ability to think; to empathize and to hope" (Goleman 1995, 34). EI is addressed using virtue ethics training.

Goleman argues that professionals can measure EI using an emotional quotient (EQ) in a manner similar to the use of the IQ. He posits that at times EQ is more powerful than IQ in terms of assessing a person's ability to function in life. He also notes that educators may find it very hard to change a person's IQ, but changing a person's EQ can be accomplished by merely developing the emotional competencies of children and even adults. Higher EQ scores should correlate to a more positive outlook for individuals and the people they serve. (See chapter 7 for a further discussion of emotional intelligence.)

FRIEDRICH VERSUS FINER DEBATE

Another landmark debate in the public administration literature was between Carl Joachim Friedrich (1940) and Herman Finer (1941). They addressed two divergent views for the best approach to secure ethical behavior and administrative responsibility in the public sector. Friedrich comes from an altruistic perspective and Finer from an egoist perspective. In the twentieth century, the clear winner of this public debate was Finer, whose views dominated the practice of public administration and remain important today. He argued for adding strict outer controls (policies and procedures) to ensure ethical behavior, such as those associated with cash internal control, oversight, and proper accounting practices.

However, the use of these outer controls also results in important negative consequences such as the reduction of organizational productivity due to the added red tape and lowering unit moral because of frustration due to complex procedures. Using complex administrative and procedural measures does not always create noncorrupt organizations but they can be helpful in doing so. Often smart but less morally developed employees and even well-intentioned employees find ways to circumvent the outer controls such as standard operating procedures. Realistically, unethical leadership and subordinates can find clever ways of being unethical regardless of how many administrative and procedural measures are used.

Friedrich's views are more appropriate for public organizations that have strong "inner controls," meaning they have a strong sense of accomplishing the public interest. Friedrich (1940) noted that "we are becoming each other's servants" (20) in the common endeavor of operating our society. Friedrich's vision of achieving public accountability was not through enforcement but through eliciting the individual's inner wisdom (Lynch and Lynch 2014). In this sense, we should view "eliciting inner wisdom" as training the individual to have a series of "inner controls" that guide their actions and behavior.

Friedrich's approach envisions creating an altruistic consciousness where employees see themselves as part of their organization, which in turn is a part of the larger society. In other words, each person sees themselves as part of the larger oneness of society and the universe, including the environment. In Friedrich's vision, unconditional love is needed, or, at least as Robert Greenleaf describes (1996, 1997), there needs to be a desire to serve each other for the greater betterment of all. This perspective encourages a greater sense of ethical responsibility within the workforce. Those who doubt whether enough employees will ever exist in any organization with the necessary "inner controls" have an egocentric perspective and therefore they question Friedrich's entire vision and his advocacy of virtue ethics.

The "outer control" approach of Finer's creates an entirely different method to address corruption and policy control than Friedrich's inner control. Finer's approach is less about creating a positive motivation to be moral and more about making it difficult— with procedures—to be immoral. Finer's approach leads to ever-increasing external controls on individuals and more administrative units that manage, audit, and evaluate others in the organization. The result probably does decrease corruption and increase managerial control but it also lowers productivity by requiring what is commonly called "red tape," meaning more administrative approvals and the filling out of time-consuming forms and reports. Bailey understood the wisdom of using procedure but also recognized the paradox that it gives public administrators who wish both effectiveness and efficiency.

The Friedrich-Finer debate tells us that there is disagreement on how public organizations should confront the problems associated with ethics. The Friedrich approach agrees with Bailey that the key to ethics within a public organization is to focus on creating and achieving a positive public servant ethic among the individuals in the organization. The Finer approach also agrees with Bailey that stronger external organizational control structures and more accounting, auditing, inspections, and evaluations units can and do create positive ethical outcomes.

In the decades since the Friedrich-Finer debate, Finer's position has dominated the practice of public administration with increased use of organizational controls and larger accounting, auditing, inspection, and evaluation units. Friedrich's altruistic reforms, such as the ones suggested by Bailey and Appleby, have existed largely on the shelves of libraries and to some extent in the activities of government. The concept of virtue ethics was largely abandoned shortly after the debate and the use of rules and procedures to achieve ethical behavior have dominated the efforts to achieve greater morality in the public sector.

CAUSES OF UNETHICAL BEHAVIOR

In a 2017 article, Nicola Belle and Paola Cantarelli conducted a meta-analysis on the question: "What causes unethical behavior?" They looked at 137 experiments published in 73 articles to address their research question. They concluded the primary causes were social influences, greed,

---

Case Study: Edward Snowden's Leak of National Intelligence Material

Working for Booz Allen Hamilton, which had a defense contract with the National Security Agency (NSA), twenty-nine-year-old former technical assistant Edward Snowden caused the biggest intelligence leak in NSA's history. He disclosed numerous volumes of top secret documents to the public via the media. He was concerned that the U.S. government was "destroying privacy, internet freedom, and basic liberties for people around the world with this massive surveillance machine they're secretly building." For him, his actions were a matter of principle. He said, "The government has granted itself power it is not entitled to. There is no public oversight. The result is people like myself have the latitude to go further than they are allowed to." He believed that the value of the Internet and basic privacy was being rapidly destroyed by ubiquitous surveillance. According to *The Guardian* newspaper in Great Britain, Snowden will go down in history as one of America's most consequential whistleblowers, alongside Daniel Ellsberg and Bradley Manning.

Snowden said he was not acting out of self-interest but rather only out of principle. As a person without a high school diploma, he was earning roughly $200,000 per year, living with a girlfriend in Hawai'i, and had a stable career and a family he loved. He gave that up to first escape to Hong Kong and later to Russia where he still lives to avoid possible charges of treason in his home country.

QUESTIONS TO CONSIDER
1. How do principles get translated into ethics? Are all principles equal? When are principles a matter of ethics?

2. The highest level officials of the U.S. government said Snowden's actions clearly hurt American diplomacy and gave useful information to the nation's enemies. How does one balance, if it all, his principles versus the hurt he caused his family, his fellow workers, and his nation?

3. Compare and contrast Snowden's thoughts with those of Appleby and Bailey.

Source: Glenn Greenwald, Ewen MacAskill, and Laura Poitras.

egocentrism, self-justification, exposure to incremental dishonesty, loss aversion, overly challenging performance goals, and time pressure. The sets of unethical behaviors corresponded to Kohlberg's moral development stages one and three and, interestingly, also to Goleman's emotional intelligence. Stage one moral development occurs in those who are extremely egocentric. The largest number of unethical behaviors fall into this category. They include greed, egocentrism, self-justification, and some of loss aversion. Three sets of unethical behaviors correspond to stage three of moral development: social influence, exposure to incremental dishonesty, and some others in the loss-aversion set. In terms of emotional intelligence, two sets of unethical behaviors are possibly time pressure and challenging performance goals. Also, some in the latter set might also be in stage one and three of moral development.

Regardless of where each set of unethical behaviors occurs in terms of moral development and EI, training and administrative procedures can largely resolve the unethical behavior. EI training clearly helps to those who have behaved unethically due to time pressures and some of those who were unethical due challenging performance goals. The Finer and Friedrich solutions would help as well as virtue ethics training, which has been suggested for police detectives and patrol officers.

The largest set of unethical behaviors cited by Belle and Cantarelli can be best addressed in reforms suggested by Finer, but Friedrich's views should not be dismissed. If the government did not hire egocentric employees or helped egocentric employees morally develop themselves to at least stage four thinkers, then Friedrich's view would be better. The types of controls suggested by Finer are costly in terms of adding more staff to accomplish the administration of those expensive controls and such controls discourage a flexible administrative approach to public problems and having creativity in the workplace.

CONCLUSION

At the beginning of this chapter, Leon asked if ethics was an illusion or a myth.

There are attempts at ethics that are illusion and certainly not real in that they do not motivate employees to behave morally in the workplace. To more insightfully address Leon's question, one need only consider what happens in a society that has laws but no ethics (see chapter 3, Ethics, Corruption, and Administrative Evil). However, noting the negative effects of unethical behavior does not directly address Leon. Unfortunately, we also know that achieving positive motivation is a complex challenge, and there are too many situations where ethical attempts failed to create the desired ethical climate.

Is ethics important, especially in the public administration setting? Although they viewed it from different perspectives, Niccolo Machiavelli and Dean Paul H. Appleby saw the connection between ethics and democracy. Appleby would have probably agreed with Machiavelli that having virtuous citizens is necessary for the continued existence of a free state, which we call a democracy today. He would have disagreed with Machiavelli that democracy would necessarily fail as a system of government because eventually a social egocentric consciousness guarantees the failure of democracy.

The U.S. Constitution, as explained by James Madison in Federalist No. 10, adopted a checks-and-balances approach to counter the influence of private interest groups that Machiavelli thought would always doom a democracy. The checks-and-balances approach accepts that Machiavelli was correct that private interests would be at play in a democracy, but the constitutional checks and balances would "mill out" the dysfunctional private interests and result in a public interest.

Thus, founders like Franklin felt that maybe and hopefully Machiavelli got it wrong. Appleby and Bailey felt that part of making Machiavelli wrong was Democratic Morality, as it would further negate the likelihood that Machiavelli's prediction would occur.

If Leon and Machiavelli are correct, democracy is doomed. The authors of this book prefer to think Franklin, Appleby, and Bailey are correct. That is, the United States can continue to be a democracy, but it is not a certain outcome, as noted by Franklin. An important but insufficient means to avoid the Machiavelli outcome is to create a viable personal ethics within public administrators and a viable social ethics within the profession of public administration and the organizations they serve. In short, ethics needs to be made real and not be an illusion. Ethics is important in public administration for the continuation of democracy itself.

Is ethics important, especially in the public administration setting? Clearly, the answer is YES, but also clearly ethics has not been a topic of primary importance in public administration except to establish a large set of rules and regulations. Friedrich's type of reform needs to be pursued aggressively. This is not an argument against Finer, but rather an argument in favor of Friedrich. These two types of reforms are not mutually exclusive. Instead, they are symbiotic. Practitioners and academics should never consider selecting one reform approach over the other, but use them together to strength each other.

Educators and managers can create intervention strategies that can improve ethical thinking and moral behavior within public organizations. Bailey's suggestion of creating a set of public servant ethics is possible. In addition, there is a good possibility that once such ethics exist in the minds of many public servants in public organizations, then the Democratic Morality social ethic is reinforced and strongly influences behavior within that organization toward strengthening democracy as suggested by Appleby and Bailey.

REVIEW QUESTIONS

1. Compare and contrast Machiavelli and Appleby in terms of the concept of public interest. Why is this contrast important in the connection between ethics and democracy?

2. Why is the definition of ethics and morals used in this book useful in the context of public administration as a profession?

3. Why is the concept of Democratic Morality important to ethics in the world today?

4. Compare and contrast Appleby with Federalist 10.

5. In what way did Bailey build on Appleby? In what way is Bailey like Fredrick and Finer?

6. What are the four essential wisdoms and why is recognizing them important to ethics for the public service?

7. What is the paradox of procedures and why is it important to public administrators? How is this related to the Fredrick-Finer debate?

8. Explain why the character traits of optimism, courage, and fairness tempered by charity are important to those who work in the public service.

9. Why is the French-Ladd debate important to ethics in public administration as a profession?

REFERENCES

American Society for Public Administration. n.d. "ASPA's Code of Ethics." Accessed January 17, 2002. http://www.aspanet.org/ethics/coe.html.

Appleby, Paul H. 1952. *Morality and Administration in Democratic Government*. Baton Rouge, LA: Louisiana State University.

Appleby, Paul. H. 1965. "Public Administration and Democracy." In *Public Administration and Democracy*, edited by Roscoe C. Martin, 17–37. Syracuse, NY: Syracuse University Press.

"Aristotle: General Introduction." 2004. *Internet Encyclopedia of Philosophy*. Accessed June 24, 2017. http://www.utm.edu/research/iep/a/aristotl.htm.

Bailey, Stephen K. 1965. "Ethics and the Public Service." In *Public Administration and Democracy: Essays Honoring Paul H. Appleby*, edited by Roscoe C. Martin, 283–298. Syracuse, NY: Syracuse University Press.

Belle, Nicola, and Paola Cantarelli. 2017. "What Causes Unethical Behavior? A Meta-Analysis to Set an Agenda for Public Administration Research." *Public Administration Review* 77, no. 3: 327–339.

Cooper, Terry. 1988. *The Responsible Administrator: An Approach to Ethics for the Administrative Role*. San Francisco: Jossey-Bass.

Finer, Herman. 1941. "Administrative Responsibility in a Democratic Government." *Public Administration Review* 1, no. 1: 336–350.

French, Peter A. 1976. *Corporate Ethics*. Fort Worth, TX: Harcourt Brace.

French, Peter A. 1979. "The Corporation as a Moral Person." *American Philosophical Quarterly* 16, no. 3: 297–317.

Friedrich, Carl Joachim. 1940. "Public Policy and the Nature of Administrative Responsibility. In *Public Policy: A Yearbook of the Graduate School of Public Policy*, edited by C. J. Friedrich and Edward S. Mason, 3–24. Cambridge, MA: Harvard University Press.

Goleman, Daniel. 1995. *Emotional Intelligence*. New York: Bantam Books.

Greenwald, Ewen MacAskill, and Laura Poitras. 2013. "Edward Snowden: The Whistleblower behind the NSA Surveillance Revelations." *Guardian*, June 11. https://www.theguardian.com/world/2013/jun/09/edward-snowden-nsa-whistleblower-surveillance.

Hamilton, Alexander, James Madison, and John Jay. 1987. *Federalist Papers*. Edited by Isaac Kramnick. Penguin.

Jordon, Barbara. 1976. "Who Then Will Speak for the Common Good?" Democratic National Convention Keynote Address, July 12, New York, NY.

Jordon, Barbara. 1995. "Citizen Focus: Accountability in Government." *Managing for Results: Advancing the Art of Performance Measurement Conference*. November 1–3, 1995, Austin, Texas.

Kohlberg, L. 1976. "Moral Stages and Moralization: The Cognitive-Developmental Approach." In *Moral Development and Behavior: Theory, Research and Social Issues*, edited by T. Lickona, 31–53. New York: Holt, Rinehart and Winston.

Ladd, John. 1984. "Corporate Mythology and Individual Responsibility." *International Journal of Applied Philosophy* 2: 1–21.

Lynch, Cynthia E. and Thomas D. Lynch. 2014. "Public Sector Value and Virtue and the OECD." In *Value and Virtue in the Public Sector*, edited by Pan Suk Kim and Michael de Vries, 241–255. New York: Palgrave Macmillan.

Machiavelli, Niccolo. 1984. *The Prince*. New York: Bantam.

Martin, Roscoe, ed. 1965. *Public Administration and Democracy*. Syracuse, NY: Syracuse University Press.

Maslow, Abraham. 1970. *Motivation and Personality*. New York: Harper and Row.

McHenry, James. 1906. "Notes." *American Historical Review* 11.

Meyers, Christopher (1983). "The Corporation, Its Members and Moral Accountability." *Business and Professional Ethics* 3 (1) 33–44.

Rest, James, Darcia Narvaez, Muriel J. Bebeau, and Stephen J. Thoma. 1999. *Post Conventional Moral Thinking: A Neo-Koholbergian Approach*. Mahwah, NJ: Lawrence Erlbaum.

Siemaszko, Corky. 2016. "Kentucky Clerk Kim Davis, Who Refused to Issue Marriage Licenses to Gays, Seeks to End Case." *NBC News*, June 21. https://www.nbcnews.com/https://www.nbcnews.com/news/us-news/kentucky-clerk-kim-davis-who-refused-issue-marriage-licenses-gays-n596476.

Velasquez, Manuel G. 1983. "Why Corporations Are Not Morally Responsible for Anything They Do." *Business and Professional Ethics Journal* 3, no. 2: 1–18.

Werhane, Patricia M. 1989. "Corporate and Individual Moral Responsibility: A Reply to Jan Garrett." *Journal of Business Ethics* 8, no. 10: 821–22.

White, R. 1999. "Public Ethics, Moral Development and the Enduring Legacy of Lawrence Kohlberg." *Public Integrity* 2: 121–34.

3 Ethics, Corruption, and Administrative Evil

PROFESSOR: *Yes, Leon?*

LEON: *Isn't corruption just natural? How can you avoid something that is normal?*

According to Transparency International, many societies and regimes have some level of corruption but few are totally corrupt. Some societies, especially well-developed Western countries, are quite clever at hiding corruption, allowing it to exist at a near legal or even legal status (Kobrak 2002). One example of legalized corruption is the "buying" of politicians by private interest groups. Sometimes successful corrupt elements win over the public by arguing that their private interest group provides the society with a valuable, indispensable service. For example, gun manufacturers and the National Rifle Association have successfully argued that the sale of guns with few regulations is indispensable to the American public.

Those causing harm often successfully argue that government regulation addressed to such concerns—such as global warming on the coal or oil burning plants to produce electricity or financial controls on the banking industry—are an inappropriate limitation on their rights in a democratic society. In some countries, corruption against the public interest is less subtle. Private interests simply offer cash bribes and in extreme cases perform violent acts to suppress anyone considered by them to be an obstacle or even "traitors."

THE CHALLENGE OF CORRUPTION

According to Webster's dictionary, "corruption" is the impairment of integrity, virtue, or moral principle. Thus, corruption can be simply breaking the law, but it is also a broader concept. For example, if a law can require every citizen in a country to eat eggplant on the third day of each week, then not eating eggplant on Wednesday is not corrupt but it is illegal. Another example is a law that allows corporations to donate an unlimited amount of money to political campaigns to ensure that the politicians they support vote in favor of the corporation's economic interests. In the latter example, campaign donations buy political influence for the corporation's material gain. This is completely legal, but that donation is corrupt because it impairs the integrity of the politician and the ability to do the will of the people he or she is elected to represent.

Why is corruption so appealing? Certainly, one reason is it often does lead to desired riches, fame, and power for those who engage in it. For the hedonists in the world, corruption can and does lead to sought-after riches. Second, corruption can satisfy the "deficit needs" and maybe even some of the "being needs" from Abraham Maslow's (1970) hierarchy of needs that was discussed in chapter 2.

Greed and deprivation are indeed great motivators, but sometimes the material and moral poverty in the whole society creates a strong incentive and even a fertile environment in which public officials and administrators turn a "blind eye" or become "morally mute" on unethical behaviors. Sometimes the prevailing social ethics and values of the culture reward excesses and preach self-advancement regardless of the cost to others, the larger society, and the environment. For cultures that value materialism, corruption is an acceptable means to an end for success "just as long as you don't get caught." In cultures where corruption is routinized, individuals easily rationalize, justify, and even legitimize it in their minds as something that has always existed and will always exist—much like Leon has at the beginning of this chapter. To them, it is simply the way business gets done and not being corrupt under the circumstances would put the individual or corporation at a competitive disadvantage and therefore it would appear to them to be entirely foolish for the individual or corporation not to be corrupt.

In some extreme cases, even legal punishment and the society's condemnation does not seem to be able to curb certain enterprises such as selling illegal drugs and participating in human trafficking, including slavery. Major factors that contribute to a pervasive culture of corruption is a lack of institutional enforcement of laws and rules. Kohlberg (1976) tells us that we can, but will not necessarily, cognitively grow in our moral development. For people who stay in the early stages of moral development, the real threat of punishment might motivate them to behave morally. Thus, a country's legal system must use forms of punishment for that set of people in order create a society of minimum levels of corruption.

If the police or judicial system do not apprehend the offenders and incarcerate or fine them, then corruption and other immoral acts become commonplace and eventually the "civil" in a civil society disappears. Typically, individual corruption is not the result of ignorance of laws and rules, but rather the result of a people, who lack sufficient will, fortitude, stamina, resolution, and persistence to confront their own and society's moral problems. Persistent and consistent corruption in a society damages and will eventually destroy the society's economic and social cohesion.

CORRUPTION AND GOVERNANCE

With public office comes power and the temptation to use power for personal advantage or gain. We find many examples of this throughout history from the ancient Chinese rulers, Hebrew kings, and Roman emperors to contemporary American presidents and legislators. Lord Acton captured this reality with his famous saying: "Power tends to corrupt and absolute power corrupts absolutely" (Payne 1975, 179). In attempts to develop a corruption-free society, there is some good news; it can be reduced and contained. But the bad news is that it is not likely to be eliminated, especially if the leadership of a country is corrupt.

Corruption exists because of the very nature and weakness of the human character. It is also due to a lack of awareness or consciousness, as discussed in chapter 1. Thus, if people are egocentric, they will not be able to even recognize their corruption as a problem and therefore it is very likely to continue until some external crisis forces action. Typical anticorruption reforms seek to establish effective legal safeguards to discourage it, lessen its occurrences, and reduce its scope. When those reforms occur in areas with a selfless consciousness and integrity, population reforms are more likely to be successful.

Over the centuries, the ancient Egyptians virtue ethics, the Code of Hammurabi, Mosaic Law, and Confucian principles were among the salient codes of conduct that defined what was acceptable official behavior for a society (Caiden, Dwivedi, and Jabbra 2001). Typically, such wisdom statements say that only the best individuals in the society should hold public office—meaning only those who are most righteous, the wisest, have the highest character and are the most highly dependable. Those ancient wisdom statements say public leaders should set an example for others with their high standards of performance, their championship of the public interest, and their compassion for all people. Such leaders should be wise, just, and sensitive. They should protect and safeguard public property as a sacred trust and be accountable for their actions to the public. This wisdom argues that there is a noble honor to promote and serve the public good (Caiden et al. 2001). In every century of human history, those wisdom statements or words like them are heard by some, but they also fall on deaf ears. Certainly, that is true in the twenty-first century.

CORRUPTION AND PERSONAL GAIN

One significant type of corruption in public organizations is intentional deviation from accepted ethical practices for personal gain. This can include bribery, nepotism, misappropriation, and granting favors to private interests over public concerns. These types of behaviors have two enormous impacts on the society. First, they lessen the effectiveness of the public service and lower the credibility of public institutions and status of public officials. Second, they lead to a breakdown in society by increasing factional interests, which sometimes results in a greater use of coercion instead of consensus to achieve a desired government objective. This type of corruption tends to be contagious and economic scarcity often encourages it.

Corruption exists throughout the world but it varies in intensity from nation to nation and sometimes even from region to region within a country. It has also varied from one era to other. Prior to American independence, several colonial governors were corrupt. Their actions created a desire in the Founding Fathers at the beginning of the republic to minimize the concentration of government power. They hoped that by making policy change difficult—requiring two chambers of the legislature to pass legislation, giving the executive veto power over legislation, and separating the branches of government—there would be less corruption. Those reforms, at the beginning of the republic, made the occurrence of corruption more difficult while making the prosecution of corruption easier.

However, despite those early efforts, the first major national scandal occurred within six years of the signing of the U.S. Constitution. The Yazoo land fraud involved forty million acres in the southern states including Alabama and Mississippi. The perpetrators of that corruption included two U.S. Senators, two Representatives, a Supreme Court Justice, and most of the Georgia legislature ("Yazoo Land Fraud" 2017). Corruption continues in America today, but often in a much subtler in form. For example, in the early twenty-first century, there were several noncompetitive contracts between then Vice President Richard Cheney's former company (Haliburton) in which the contract work was remarkably overpriced. Those contracts involved supplying the U.S. Army during the second Iraq War and the reconstruction of Iraq (Rosenbaum 2004).

A WORLD OF CORRUPTION

As economic commerce and relationships become more and more globalized, the impact of corruption in one part in the world has a direct impact on the rest of the world. International trade takes goods manufactured in one country and sells them in other countries, usually to the benefit of consumers unless corruption reduces that benefit. For example, an importer might be able to import goods into his or her country at a significantly lower cost than the country can produce those goods themselves. The cheaper availability of those goods upgrades the quality of life for the people of that country.

However, if the port director and police officials of the country are corrupt and demand bribes for doing their jobs of unloading the shipments and protecting the port, the cost of those goods will increase. Or the corrupt officials can entirely prevent the goods from entering the country. Both results negatively impact consumers and reduce their quality of life because they cannot access the goods at the optimal price or in some cases not at all. It also hurts the trade possibilities of the exporting country.

CENTRAL AND EASTERN EUROPE

Russia and other former Soviet Union countries experienced considerable corruption in the 1990s as well as in the new millennium (Friedman 2012). The public recognition of the problem and the strong anticorruption efforts of the Organisation of Economic Co-operation and Development (OECD) and other world organizations helped the Eastern European countries lessen their corruption problem, but with limited success. There are many cultural causes that contribute to unethical behavior in that part of the world.

For example, in Kyrgyzstan, public employment appointments are made on the basis of tribal relations, a form of cronyism, rather than using the merit and capability of individuals as the criteria for employment. The shift toward a democratic capitalist system from a communist party system, which involved strict controls, created civil uncertainty in Kyrgyzstan and in other former Soviet Union countries. The uprooted previous bureaucratic control mechanisms and the selling of public enterprises to private companies created an environment that was essentially wholesale corruption. Moving to a more capitalist economic system allowed the countries' new leaders to reward tribal loyalty, which encouraged corrupt behavior such as extra judicial violence, cronyism, and nepotism (Freedom House 2017a).

A major change in society, such as moving from one economic system to another, is often a social environmental opportunity for widespread corruption. In the previous example, the opportunity was created by moving from a communist system to a somewhat democratic free enterprise system. In this example, eliminating tribal controls was a major change that led to widespread corruption. In Central and Eastern Europe, contemporary negative factors that foster corruption are modernization and globalization coupled with changing from a totally socialist to a capitalist system.

Rapid modernization industrialized urban centers but limited the social control of the once rural agrarian societies. Limited social control in the expanding urban centers fostered greater opportunities for corruption as the previous tribal controls no longer prevailed in the changing social and political setting. Positive social ethics for a new civil society did not develop at the same rate as the negative consequences of fast modernization. This spread and increased corruption handicapped many countries in their attempts to catch up with the Western economy.

Often, democratization means that government jobs are no longer controlled by a civil service authority with job security and high social standing. Instead of experienced civil servants performing the work of government, hiring and firing are based on family blood lines, tribal connections, or political affiliations. The concept of a professional civil service and its commitment to the abstract notion of "public interest" is lost. As the public service's essential ethic is undermined, there is greater likelihood that civil servants will use their positions for personal gain, such as demanding money from the public for performing or not performing the normal government functions that should be a part of their job description. As noted in chapter 2, Appleby's Democratic Morality would consider this to be bribery and make the development of positive social ethics impossible to create without remarkable political reform from the highest levels within the country.

A twofold relationship exists between democratization and public administration reform. A viable democracy needs a well-functioning state with an effective bureaucracy to implement the decisions of the elected government. As demonstrated by Central and Eastern European nations, new and rapid democratization can weaken a society and cause dysfunction, making it difficult to create a positive social ethics. Such conditions create a moral wasteland for civil servants with little to prevent and much to encourage their corruption.

The incomplete market reforms of Eastern Europe created monopolistic structures that gave government officials opportunities for discretionary decisions and increased preexisting corruption. For example, in the Ukraine, after the fall of the Soviet Union, a firm owner spent 30 to 40 percent of his or her time dealing with public officials due to the multitude of required state regulations and licenses plus high taxes required to operate a business in the Ukraine. The result was extensive "bargaining," often in the form of bribes, to reduce the burdens of regulations, licenses, and high taxes. Eventually, these conditions lead to a rebellion that overthrew the existing government followed by a successful Russian invasion in the eastern part of Ukraine (Freedom House 2017b).

THE MIDDLE EAST

Between colonial independence and the Arab Spring rebellions of 2010, there was an increase in the size and importance of government bureaucracy accompanied by an increase in the importance of civil service in many countries in the Middle East. This condition increased the opportunities for corruption, unethical conduct, and misuse of public office for personal profit. The overcentralization of structure and the overconcentration of authority established a bureaucratic nightmare with crowded offices where civil servants accomplished little of substance. The result was an unsystematic flow of information, poor coordination, lack of comprehensive planning, difficulty of control and supervision, red tape, and gross inefficiency. Such a social environment encouraged influence peddling, corruption, and eventually revolts. In this area of the world, family loyalty is also important resulting in nepotism and family favoritism (Gumede 2012).

After World War I, the winning European nations created the countries of the Middle East from the remains of the Ottoman Empire. To create national and regional peace and reasonable prosperity in the region, the Europeans created many of the current nations of the Middle East based on their own geopolitical needs of the moment rather than on the tribal and religious realities of the region. Little effort was put into nation building and as a result the national identity of these new nations was weak, with people reduced to seeking protection from powerful patron families rather than the state. Such a social environment encouraged patronage, influence selling, corruption, and other unethical conduct (Zughayar 2014).

For example, in the Arab Republic of Yemen, officials and business people operated their own market mechanism to circumvent government import restrictions, price controls, and the sales of food and other commodities that at the time were established as state-owned companies. They did this to offset private sector exploitation, but their actions hindered the government's efforts to deal with the national economic problems and thus civil war broke out (Dbwan 2014).

AFRICA

In many African countries, the struggle with corruption is a result of failed states, whose political or economic systems have become so weak that the government is no longer in control. Petty corruption of a universal nature by individual civil servants is particularly present in West Africa, but more significant is the systemic corruption that occurs at the highest levels of government. When state leadership pursues private rather than public interests, the result is institutionalized corruption. Sometimes direct anticorruption activities are not effective in combating systematic corruption because the leadership of the government itself creates the corruption. In addition, new emerging regimes devote inadequate resources to deal with corruption and do not have strong enough institutional leadership to promote the necessary positive ethical behavior within the institution (Atuobi 2007).

The most effective anticorruption practices are those linked with other reforms such as democratization, decentralization, and public sector reforms. Without developing effective local government systems, the negative social ethical culture of graft persists. The likely first step to anticorruption lies in developing effective community level systems of accountability that are backed by state leaders and state institutions committed to public rather than private interests.

Of great concern in the past decades in the regions of the Middle East and North Africa are the increasing number of stateless nations. The Arab Spring of 2010 did not go well for many countries such as Egypt, Tunisia, and Libya. In fact, they have fewer freedoms now than when the Marches for Democracy began. Endless wars, drought-related climate change, famine, and pandemic viruses have also taken a toll on this part of the world. For long periods of time, Somalia, Congo, Libya, Syria, Liberia, and others have lacked functioning governments. Others like Rwanda have fledgling governments that need assistance over time until they are strong enough to maintain a state. Stateless countries are not only ripe environments for corruption, they are also safe havens for violent organizations to do even more damage by terrorizing the local population and harboring safe zones for pirates and international terrorists (Abd-El-Hafez 2015).

Asia

In Asia, corrupt practices vary, from Singapore, which has very little corruption, to China, which struggles with serious corruption problems. Singapore changed from a seriously corrupt society in the 1950s and 1960s to being one of the least corrupt by the turn of the century largely due to strong political leadership. In 1959, the People's Action Party came to power and by 1960 introduced a comprehensive anticorruption strategy. Not categorized as a democratic government, the leadership strengthened the existing anticorruption laws by decree to reduce the opportunities for corruption and increased the penalties for offences. These measures created a deep mind-set in the whole population that supported the "public good."

The key anticorruption agency in Singapore is the Corruption Practices Investigation Bureau (CPIB). A small staff of seventy-one persons includes forty-nine investigators. The unit receives and investigates complaints of corruption in both the public and private sectors and scrutinizes malpractice and misconduct by public officials. In addition, it examines the practices and procedures in the civil service to minimize opportunities for corrupt activity. The CPIB reports directly to the prime minister and its legal powers enable it to obtain the required cooperation from both public and private organizations (Salleh 2017).

Places like Singapore and to a lesser extent Hong Kong demonstrate that reformers can minimize corruption when political leaders are sincerely committed to the task and they implement comprehensive anticorruption measures impartially, regardless of the form of governance in the country. Minimizing corruption is necessary, but it is an insufficient precondition of good governance. Of note is that the extent of corruption is inversely related to the quality of governance. Anticorruption agencies, which have highly capable staff, need independence from political leadership while also having strong support of the nation's top leaders in order to maintain their integrity. A focus on the public rather than the private interest is essential in establishing a strong public interest attitude that demands good ethical practices throughout the society and culture. The government must provide the support for anticorruption policies from the top while strongly encouraging the same support throughout the society.

China is the most populous nation in the world with an economy that is likely to soon surpass that of the United States. Most of its remarkable economic boom occurred in the late twentieth and early twenty-first centuries by moving away from a strong socialist economic system to free enterprise. The country kept its communist political system, but remarkable economic reforms opened opportunities to massive corruption. Clearly, the Chinese Communist Party can take credit for economic success that greatly improved the Chinese economy and the standard of living of its people. However, it must also take the blame for the very large boom in corruption.

"Bean curd" projects in China are construction efforts that result in engineering accomplishments that easily fall apart soon after the public officials construct them. Unfortunately, they exist in China on a grand scale, with new bridges, roads, dikes, buildings, and dams collapsing all over the country due to shoddy work, improper use of materials, poor engineering designs, and corruption.

For example, engineers used mud rather than concrete when building dikes and weak foundations meant that new buildings fell apart soon after completion (Hays 2008).

This particular type of corruption in China is also found in places such as Eastern Europe. Public officials give contracts to relatives or friends of the local communist party bosses where the project is to be built. They, in turn, subcontract the job to inefficient state-run firms that divert resources to their own private self-serving projects. For example, the Chinese National Audit Office noted that the Three Gorges Dam set aside around 279 million yuan (USD 45.5 million) for the relocation of persons due to the dam and that money was misused or misappropriated. The country's leadership recognized the problem but it was not able to effectively confront this endemic corruption and its virulent underground economy (Adams and Balfour 1998). More recently (2012) under the leadership of Secretary General Xi Jinping, a comprehensive anti-corruption campaign was launched to crack down on what he called the "tigers and flies," which is a reference to high-level officials and local government employees (*The Economist*, 2015).

LATIN AMERICA

The Iberian capitals of Madrid and Lisbon ruled Central and South American until the early eighteenth century. European conflicts, such as Napoleon's invasion of the Iberian Peninsula (Portugal in 1807 and Spain in 1808) kept both countries involved in home front wars and thus distracted them from controlling their own colonies and permitted Latin American independence. For example, Venezuela won independence in 1811, Chile in 1818, Peru in 1821, Mexico in 1821, Brazil in 1822, and Ecuador in 1822. In addition, the 1823 Monroe Doctrine of the new United States strongly discouraged European military influence in South and Latin America.

A patrimonial legacy largely explains Latin America's corruption. Unlike revolutions based on liberty, equality, and civil rights, Latin American liberation left in place the property and privileges of the landed oligarchy that originated in Spain and Portugal, who had profited from colonialism. From this, the political systems evolved into autocratic republics rather than popular democracies. Government jobs resulted from loyalty to the current patrimonial powers and not to the notion of public interest. The state administrative culture, which dominates the society, reflects aristocratic values with the education of this class focused on socialization to those values rather than acquiring managerial, technical, or clerical skills. These conditions combined with economic realities fostered a culture of corruption that reformers can only address with significant attitudinal and value changes.

Mexico has a long history of elections being "fixed" by the Partido Revolucionario Institucional (PRI) political party. For decades in the twentieth century, the PRI won almost 100 percent of all votes. The party deployed the police, the army, and other powerful forces to achieve their political results. They succeeded by physical seizures of voting booths, buying votes, multiple voting by PRI supporters, intimidation, harassment, and hindering the opposition by preventing their meetings and even their voting. The 2000 movement to a true two-party system with the election of new leaders like President Vicente Fox significantly altered politics in Mexico. However, the decades-long drug war has compounded the challenged Mexican democracy. In President Fox's 2007 book, *Revolution of Hope: The Life, Faith, and Dreams of a Mexican President*, he notes that his immediate predecessor, President Ernesto Zedillo, was the first Mexican president who did not steal his country's resources in his final year in office. As evidence of this, he pointed out that both he and Zedillo have had to continue to work since they left office and neither man was exiled from the county (Fox and Allyn 2007).

DEMOCRACIES

Corruption severely damages the credibility of government in general, the people's confidence in democracy, and the creditability of the government's leaders. This is a problem in newly emerging democracies as well as those that are more established. By definition, emerging democracies have little to no experience with democracy and any setbacks due to corruption give ammunition to antidemocratic forces that wish to return to the "good old days" that had less publicized corruption. Reformers realize that corruption existed before current attempts to establish democracy but that the cast of villains changes. Unfortunately, law and order can collapse, as crime radically increases with newly created underground wealth. Given that history is often overlooked, people in new democracies do not realize that established democracies went through similar periods of corruption, such as the United States in the early 1800s to the mid-1900s.

In established democracies, corruption exists but may be localized; however, vast problems such as epidemic drug addiction or a national disaster can foster corruption on a national and international scale. The simpler forms of corruption common in other regions of the world exist but typically involve fewer people. For example, in Louisiana in 1996, the Federal Bureau of Investigation (FBI) learned of a payoff scheme involving then Louisiana Governor Edwin Edwards and Bobby Guidry, a tugboat owner and regular guest at the governor's mansion for the governor's Thursday night poker game. As a result of a payoff for a gambling debt, Guidry won a riverboat casino license from the governor's riverboat casino board. The federal court convicted Governor Edwards on sixteen counts of money laundering related to the Guidry payoff (Gott 2000).

Established democracies, such as the United States, are more likely to exhibit more sophisticated forms of corruption such as kleptocracy, which is viewing public resources as private spoils. Private interests request funds from public officials in the hope of using public resources for their personal or corporate benefit. For example, corporations can and do ask politicians for tax relief that excludes them from paying all or a major portion of their taxes. The result is the many extremely wealthy Americans pay little or no taxes and the burden of the nation's taxation falls on the middle class.

Another example of kleptocracy is when a state or local government wishes to attract a major manufacturing company to relocate a plant or factory to their area. The company will shop around from state to state looking for the best deal and leveraging one state against the others to get the best bargain. Often, governors and state legislatures will offer the company many incentives to choose their state. Benefits include decades of tax exemptions on manufactured items, giving the land to the company as a gift, or offering a share in the construction fees in a public-private agreement. Typically, the rationale for public gifts to a private company is that this new company will create jobs for the local economy, but often the jobs are few in number while lost taxes and public expenditures are great.

Another example of legal corruption often used in the western United States, such as Washington, Idaho, Wyoming, Nevada, Montana, Utah, New Mexico, and Oregon, is for private companies to ask the federal government to give multimillion-dollar deals in reduced fees to access public grazing land for ranchers or forests for loggers. In these cases, timber companies get the logging rights to trees on public lands or corporate ranchers get land leases for grazing their animals on public lands well below market value. In Nevada and other states, the federal government gets nothing for minerals such as gold found on federal land. The result is higher corporate profit margins and often the abuse of public lands.

Whether or not kleptocracy is legal or illegal, it is all corrupt. In more sophisticated democracies, supporters of kleptocracy cleverly sell these sweetheart deals to politicians by hiding the negative side of this form of corruption, overstressing the public value of the legislation, and giving significant campaign contributions to the correct influential members of Congress. Legal corruption occurs when the language of the law is changed by politicians to benefit key private interest group that have invested in those politicians. In some situations, congressional committees have asked representatives of a key interest group to join them in writing legislation. Exhibit 3.1 is one example of that type of legal corruption.

Exhibit 3.1. Political Revolving Door: Congressman to Lobbyist

From 1980 to 2005, Wilbert Joseph (Billy) Tauzin II was a U.S. Congressman. From 2001 until 2004, he was Chairman of the Energy and Commerce Committee, which had oversight of the drug industry. In the final days of his chairmanship, he played a key role in shepherding the Medical Prescription Drug Bill through Congress, which prohibited the government from negotiating lower drug prices and banned the importation of identical, cheaper, drugs from Canada and elsewhere. In the days after his term in Congress ended, he became the head of Pharmaceutical Research and Manufacturers of America, which is a powerful trade group for pharmaceutical companies. His annual salary was two million dollars.

Source: Dan Eggen, "Billy Tauzin, Key Player in Health-Care Push, Leaving PhRMA," *Washington Post,* February 13, 2010.

Public interest groups, funded by drug companies, legally provide congressional members with large sums of money in campaign contributions for years, which the politicians can spend as they wish. The interest group's contributions are legal if the corporation adheres to campaign finance law, but this action nevertheless allows for and even encourages the legal existence of corporate corruption that harms the public good. In their defense, corporations argue that there is no such thing as "public good" or "public interest" and therefore the very existence of something called kleptocracy is nonsense. They also argue that an act of Congress can simultaneously benefit a private interest while still being for the public good that they before argued did not exist. Sorting out whether an act of Congress was motivated solely or substantially for private interests to the disadvantage of the public good can be difficult and that is why kleptocracy is such a difficult ethical problem to address.

Clearly, this ethical challenge is seriously compounded when there is no limit to corporate giving to campaign financing. Thus, gaining larger profits motivates private interest groups, and they use kleptocracy to buy American politicians legally. Given the personal benefit to politicians and private interest groups, the likelihood of an effective reform to stop this form of corruption is slim to none.

Only if the electorate rebels at the ballot box will this from of corruption stop. The electorate must decide that the wealthiest individuals, who are capturing the major portion of the nation's wealth, are engaging in corrupt practices to the disadvantage of the public interest (Kobrak 2002).

The subject of legal corruption needs to go beyond kleptocracy to include inappropriate use of administrative discretion (see Exhibit 3.2, for example). In an attempt to mirror the private sector, governments use bonuses to reward excellent employee performance, but those programs can easily be corrupted. Other examples of "legal" corruption include racial profiling, in which police target people due to their race, or communities providing fewer municipal services in minority neighborhoods.

Exhibit 3.2. Bonus Pay for Poor Performance

The U.S. Department of Veterans Affairs uses a bonus system to reward outstanding work, but that objective is questionable given its actual implementation. For example, a former top VA official in Ohio was given a bonus the same day he received notice that he was going to be fired and subsequently retired. More than 300 senior executives received $3.3 million in bonuses for an average of $10,000 each. More than half the agency received a bonuses that was 20 percent higher than that of the previous year. Rep. Jeff Miller, chair of the House Committee on Veterans Affairs said, "Whether it's shuffling problem employees from one location to another instead of disciplining them or repeatedly paying out bonuses with reckless abandon, VA's habit of coddling those who can't or won't do their jobs is as well documented as it is disgraceful."

Source: Bill Theobald, "More Bonuses for VA Employees Despite Ongoing Problems at the Agency," *USA Today*, October 28, 2016.

INTERNATIONAL ANTICORRUPTION EFFORTS

Caiden, Dwivedi, and Jabbra (2001) noted that "corruption hollows out governance just like termites weaken wood" (245) and that in the last quarter of the twentieth century corruption spread to places once thought to be immune. Fortunately, in reaction to the spreading and increasing infestation, the international community finally broke the social taboo of not discussing corruption openly. By 1996, the trickle of concern about corruption turned into a flood resulting in numerous agreements, conventions, declarations, and resolutions of international agencies on ethics. However, like any other flood, when the water recedes underlying damage remains. Corruption causes failed states, sometimes failed revolts, and remarkable hardship for the citizens of those states.

TRANSPARENCY INTERNATIONAL

Transparency International (TI) is a transnational nongovernmental organization founded in 1993 to expose and thus discourage worldwide corruption. Its fundamental assumption is the simple thesis that corruption cannot survive if there is an open awareness of its existence. In the remarkably short period of its first ten years, the organization grew to eighty national chapters.

TI publishes an influential corruption score card that shapes public opinion largely by publicly shaming leaders around the world, forcing them to address their corrupt practices. Its most impressive tools are its transparency indexes, which are national rankings that comparatively assess corruption in its various manifestations.

The publication and wide distribution of the indexes influence the behavior of decision makers often in ways that reduce corruption. TI effectively focuses on citizen empowerment through active participation within the nation. It uses insider insight from local chapters to suggest and develop adaptive, tailor-made anticorruption strategies that typically offer more carrots than sticks. Rather than confrontation, TI stresses diplomacy and the use of a combination of local and global perspectives.

TI also asserts that the role of civil society was the missing factor in previous efforts to curb corruption. Those efforts focused on solutions imposed by governmental or international agencies. TI's training and development work seeks to empower the authority of civil society often with an emphasis on the general public's aspiration for improved ethics. TI believes that chronic, collective shame and disappointment is a strong motivation for reform. Their specialists assure that leaders of public systems can run for office more ethically and fulfill their public roles more effectively under the bright lights of public scrutiny.

THE UNITED NATIONS

Many think of ethics only terms of corruption, but human rights are an equally important component. At the very founding of the United Nations in 1948, it voted on and created the Universal Declaration of Human Rights, which addressed that aspect of ethics. In the 1990s, the UN led a large anticorruption campaign that stressed the urgency of restoring and reinforcing ethical values in the professional public service by enhancing the role, image, performance, and professionalism of the civil service. The UN believes that the use of sanctions imposed against rule violators alone do not produce the desired results. In fact, the rule approach often creates other serious problems, such as lowering morale and creating inflexibility in government administrations, as they attempt to deal with complex public policy problems in society. An important step in fighting corruption internationally was the adoption of a Code of Ethics for Public Officials under the UN's 1996 Resolution 51/57 titled "Action Against Corruption."

In 1997, the UN's General Assembly called for action against corruption and created the United Nations Development Programme (UNDP) to do just that. The UNDP Global Anti-Corruption for Development Effectiveness program from 2008 to 2013 was followed by the UNDP Global Anti-Corruption Initiative from 2014 to 2017. The UNDP Program for Accountability and Transparency aimed at building and strengthening capacities of financial management and accountability systems in the tradition of Herman Finer (see chapter 2). In 2007, the UN changed the program to the UN Transparency and Accountability Initiative, which stresses the following purposes in member nations:

- Availability of internal audits and other reports.

- Public access to all relevant documentation related to operations and activities including budget information and procurement activities.

- "Whistle-blower Protection" policies.

- Financial disclosure policies.

- An effective Ethics Office.

- Independence of the respective internal oversight bodies.

- Adoption of international accounting standards in funds and programs.

- Transparent administrative support costs for voluntarily funded activities.

    Since then, there have been additional iterations of the program.

ORGANIZATION OF AMERICAN STATES

Around the world, ethics is considered part of good governance and essential for regional and national sustainable development. Essentially, there is a widespread urgent need to bring integrity into public life. For example, the 1996 Inter-American Convention Against Corruption said that the purpose of the Organization of American States was to promote and strengthen the development of the mechanisms needed to prevent, detect, punish, and eradicate corruption. In addition, that effort was to promote, facilitate, and regulate cooperation among the states to prevent, detect, punish, and eradicate corruption in the performance of public functions.

International institutions and national leaders see the wisdom of codifying and making illegal their more serious corrupt practices. Many nations of the world have taken other positive steps including the widespread overhaul and reform of legal and judicial systems, installation and implementation of professional education and training on ethics, creating of extra-legal arrangements such as special prosecutors, and new legal and investigatory tools such as inspector generals, establishment of novel information-gathering protocols such as hotlines and protection of whistle-blowers, and increasing focus on and even attacking organized crime.

Of particular importance to deontological (rule-based) ethics is the Caiden and Dwivedi statement (2001) that no amount of laws, codes of conduct, and threats can force public officials to behave ethically. The ultimate answer *must* include a virtue ethics approach, which focuses on creating the correct mind-set in the public officials. They argue that public officials must see government as a public trust and the public service as a professional vocation. In the words of the authors: "Morality requires self-discipline, humility, and resistance to the arrogance that can come with holding a public office. It enables people to center their values upon notions of a cosmic ordinance and a divine law that must be maintained. Spirituality serves both as a model and operative strategy for the transformation of human character by strengthening the genuine and substantive will to serve the common people" (Caiden et al. 2001, 253).

ORGANISATION FOR ECONOMIC AND CO-OPERATION DEVELOPMENT (OECD)

The OECD is an international organization of thirty member nations plus some nonmember states. Its thirty member democracies represent 70 percent of the global markets, 59 percent of the world's GDP, 95 percent of the world's development assistance, and consume over half of the world's energy. However, its members represent only 18 percent of the world population. The organization is an outgrowth of the post–World War II Marshall Plan for the reconstruction of Europe. OECD was organized in 1961with the vision "to build strong economies in member countries, improve efficiency, hone market systems, expand free trade and contribute to the development in industrialized as well as development countries" (2009). Part of that mandate involved addressing the problem of corruption.

For many years, the department responsible for researching and developing programs for the civil service was the public management service known as PUMA. It was responsible for helping member countries achieve high standards of effective and good governance, analyzing how governments manage the public sector, improving service delivery and making policy implementation more coherent, and developing recommendations for best practices (OECD 2002). PUMA produced several important recommendations on ethics in public management including Public Management Occasional Paper No. 14, "Ethics in the Public Service: Current Issues and Practices" (1996), and Public Management Brief No. 4, "Principles for Managing Ethics in the Public Service" (1998). Their recommendations used a rule-based policy approach to attaining transparency, avoiding conflicts of interest, antibribery, anticorruption, and the fight against money laundering.

ADMINISTRATIVE EVIL

THE EICHMANN DEFENSE

In the foreword to *Unmasking Administrative Evil* by Guy B. Adams and Danny L. Balfour, Curtis Ventriss presented a story about Hannah Arendt, who attended the famous trial of the Nazi war criminal Adolf Eichmann. At the trial, she sat in the back of the room and heard Eichmann repeatedly claim that he was also sickened by the Third Reich concentration camps that carried out the mass murder of so many Jews. In an almost eerie calmness in his bulletproof glass case, he reiterated that he had nothing personal against the Jews and then admitted that he organized with remarkable administrative care the deportation of hundreds of thousands of people to their deaths. He claimed that on visiting those camps that they were repugnant to him, but that he never let those feelings interfere with the administrative duties that the Third Reich commanded him to do. In other words, he was just following orders like any other soldier.

Of note is that Eichmann invoked Immanuel Kant's famous deontological categorical imperative (see Kant in chapter 5 on contemporary ethics) to justify his behavior. His argument was that if he had disobeyed these administrative orders, then every soldier (from any army) would have the right, if not the obligation, to disobey any order found to be personally objectionable. The trial took place in 1961. In 1992, Thomas Lynch, one of authors of this book, was in Beijing after the famous 1989 tragedy at Tiananmen Square in which Chinese troops killed protesters, most of whom were college students. In a presentation to the political science department at the elite Peking University and in response to a critical observation about the tragedy, a PhD student in the audience used Eichmann's same argument to justify the action of the Chinese army at Tiananmen Square.

Clearly, this student and others find this argument persuasive, even rational. In making his case, the student said, "Surely, the American army would not permit such disobedience." Lynch answered by saying that the U.S. Army does allow such disobedience as a defense at a court martial or other hearing if the order was unlawful (Article 92 of the Uniform Code of Military Justice). If a superior American officer orders a clearly wrongful action such as the killing of peacefully protesting students, then the solider has the duty not to obey such an order. If that occurred, the military should not prosecute him for failure to obey the officer under Article 92. That answer greatly surprised the Chinese audience. American military policy on unlawful orders has a laudable history that runs counter to the Eichmann defense.

Eichmann's defense reflects a mechanical thoughtlessness as well as inability to consider the wisdom of having independent critical thinkers at all levels of government service (see chapter 8). As Adams and Balfour suggest, Eichmann represents a type of *administrative evil,* which public officials apply within their organizations. Another form of administrative evil is making the acceptance of bribes almost necessary and certainly acceptable. As noted previously, in many countries public officials are paid poorly and view accepting bribes as merely a reasonable entitled supplement to their salary.

In fact, some societies formally and informally expect corruption and other unethical behavior. For example, government employees are expected to hire relatives, and give favored contracts to friends' family or clan members. In many countries, a person seeking a contract would naturally give a very nice gift to the public official because in their minds it is the polite thing to do and such a practice might be quite legal in those country. In some countries, the administrative evil of "enhanced interrogation" (torture) is an accepted police practice. In other countries where such practices are illegal, government officials simply transfer prisoners to other countries to obtain their desired information. Another ploy is to redefine an unethical act, such as waterboarding, as not torture but instead merely an "advanced form of interrogation." But whether or not such actions are illegal, they are always unethical.

SEMANTICS MASKS INTENTIONS

Modern public service ethics uses a technical and rational approach to decision making that does not offer much of a bulwark against such administrative evils. With the use of words such as "evacuation," "resettlement," and "labor in the East," Germany's Third Reich justified the extermination of Jews and others that they proclaimed to be society's misfits. Other regimes mask their actions with their own more up-to-date words that connote their true intention. For example, the U.S. government can hold prisoners indefinitely, without a hearing or trial, if the government labels them as "war combatant not under the Geneva Convention" or a "material witness." But if the label "prisoner" were changed to "defendant," the detainee would get a pretrial hearing and a trial. This legal use of various words with different results makes the ethics of this treatment confusing to civil servants, including federal law enforcement officers. It also hollows out the meaning of ethics in the public sector.

Public disclosure and transparency reveal the true nature and extent of administrative evil that results from public access to information and documents, which hopefully unmasks the evil. For example, the U.S. Public Health Service for many years ran syphilis experiments on infected black males in Tuskegee, Alabama. The experiment started in 1932. Of the 600 subjects in the experiment, 399 were infected and 201 were not. The researchers knowingly *withheld* the information from the inflected members of the experimental groups even after penicillin was discovered as an effective cure for the disease. In other words, the men were never told they had the disease. The purpose of the experiment was to observe the natural course of the disease. While experimentation is an important part of medicine, once a cure is found, ethically the scientists must give it to the subjects. In this case, experimentation continued for more than twenty years after a cure was known. Only in 1972 when a whistle-blower informed the *New York Times*, a story on this long-term program terminated that experiment.

A fundamental rethinking of public administration's fixation on technical and scientific rationality is essential if reformers are to successfully confront administrative evil. For example, efficiency is a key value of public administration. Therefore, does the fact that the Nazi's concentration program was remarkably efficient at killing people make it right? Unfortunately, a fixation on technical rationality can lead to such conclusions. To confront administrative evil, public administrators need an understanding of both normative and descriptive ethical theories, but they also need a clear understanding of how to employ critical thinking and emotional intelligence to their situations. There is a need to bring a greater ethical awareness to the person and the workplace. This requires training to upgrade the level of consciousness in society and certainly in the public service.

For the past 100 years and more, technical rationality has been the dominant Western cultural method of thinking. Its emphasis is on the scientific-analytical mind-set and belief in technological progress. This mind-set helped create higher standards of living but it also introduced what Adams and Balfour (1998) termed "administrative evil." Public officials engage in evil without being aware that they are acting unethically because in their minds they are certain that their actions are legal. Being legal is not necessarily being ethical. Having an administrative bonus award system that rewards poor performance as mentioned in Exhibit 3.2 is another version of administrative evil.

Under conditions of moral inversion, society convincingly redefines evil as good, civil servants engage in unethical conduct while believing that what they are doing is correct and appropriate behavior. For example, a group of elite U.S. Navy combat pilots attended a "Top Gun" aviators' annual conference in 1991. Excessive drinking occurred and some attendees engaged in sexual misbehavior toward women. The macho culture of the military at that time and place permitted the pilots to "let their hair down" and accept that "boys will be boys." The military even gave the name "Tailhook" to the activity to glorify this annual dinner party that celebrates their status as accomplished alpha male pilots (Winerip 2017). A moral inversion occurred that sanctioned and even encouraged unwanted and inappropriate sexual behavior toward women. After great media coverage and several lawsuits the practice was curtailed.

Why does this phenomenon of administrative evil occur? First, in a postmodern culture we easily "unname" evil because ethics is considered to be relative and nonsensical. In other words, in the influential world of marketing and politics unnaming is normal, as are word spinning and gas lighting. For the male pilots involved in the Tailhook scandal, it was "just having a little fun" and "letting off some steam." However, for the women involved, it was a demeaning sexual assault. Second, the movement away from hierarchy and toward weblike organizations diffuses individual responsibility and requires the compartmentalized accomplishment of role expectations in daily work. Thus, administrative controls that previously could facilitate ethical conduct are no longer possible to employ. In the case of Tailhook, the annual meeting was a "private party" where the official "on-the-job" military ethical code of conduct did not apply.

Third, the culture of technical rationality narrows the processes of public policy formulation and implementation so that moral inversions are more likely to occur. In Tailhook, no one seemed responsible for the public policy that created the situation that invited misbehavior on the part of these young men. Ethics requires a developed consciousness and holistic thinking and that becomes more difficult in a narrow process of public policy making. Finally, the roles assigned in government have buried ethical assumptions within them that mask public officials and inhibit critical thinking about their actions. Somehow, being an "elite pilot" excused behavior that would be totally inappropriate for anyone else in society. In this case the uniform, and in other cases the desire to accomplish objectives, distorts higher reasoning functions and decision making becomes dysfunctional for good ethical conduct.

Administrative evil poses a fundamental challenge to the ethics used in public administration. Such ethics need to include a coherent justification for an individual's personal consciousness in which higher values guide them to first recognize the potential danger and second resist the temptations of administrative evil. There are occasions in which an ethical administrator must resist the hierarchy of authority, prevailing public policy, and the requirements of the job or profession. It is on those occasions that public administrators realize or should realize that they are abdicating personal and social responsibility for the content or effect of their administrative actions. Ultimately, responsibility rests with the individual public administrator, as an ethical person, regardless of the title or position held in government, including the President of the United States.

CONCLUSION

To some extent, Leon's comment at the beginning of this chapter is correct, but not entirely. Corruption is remarkably common in many places in the world, but it need not be the prevailing condition or a significant condition in a society. In some places in the world, corruption is an institutionalized habit such as gift giving that is part of the social fabric, involving both the public and private sectors. In such places, everyone in the society expects that behavior and citizens are genuinely puzzled when an outsider calls it corruption and considers it a problem that should be addressed. Reformers, who argue such practices are ethically improper, often use voluntary codes of ethics to remedy the problem as they see it. Not surprisingly they meet resistance and thus the repeated failure of their reforms.

When cultural norms are strong, these types of reforms will fail and the ethical problems they address will persist for decades and even generations until conditions become so bad that the whole government system is corrupt and a national political crisis occurs. At best, when extreme corruption becomes systemic in politics and economics, it brings about a loss of trust in government and typically government leaders resort to suppression of institutions and individuals. At worst, it means civil unrest, revolt, and in some cases, bloody revolution.

Like Adams and Balfour: "We begin with the premise that evil is inherent in the human condition" (xix). Corruption is natural but there is clear evidence that some societies have avoided almost all corruption or at least the worst versions of it. Empirical evidence demonstrates that societies cannot completely avoid corruption, but reformers can confront most of its forms with significant success. Empirical evidence also tells us that many anticorruption reforms fail but that some are very successful. Public organizations can be run ethically but this often requires strong leadership at the highest levels and a keen understanding of how an ethical context can be intelligently created.

Corruption is a major and even an increasing challenge to modern civilization as technology creates more ways to be corrupt. Clearly, the position and financial "benefits" from corruption are a motivator to many. Unfortunately, government, with its remarkable power and large sums of money, is an ideal target for someone motivated by the "benefits" of corruption. Thus bribery, nepotism, misappropriation, and other public sector wrongs, including granting favors to private interests over public concerns, become common in many governments in the world. This quest for hedonistic and egocentric power, favor, and pleasure leads to a breakdown in shared concerns, increased factional interests, and an increased use of coercion rather than consensus in a society. To compound matters, corruption is contagious and in the presence of economic scarcity it is often encouraged.

Not surprisingly, corruption in the world is common as are the harmful effects of corruption on society. In many countries, the corruption is simple, obvious, and omnipresent. It exists in communist societies, former communist countries, developing nations, emerging democracies, and established democracies. Corruption is an equal opportunity contagion and is well understood worldwide. A myth exists that viral corruption does not exist in a democracy but the kleptocracy version of corruption not only disproves that myth but seems to validate the 1532 Niccolo Machiavelli prediction in *The Prince* that democracies will eventually fail to endure due to the existence of private interest groups that place their concerns ahead of the public good.

When public servants lose sight of the larger public interest, which includes everyone in the society and not just the wealthiest citizens, administrative evil and moral inversion can occur. The administrative excuse of "I was just following orders" is unacceptable. Regardless of position, rank, uniform, or other trappings of office, each public administrator is personally responsible for his or her ethical conduct. This means that each person—particularly more senior ranked officials—must holistically understand normative and descriptive ethical theories and know how to effectively make their decisions about right and wrong behavior beyond what is legally correct.

REVIEW QUESTIONS

1. Why is corruption in government harmful to the national and international economy? Why is it harmful to the culture and society of the country and the international community?

2. Why does corruption exist in government? Cite as several reasons for the existence of evil in government and the negative implications of those reasons. For each, explain a means for stopping that cited evil or at least a way to minimizing the problem.

3. Compare and contrast the types and character of corruption in the various regions of the world. For example, what is the importance of the patrimonial legacy in terms of corruption?

4. Why is kleptocracy dysfunctional to a democratic society? In what why does it exist in your national, state, and local government?

5. Why is Transparency International a useful tool against national corruption? What are the implications of TI's success in terms of curbing corruption in government?

6. What types of ethical reforms seem to have more success than others? Why?

7. What is the Eichmann defense? Why is this important to a public administrator?

8. What is moral inversion? Compare and contrast it with administrative evil?

REFERENCES

Abd-El-Hafez, Manal. 2015. "Lessons from the Arab Spring." New York: CUNY Academic Works. http://academicworks.cuny.edu/cc_etds_theses/362/

Adams, Guy B., and Danny L. Balfour. 1998. *Unmaking Administrative Evil*. Thousand Oaks, CA: Sage.

Adams, Patricia, Brady Yauch, Dai Qing, Fan Kiao, Lawrence Solomon, Mu Lan, and Lisa Peryman. 2013. "$45.5 million of Three Gorges Relocation Fund Misused: Audit." *Probe International*, June 8. https://journal.probe international.org/2013/06/08/45-5-million-of-three-gorges-relocation-fund-misused-audit/.

Atuobi, Samuel. 2007. "Policy Brief: Corruption and State Instability in West Africa." *Africa Portal*, December 1. https://www.africaportal.org/publications/policy-brief-corruption-and-state-instability-in-west-africa/.

Caiden, Gerald E., O. P. Dwivedi, and Joseph Jabbra. 2001. *Where Corruption Lives*. Bloomfield, CT: Kumarian Press.

Carroll, Stephen J., and Martin J. Gannon. 1997. *Ethical Dimensions of International Management*. Thousand Oaks, CA: Sage.

Dbwan, Abdulmoez. 2014. "Fighting the Culture of Corruption in Yemen." *World Bank*. December 4, http://blogs.worldbank.org/arabvoices/fighting-culture-corruption-yemen.

Donaldson, Thomas. 1989. *The Ethics of International Business*. Oxford, UK: Oxford University Press.

Eggen, Dan. 2010. "Billy Tauzin, Key Player in Health-Care Push, Leaving PhRMA." *Washington Post*, February 13. http://www.washingtonpost.com/wp-dyn/content/article/2010/02/12/AR2010021205129.html.

Fox, Vicente, and Rob Allyn. 2007. *Revolution of Hope: The Life, Faith, and Dreams of a Mexican President*. New York: Penguin.

Freedom House. 2017a. "Kyrgyzstan" https://freedomhouse.org/report/freedom-world/2016/kyrgyzstan.

Freedom House. 2017b. "Ukraine: Freedom in the World 2017." https://freedomhouse.org/report/freedom-world/2017/ukraine.

Friedman, Misha. 2012. "For Russians, Corruption Is Just a Way of Life." *New York Times*, August 18. http://www.nytimes.com/2012/08/19/opinion/sunday/for-russians-corruption-is-just-a-way-of-life.html?mcubz=0.

Gott, Natalie. 2000. "Casino Operator Details Alleged Kickback Scheme in Louisiana Trial." *Las Vegas Sun*, January 31. https://lasvegassun.com/news/2000/jan/31/casino-operator-details-alleged-kickback-scheme-in/.

Gumede, William. 2012. "Why Fighting Corruption in Africa Fails." *Pambazuka News*, November 14. https://www.pambazuka.org/governance/why-fighting-corruption-africa-fails.

Hays, Jeffrey. 2008. "Infrastructure in China: Bridges, Large Projects and Bean Curd." *Facts and Details*. http://factsanddetails.com/china/cat13/sub84/item326.html.

Kobrak, Peter. 2002. *Cozy Politics*. Boulder, CO: Lynne Reinner.

Kohlberg, L. 1976. "Moral Stages and Moralization: The Cognitive-Developmental Approach." In *Moral Development and Behavior: Theory, Research and Social Issues*, edited by T. Lickona, 31–53. New York: Holt, Rinehart and Winston.

Machiavelli, Niccolo. 1984. *The Prince*. New York: Bantam.

Maslow, Abraham. 1970. *Motivation and Personality*. New York: Harper and Row.

Payne, Pierre S. R. 1975. *The Corrupt Society: From Ancient Greece to Present-Day America*. New York: Praeger.

Richter, William L., Francis Burke, and Jameson W. Doig. 1990. *Combating Corruption: Encouraging Ethics*. Washington, DC: American Society for Public Administration.

Rosenbaum, David E. 2004. "A Closer Look at Cheney and Halliburton." *New York Times*, September 28. http://www.nytimes.com/2004/09/28/us/a-closer-look-at-cheney-and-halliburton.html?mcubz=0Kobrak.

Salleh, Nur Asiqin Mohamad. 2017. "Singapore Climbs to 7th on Global Least-Corrupt Index." *Straits Times*, January 26. http://www.straitstimes.com/singapore/singapore-climbs-to-7th-on-global-least-corrupt-index.

The Economist, "Robber Barons Beware." October, 24, 2015. https://www.economist.com/china 2015/10/22robber-barons-beware. Retrieved on July 17, 2018.

Theobald, Bill. 2016. "More Bonuses for VA Employees Despite Ongoing Problems at the Agency." *USA Today*, October 28. https://www.usatoday.com/story/news/politics/2016/10/28/more-bonuses-va-employees-despite-ongoing-problems-agency/92837218/.

Tiihonen, Seppo, ed. 2003. *The History of Corruption in Central Government*. Amsterdam, the Netherlands: IOS Press.

Transparency International. 2016. "The Global Anti-Corruption Coalition." http://www.transparency.org/.

"Tuskegee Syphilis Experiment." n.d. http://www.thetalkingdrum.com/tus.html. Retrieved on June 15, 2004.

United Nations Development Programme. 2004. *Human Development Report 2004*. hdr.undp.org /en/content/human-development-report-2004. Retrieved on June 15, 2017.

United States Mission to the United Nations. n.d. "UN Transparency and Accountability Initiative." usun.state.gov. Retrieved on June 13, 2017.

Winerip, Michael. 2017. "Revisiting the Military's Tailhook Scandal." *New York Times*, May 13. https://www.nytimes.com/2013/05/13/booming/revisiting-the-militarys-tailhook-scandal-video.html.

"Yazoo Land Fraud." 2017. *New Georgia Encyclopedia*. http://www.georgiaencyclopedia.org/articles/history-archaeology/yazoo-land-fraud.

Zughayar, Ghada. 2014. "Middle East and North Africa: A Region in Turmoil." *Transparency International*, December 3. http://blog.transparency.org/2014/12/03/middle-east-and-north-africa-a-region-in-turmoil/.

4 History of Ethics[1]

PROFESSOR: *Yes, Leon. You have a question?*

LEON: *You have been reviewing the history of ethics for us, but let us get REAL. Honestly, aren't these just old dead white guys not relevant to what real people are doing today?*

As human beings, we make decisions—some small and others profound—every day. How do we know what is right and what is wrong? The short answer is ethics and the long answer has been the subject of some of the greatest philosophical writings in human history. In the public sector, administrators make or recommend how to address ethical questions and they must always be able to clearly articulate their reasoning for their recommendations and actions. This chapter reviews how a selected sample of great thinkers in Western culture have addressed the topic of ethics and related matters over the past 2,500 years. They were selected on the basis of whose work would be the most useful in presenting the evolving understanding of ethical thought as a tool to achieve desired moral conduct in organizations and within professional public administrators.

Although making moral decisions is a part of what public administrators do, they often have little education concerning the depth of ethical thought from the past great thinkers and how their ethical ideas might help today's public servants with their decision making. A quick overview of some historic thinkers is followed by a discussion of how their ideas relate to modern attempts by Lawrence Kohlberg, Carol Gilligan, and others to create a descriptive theory of moral development.

As noted in chapter 2, ethics is the study of right conduct and the good life. Almost all of the ethical theories addressed in this chapter are normative; whereas, the Kohlberg's and Gilligan's theories of moral development are descriptive. Descriptive theories, as the words suggest, are about what is or is likely to happen, whereas normative theories reflect on what *ought to be*. In other words: How *should* you act if you are an ethical and moral person? As mentioned in chapter 12, descriptive theory help refine normative theories that are the tools to achieve desired moral outcomes.

---

[1] In writing this chapter, the authors extensively used *Ideas of the Great Philosophers* by William S. Sahakian and Mabel Lewis Sahakian (1993).

GREEKS AND ROMANS

HERACLITES

Heraclitus (537–475 BCE) of Ephesus (a city in Asia Minor that is now in Turkey) articulated what is currently called process philosophy. Later, other Greek philosophers such as Parmenides, Zeno, the Atomists of pre-Socratic Greece, Plato, and Aristotle, built on and in some cases ignored or disagreed with the work of Heraclitus. Unfortunately, almost all of his written work is lost, but fragments survive in quotes and references from other authors. For example, in *Cratylus*, Plato said, "Heraclitus, you know, says that everything moves on and that nothing is at rest; and comparing existing things to the flow of a river, he says that you could not step into the same river twice" ("Heraclitus," *Stanford*).

Heraclitus contributed two important concepts to philosophy: (1) everything that is considered reality should be thought of not at being at rest but always moving through time, and (2) almost all concepts considered to be dualistic are instead unities of opposites. Most philosophers, including Plato, assumed everything was at rest when thinking about reality. Heraclitus took another view, that everything in reality is in process. A chair, for example, started as a tree, then became a chair and, later, fuel for a fire. In other words, everything we think of as a reality is undergoing a fast or slow process of change. Thinking of reality as something in process makes for more dynamic and useful understandings of that reality. This fundamental concept is the building block of modern day process philosophy. The advantage of Heraclitus's concept is that it directs the mind to think about how the process works and how it can be improved from the perspective of someone that is using or is affected by process.

Heraclitus's concept of unities of opposites can apply to many apparent dualistic pairs—such as "men and women," "north and south," and "good and evil." In Heraclitus's view, each pair is not made up of separate discrete elements, but rather is linked thus not dualistic but is unified. Any one of the elements in a pair cannot be correctly understood without an awareness of the other because one defines and helps explain the other. The advantage of that concept is that in thinking about how the opposites relate as a unity enables and encourages more useful theory building about reality. For example, thinking of men and women as a unity of opposites allows one to accept the unique qualities of each while stressing the importance of harmony between the equal elements of the unity. (This concept will become particularly relevant in chapter 12, on creating public organizational ethics.)

HEDONISM

Hedonism is commonly used today as an ethical philosophy and moral practice called "egoism." For Hedonists, the purpose of life is to seek pleasure and avoid pain. In the ethical theory of hedonism, the only moral obligation a person has is to gratify his or her desire for pleasure and to eradicate or at least minimize pain whenever and wherever possible. Several ancient Greek philosophers and others, each with their own set of followers advocated this theory with several important variations. However, today, most people who adhere to this theory, are not aware of the development of these ancient theories and merely practice immediate gratification with little understanding of its earlier roots and developed logic.

Epicurus says:
"Life is good!

Make sure to
enjoy it."

Epicurus on the Cyrenaic School

Some hedonists emphasized momentary sensual pleasures, while others devoted their attention to avoiding pain. For example, the Cyrenaic School, founded by Aristippus (435–356 BCE), argued that a person should enjoy every momentary pleasure to the fullest, lest that person loses the opportunity for such an experience forever. A modern aphorism that capsulizes this theory is "make hay while the sun shines." Hedonists reasoned that since pleasure was the only good, then everyone should take advantage of *all* opportunities to enjoy pleasure and postpone nothing. With a carpe diem (or seize the day lest you die tomorrow) mentality, these hedonists were not concerned about the future or their impact on others.

Epicurus (341–270 BCE) disagreed with the Cyrenaic School's indiscriminate pursuit of all pleasures. He argued that many immediate pleasures are eventually detrimental to the person and those pleasures should be avoided. Hedonism often results in disaster because one does not die but instead suffers the consequences of excess or ill-chosen pleasures (e.g., gluttony or substance abuse) and hurts others by their behavior. Therefore, Epicurus argued for the use of discrimination in the selection of pleasures. For Epicureans, prudence is the best criterion to use in life. The avoidance of pain was much more important than the pursuit of pleasure. The Greek Hedonist Ideal Utilitarian School argued for indulging in only those pleasures to which a person is rightfully entitled and advocated a goal of the greatest possible benefits for all humankind (see the section on utilitarianism).

Socrates (470–399 BCE) disagreed with hedonists almost entirely. He argued that all life events affect a person and are of great importance. All events in a person's life need to be carefully examined (reflected upon) because an unexamined life is not worthy of being lived. He felt that to know oneself completely, including the conscious and unconscious self, allowed one to achieve power, self-control, and success in its deepest sense. As humans, we encounter what we call *problems* because we truly do not know ourselves, our true nature, limitations, abilities, motives, or personalities. Socrates felt that we commit wrong moral actions because of our personal ignorance.

In this school of thought, to be successful you need to see your spiritual inner-self. Knowing your inner-self intimately allows you to know what to do to achieve success. Unfortunately, proximity to oneself does not guarantee insight into your inner-self. It takes additional knowledge, or wisdom (sometimes referred to as "spiritual wisdom." To Socrates, self-knowledge was an essential good and

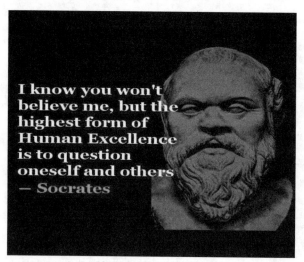

I know you won't believe me, but the highest form of Human Excellence is to question oneself and others — Socrates

valuing self-knowledge was a critical virtue. The virtuous find happiness (or what Maslow later called self-actualization) because if what you are doing is right, you are acting morally, which is always in your own best interest.

Aristotle and Self-Realization

Influenced by Socrates and Plato, Aristotle (384–322 BCE) developed a system of ethical thought focusing on self-realization similar to what Maslow argued many centuries later as the highest point on the human hierarchy of needs (see chapter 2). Maslow said that as humans we first must satisfy physiological needs, next security needs, then needs for esteem from others, then the need for self-esteem from a sense of competence, and finally a need for self-actualization. Many centuries earlier, Aristotle reasoned that a "good life" gives you pleasure as the result of fulfilling your potentialities, character, and personality. Each person must convert his or her potential into actualities. If not, the person will feel lost and frustrated, which is often manifested in illness and unhappiness.

Aristotle felt that the attainment of happiness depended entirely upon self-actualization. He argued that man's highest nature is found in the realm of the mind. For example, the fullest expression of scientific or philosophic thought produces the greatest happiness. Thus, reflection and contemplation produces a person's highest satisfaction. Each of us has a threefold nature: the physical, the emotional, and the rational. Aristotle argued that we must fulfill all three. For example, good physical health induces a sense of well-being. Proper exercise helps sustain the body. Enjoyment of the senses, such as appetites and instincts, brings emotional fulfillment. However, rational thinking brings the greatest happiness that anyone can achieve as it fulfills the potential of the mind and prevents us from engaging in excesses that result from physical and sensual appetites.

Aristotle's Rationality and Virtue

Knowing yourself is the beginning of all wisdom.

—*Aristotle*

Aristotle associated the highest nature of rationality with virtue. Habitual practice of the moderate virtues allows us to "program" those virtues into our lives. We understand this now as training the brain for a heightened awareness or consciousness. Aristotle considered almost any virtue done to both extremes—minimum to maximum—as probably evil and inappropriate; thus, he argued for virtues that were in the zone of the *mean* between extremes. This mean is normally near what statistically is called the average. For example, the ideal virtue of courage is in the mean between cowardice and recklessness.

Aristotle

To be correct, each virtue should be practiced over a lifetime and developed into a habit. That is to say it becomes a part of the personality and a way of being rather than applying it to a single act such as heroism. However, these habits require the understanding that applied virtue is not applicable to all situations in the same way. Rather, it should be applied contextually. For example, if you are in a bank when six men with guns came in to rob it, perhaps the most "courageous" thing to do is to follow the orders of the robbers in order to help keep everyone—bank employees, clients, and robbers—calm. In contextual contrast, if you find yourself on a bus and someone is bullying a young girl for her religious attire, perhaps the most "courageous" action is to stand next to her and compliment her sincerely in a loud voice. Some of the more important virtues in an infinite list of virtues include temperance, magnanimity, gentleness, truthfulness, friendliness, modesty, and righteous indignation. The sum of all the virtues in the mean is justice.

For Aristotle, happiness meant a life well lived, which he believed naturally resulted from acting with the highest virtues in mind. Making moral decisions is simple but not easy. A person makes those decisions based on an inner-self programmed set of moderate virtues that are repeated so many times they become habitual. That is the "simple" part. However, to Aristotle, virtue means doing the right thing, in relation to the right person, at the right time, to the right extent, in the right manner, and for the right purpose. That part is not so easy. Aristotle's concept of "mean" is very similar to the Buddha's teaching on the Noble Eightfold Path of Right Understanding, Right Thought, Right Speech, Right Action, Right Livelihood, Right Effort, Right Mindfulness, and Right Concentration.

STOIC PHILOSOPHY

The great stoic philosopher Epictetus (55–135 CE) believed that life's greatest value was contentment created by a life of tranquility, serenity, and composure. What was important to the Stoics was the peace of mind that a person gained through disciplined self-control or self-mastery. The goal of self-mastery was harnessing one's desires and ap-

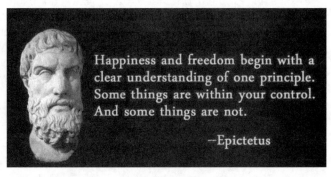

Happiness and freedom begin with a clear understanding of one principle. Some things are within your control. And some things are not.

—Epictetus

petites and commanding them instead of allowing them to command you. He believed that to permit another to disturb your mental equilibrium was in effect offering yourself to that person as a slave because you made your soul servile to the other person. He reasoned, as in the Hindu and Buddhist traditions, that finite things—such as clothes, cars, houses—can have a tenacious hold on a person. To gain freedom, you need to extinguish your desire for all things, including life itself.

If a person stole your watch, which you bought for $2,000, you would be upset. However, if you considered it old and worthless, then you would probably be less upset. Buddhists use the concept of "nothingness" to say there is no inherent value in a thing, which in this case means you place no value on the watch other than that it can tell the correct time. As the owner of the watch, you can place an emotional, social, or cultural value on the watch, but such values are extrinsic. Other than the watch telling you the time, the watch really has no value. If all you need the watch to do is tell the time, you can find an inexpensive replacement. If you place no other value on the watch, then you need not be upset that it was stolen. In other words, you can choose to exercise self-control or self-mastery and with it you can maintain your life in contentment.

Stoic philosophy teaches us to accept what we cannot change. By learning to live with unavoidable disappointment, its sting diminishes and fades away. Because most of our "misery in life" comes from valuing something, our refusal to place value on it significantly adds to our tranquility, serenity, and composed lifestyle. As in the case of Epictetus himself, who was born a slave and was handicapped, physical impairments became endurable because he accepted his misfortunes as part of life. Exhibit 4.1 provides an example of knowing what you can and cannot control.

Exhibit 4.1. A Stoic Approach to Loss

A family moved from Mexico to Texas using a Mexican mover. The family and the mover had a contract with an agreed time of arrival of the goods and the price for the move, which had to be in cash upon delivery. The movers arrived with half of the goods and demanded the full payment in cash. In fear that the movers would not release the half of their goods they could see, the family paid the movers and got half of their goods. However, the other half never arrived.

The mover agreed to send the rest of their goods for a significantly larger amount than the contract amount and only if the family would pay in advance. The family declined the suggestion and the movers keep the goods. Later they contacted the Mexican government authorities to resolve this problem, but that effort provided no results. They contacted their American insurance company, which earlier had told them they were covered. The company required a full list of the goods and the individual value of each stolen item. Upon finding the goods were worth about $50,000, the insurance company ruled that they were not liable because the family had voluntarily turned the household goods over to the movers.

The family reasoned that they should downsize anyway, and decided the movers had done them an unexpected favor. However, they did note the loss on their American IRS statement for the year and paid less taxes in that year.

Source: Thomas and Cynthia Lynch, 2018.

Like modern era existentialism, stoic philosophy stresses that you must keep your individual will inviolable and autonomous. You must own it and never allow others to control it. By remaining an independent invincible spirit, no one has true power over you even if you are imprisoned. Socrates illustrated that spirit when he was awaiting death by order of his enemies. He said, "Anytus and Meletus have power to put me to death, but not to harm me." To a Stoic, the secret of dying is to give up that which, in reality, belongs to God. In death, we return to God or the larger universe.

Epictetus tells us not to resist difficult problems of life but to embrace them. These experiences lead to spiritual growth. For the faithful, God is merely wrestling with you so that you become stronger through experience. Epictetus believed that just as the body needs physical exercise to remain in good condition, the problems that life provides you are what God makes available to you in order to strengthen your spiritual inner being.

WESTERN PHILOSOPHERS

KANT

Immanuel Kant (1724–1804) created his theory based on rational good will. To him, where there is no will (understood as intent), there is no freedom to choose and this precludes the ability to make a moral choice. Unlike Jeremy Bentham and John Stewart Mill (discussed later), who both thought an inherent value rested in objects, Kant believed that morality rested entirely within the individual. Moral values arise from a person's will and purpose rather than from an overt action that is dependent on a consequence of an overt action.

The will of an individual has the only value regardless of the results of the overt actions. Actions are morally neutral. This theory says that as long as your intention is right then action is right regardless of the consequences. Boiled down, this means that if you throw a ball and it accidently breaks your neighbor's window, as long as you didn't throw it intentionally to break the window, you are not morally guilty. However, as a practical legal matter, you may need to pay to repair the window.

The "categorical imperative" was Kant's criterion for making moral decisions. His view was that any action is moral if the principle from which you acted was a universal law of nature. To determine if an action is moral, a person need only conclude that the moral law applies to everyone including the person making the observation. For example, let us say you are about to break a promise that you made to your parents or spouse. The categorical imperative requires that you can only break that promise if you conclude (i.e., will it) that everyone else can also break their promises if they choose to do so. If the conclusion is negative (e.g., people should not break promises), then the proposed action is immoral. For Kant, this test is unconditional and must hold true regardless of the condition. Interestingly, the categorical imperative is a form of the Golden Rule—"Do unto others as you would have them do unto you."

Kant maintained that there was a "rational good will" in human beings and morality is possible because of it. He maintained that free choice, which is when nothing coerces a decision, does exist. He believed that all things, except human beings, have an exchange value where a meeting of the minds occurs (that is, there is agreement by both parties). In addition, the two parties must engage in bargaining freely and come to an agreed purchase price.

Kant's exception of human beings was important because he argued that we must treat people as an *end* in themselves and never as a *means*. Thus, to Kant, slavery was wrong under all circumstances. In addition, he believed that people are moral agents and that moral values exist in and for persons only. We must all respect each other because each of us possesses infinite intrinsic worth. Kant was an optimist and considered the universe essentially moral. To him, moral laws make it impossible for any person or institution to continuously act morally because those laws will eventually frustrate the person or institution and out of that frustration, they will choose the correct action.

Arthur Schopenhauer

SCHOPENHAUER

Arthur Schopenhauer (1788–1860) and Thomas Hobbes (1588–1679) were both pessimistic about the human condition. Hobbes declared that humans are "mean, nasty, and brutish" (Hobbes1651). Essentially, he thought humans were untrustworthy, corrupt beings who must protect themselves from other persons just as the animals in the wild protect themselves from other animals. Schopenhauer agreed that the world was basically and inherently evil. He believed that happiness is experienced only as momentary respites between periods of unhappiness. He felt that the world was an irrational blind force acting without guidance because there was no God to direct it.

Similar to the Stoics and to Buddhist teachings, Schopenhauer considered suffering inevitable. He understood evil as a positive rather than a negative force in life and believed that human wanting comes from deficiency, which results in suffering. He reasoned that our desires and appetites remain with us throughout our lives and our demand for desires is necessarily infinite, therefore we can never satisfy them. Satisfaction derived from the fulfillment of desires is necessarily short lived and a new desire takes its place in a never-ending cycle. No desire can be satiated to give a lasting satisfaction. His answer to escape the misery of this world was to eliminate desire through object denial. Essentially, he argued that a person needs to annihilate the will, suppress desires, and transcend all natural instincts by always being content with nothingness.

Schopenhauer thought we should pity each other because each person's life is tragic with each having its own special torments. Thus, to him, compassion was necessary as we are all in the same boat of misery and showing compassion helps to temper that unhappiness.

UTILITARIAN PHILOSOPHY AND SOPHISTICATED HEDONISM

The modern philosophy of utilitarianism is remarkably influential not only in our lives but also in contemporary democracy and economic thought. Jeremy Bentham (1784–1832) and John

Jeremy Bentham

J. S. Mill

Stuart Mill (1806–1873) are credited for developing it. Like ancient hedonism of the Greek Ideal Utilitarian school, modern utilitarianism defines "good" not in terms of the "good life" or as "a life worth living" but rather in terms of pleasure. Its basic aim is the greatest good for the greatest number. Bentham used the principle of utility to define an inherent value for every object and act. He defined utility as any source of pleasure, happiness, benefit, good, advantage, or any means of prevention of pain, evil, and unhappiness.

Bentham was a quantitative hedonist because he believed that there is only one kind of pleasure, which is physical, sensual. To him, the term "pleasure" differed only in amount, duration, and intensity, and not in quality. For example, there is no difference between enjoying an ice cream cone and winning the lottery. Bentham rejected any pleasures derived from a religious or spiritual experience because they are intangible internal experiences that he regarded as only pseudo-pleasures.

Like the hedonists, Bentham believed that physical pleasures were the greatest good attainable in life. One's primary and perhaps sole objective in life should be the pursuit of pleasure. Much of contemporary economics uses the "rational man" assumption, which assumes much the same thing—that everyone acts to maximize their own interests and desires. From this assumption, academic theorists and economists developed microeconomics and the market system.

Utilitarian Hedonist Calculus

Bentham created a hedonist calculus using specific criteria to help determine the correct choice between pleasures. He did this because he felt most people were not sufficiently analytical to correctly choose the best possible pleasure for themselves. The hedonist calculus greatly influenced the creation of modern day benefit-cost analysis used in economic decision making and crafting public policy.

In order to save us from ourselves and prevent immoral excess of gratification, Bentham defined four sanctions or deterrents: physical, political, moral/popular, and religious sanctions. An example of a physical sanction is when a person overeats he experiences the physical sanction of becoming nauseated and ill. If a person finds pleasure in stealing and gets caught, he experiences the political sanction of imprisonment. If a person engages in an unjust pleasure, then he experiences the moral/popular sanction of society ostracizing him. If a person indulges in immoral pleasures, then God punishes him. Given that Bentham was an atheist, he may have cited the latter sanction with irony, as he clearly did not think it was a real or relevant deterrent. However, he may have thought that some considered it real and thus included it in his sanction.

Both Bentham and Mill used the democratic dictum happiness and the good of each person are essentially equally and should be considered equal. But, John Stuart Mill disagreed with Bentham's quantitative hedonism and developed qualitative hedonism. Instead of using the hedonistic calculus, Mill advocated the use a "hedonic expert." These experts could decide between the better of two pleasures because they had experienced both, thus making them "experts." If two Hedonic experts disagreed, then the more intelligent person's opinion would prevail. However, the question remains: How does one determine who is the more intelligent?

NIETZSCHE

Friedrich Nietzsche (1844–1900) agreed with Schopenhauer that life instincts controls man's nature. However, to Nietzsche, the task of life was not to inhibit man's instincts, as suggested by Schopenhauer, but rather to fulfill them. He said that two moral codes dominated the world: one was the code of the enslaved and the other was the code of the dominant elite. The slave morality, as Schopenhauer suggested, requires people to accept subjugation and obedience and thus repress their individual will. The elite moral code applied to the "Aryan race of conquerors." For the elite, peace comes with the acknowledgment of the natural rights of the strong to rule the weak. Nietzsche noted that "might makes right," as it is the verdict of nature. He asserted that the traditional Judeo-Christian culture and its ethics of renunciation is appropriate only for slaves.

Nietzsche called for a reevaluation of all values and argued for a race of supermen who were moral giants endowed with physical superiority. Supermen would combine the might and majesty of Caesar with the moral superiority of Jesus. Ironically, while he repudiated Judeo-Christian values and was particularly anti-Semitic, he considered Jesus, who was without question a Jew, a morally superior superman. As an atheist with strong feelings of superiority over religious believers, he mocked persons of faith by noting that both Jews and Christians continued moral misbehavior despite the teachings of their faiths.

To Nietzsche, this hypocritical behavior and lack of adhering to one's faith with impunity indicated that the concept of God must be irrelevant because true believers would not dare to misbehave so abominably. Clearly their actions communicated that they did not truly believe in God. He reasoned that without people believing in a deity, the concept of the deity ceases to exist. God was to Nietzsche merely a concept and if the concept of God no longer exists, God no longer influences human conduct. Given that reality, any vestige of "God" ceased. Thus, Nietzsche made the famous and often quoted pronouncement that "God is dead."

To Nietzsche, the purpose of life was self-realization and the act of Jesus dying on the cross merely pointed out the foolishness of loving others. Considerations of sentimental attachments must not dissuade individuals from self-realization. For Nietzsche, Jesus foolishly died for an unworthy segment of humankind that was capable of only committing incorrigible behavior. In the 1930s and 1940s, the Nazi Party in Germany adopted his philosophy, which may have been because of a possible misunderstanding. Nietzsche spent the last years of his life in an asylum for the mentally ill, and his sister rewrote some of his key writings in order to gain favor with the Nazi Party. Of significance is that either his or her words greatly influenced Germany and helped give rise to the Nazi Party prior to World War II and neo-Nazi parties later on.

Friedrich Nietzsche

ROYCE

The American philosopher Josiah Royce (1855–1916) took as his central theme the virtue of loyalty rather than the good life. For Royce, loyalty represented the supreme good in life. Loyalty meant the willing, practical, and thorough devotion of a person to a cause. He felt that loyalty contained all other virtues; and where conflict arose, then one should choose the superior virtue of loyalty. To Royce, it was the greatest good that a man can experience because it is always pure regardless of the cause one supports. If one happens to be loyal to an unworthy cause, then it is the cause that is deficient not the pure devotion of the individual. To Royce, one should seek to associate with a cause worthier of one's devotion. He said it was the spirit of loyalty rather than loyalty itself that was good. The cause selected was up to the enlightened intelligence of each person.

MODERNISTS AND POSTMODERNISTS

In the twentieth and twenty-first centuries, the dominant and most influential philosophy has been modernism, which gave us modern science. However, postmodernists began in the twentieth century and had great influence in the arts, humanities, and communication. For example, following the influence of postmodernism, news organizations try to present both sides in a political election even if one side primarily presents lies, assaults on the character of his opponents, and presents policies that are unworkable.

Josiah Royce

René Descartes

DESCARTES

French philosopher René Descartes (1596–1650) is thought of as the founder of modernism. Descartes argued that reality consisted of two elements: matter and mind. He defined matter as occupying space and being corporeal (physical) in nature. In contrast, the mind is incorporeal and nonmaterial, or what we might call "spiritual," in nature. Thus, the nature of the soul is the mind; whereas the nature of the physical body is matter. For Descartes, matter and its existence were incapable of a final proof, whereas mind could be conclusively proven. He did so with his famous statement: *cogito ergo sum*, loosely translated as "I think, therefore I am" or "I am aware, therefore I exist." Although the difference of the two translations seems negligible, being "aware" stresses the importance of consciousness in the proof of a person's existence, which can become significant in understanding the nuances of his statement.

Descartes started his reasoning process by arguing that all you can say with absolute certainty is that you exist because everything else that might be happening to you could be a dream or your poor perception of "reality." Therefore, no one can absolutely say that "matter" exists but you can say that you exist as a mind because the very act of thinking proves your existence. While this may sound redundant, this reasoning is the basis for why researchers say that a hypothesis about reality can only be affirmed or rejected but never proven. Descartes then reasoned that if he did not exist, then "who is doing the doubting?" Since there is doubt, then he must exist because he could not doubt if he did not exist. What is important in this collection of negative statements is that a person who doubts has to exist. However, in terms of absolute certainty on other matters, there is no certain absolute proof.

From Descartes's perspective and that of modernism, the concept of intersubjectivity is important. This is when two or more people look at the same object and each identifies it in a same manner. For example, if two persons subjectively identify an object as a "chair," their parallel thinking and conclusion are intersubjective and that makes communication and agreement possible. Each person understands the perception of the other through language and comes to believe that they share the same understanding. However, intersubjectivity is only the "apparent" sharing. Neither person can be absolutely sure that intersubjective reality exists, but each assumes it does on the basis of faith that they share what each thinks is the same understanding of the object in question.

LOCKE AND MODERNISM

John Locke (1632–1704) disagreed with Descartes on an important point in the process of the development of modernism. Descartes argued people reason—that is, think—without depending on facts or experience of any sort. Nevertheless, a person can and does reach conclusions about what is "reality" without needing any external proof. Descartes concluded that knowledge exists within a person at birth as an inner awareness or innate ideas. That is to say some thinking exists without requiring experience and is thus innate. In simple language, we know something because our gut tells us so.

Locke disagreed and insisted that a person derives knowledge only from experience. He said that at birth the human mind is a tabula rasa, meaning a "white paper" or a blank tablet. At birth, a person starts receiving sensations that the mind registers. Over time, experiences build and accumulate into knowledge and possibly even wisdom and insight about reality. The following quote from Helen Keller, first presented in chapter 1, seems to confirm John Locke:

John Locke

Before my teacher came to me, I did not know that I am. I lived in a world that was no-word. I cannot hope to describe adequately that unconsciousness, yet conscious time of nothingness. . . . Since I had no power of thought, I did not compare one mental state with another. (Dennett 1991, 227)

Exhibit 4.2. Wittgenstein versus Socrates

There is a logical snag or difficulty with Wittgenstein position, which the following fictional dialogue illustrates:

WITTGENSTEIN: Ethics is relative; it is only a matter of opinion between sets of people who hold differing logical value paradigms.

SOCRATES: You mean that ethics is merely subjective opinion across groups.

WITTGENSTEIN: Exactly. For example, what is ethical for you in Greece and what is ethical for me in England is ethical for both of us in spite of the fact that we have fundamentally different values. Ethics is subjective.

SOCRATES: Do you really mean that? That my opinion on ethics is true by virtue of my opinion being consistent with those in my country rather than it being true in general?

WITTGENSTEIN: Indeed I do.

SOCRATES. My opinion is the people of Greece believe Ethics is absolute and that you, Mr. Wittgenstein, are absolutely in error. Since this is my opinion within my group paradigm, then you must grant that it is true according to your philosophy.

WITTGENSTEIN: Ah, you are quite correct, Socrates. However, for you alone and the others in your paradigm.

SOCRATES: So, both moral relativism and moral absolutism are correct in spite of the fact that they are logically the opposite of each other?

WITGENSTEIN: Ah, you are quite correct again.

Source: Thomas and Cynthia Lynch, 2018.

Before her teacher, she knew she "did not know that I am." Nevertheless, in that period of what she called nothingness, she knew she seemed to be unconsciousness or at least in a period of conscious time of nothingness. With her teacher, her nearly blank tablet filled with words and the power of thought that even apparently taught her the words of Descartes and a sophisticated understanding of those words.

Locke argued that the stimulation of the senses helps the mind to create mental images that permits "understanding." As a person ages, more sense stimulation occurs that challenge the correctness of the former mental images for reasons such as accuracy, relevance, and inconsistency. In a continuous process, the mind updates the former mental images and uses the new images to understand even more input, which in turn refines the previous mental images. Contemporary statisticians adapted this concept and call it Bayesian updating. As new data is received and added to the equation, the probability for the hypothesis is updated for accuracy.

Eventually, the mental images permit a child to think in terms of language and start sharing concepts with others using language. The process of having mental images or words, receiving input from our senses, and re-creating mental images or creating new mental images continues until we die. Typically, the early mental images are powerful and abandoning them for new ones is difficult.

Plato had explained the latter phenomenon centuries earlier with his allegory of the cave. In the story, several men were held captive in a cave and were bound together so that they could not move. They could not see the outside world but they could see the shadows of the outside world on the cave wall. None understood what the shadows were about or why they appeared on the wall of the cave, however, each felt confident he understood what the shadows meant. Eventually, one man escaped and ventured outside to see sunlight, green grass, and people moving casually in front of the cave. He realized that these passing travelers caused the shadows on the cave wall. He returned to his friends and explained what he had discovered, but they refused to accept his explanation of the shadows and declined the opportunity to escape from the cave to see for themselves.

Locke believed that ultimate reality was unknowable. He thought that matter existed but that a person could not fully understand it. Doubt was always present and the mental images we use to comprehend can be incorrect and thus can limit our awareness. The primary and secondary qualities of reality are not inherent within the real object because they are the creation of the mind. For example, does a red rubber ball have an underlying substance? Locke would say that we might think it does but that thinking is a creation of our mind. It might have such a substance, but ultimately we cannot know it.

Let us turn to Descartes's concept of the intersubjective. Two or more people can agree that an object is a red rubber ball with certain characteristics and thus have intersubjective agreement that exists among them. As mentioned earlier, they cannot completely know that intersubjectivity exists between them, but with an easy leap of faith they make that assumption. They can even narrow that leap with careful observation and experimentation, which seventeenth-century philosophers called the "scientific method," which is using a careful methodology to observe something.

Furthermore, one person could examine many red rubber balls and others could confirm the first person's tentative findings on the nature of "red rubber ballness," which explains the common essence of red rubber balls. Scientific inquiry requires careful thinkers to use a rigorous approach to define "certain knowledge" in order to minimize doubt about its certainness from an intersubjective point of view. In other words, such an inquiry could consider the quality or hue of the red color, the density and type of rubber, the smoothness of the surface, the roundness of the ball, and so on. The study of what the scientific method and other approaches define as "acceptable knowledge" is called "methodology."

Locke noted that all morality rests within the individual who *can* control his or her mind. The individual does that with will, intention, and predisposition, as Helen Keller did. To Locke, the potential for individual control was important and greatly influenced his philosophy, which, in turn, significantly influenced the founding fathers of the new American republic.

UTILITARIANISM AND MODERNISM

G. E. Moore

G. E. Moore (1873–1958) is remembered as a champion of common sense realism or the "ordinary view of the world." His philosophical thinking was similar to that of Bentham's and was clearly opposed to the set of philosophers who argued for intuitionism, such as John Locke, Immanuel Kant, and Arthur Schopenhauer. As a utilitarian, Moore assumed there is a reality. Bentham's utilitarianism described the moral realm in terms of overt actions, consequences, and external events. Moore's utilitarianism defines moral actions as right or wrong because of the total effects caused by the act regardless of the doer's good intention. If the total consequences make the world a better place to live, the act is moral; if not, the act must be wrong. The test is "Does the act produce the best possible consequence?"

Moore argued that terms such as "goodness," "values," and "beauty" cannot be defined. They can only be demonstrated or grasped. Moore disagreed with Kant, who said the intention was important and not the consequence of the action. Moore's position was that only consequences matter because those consequences exist in reality and the person's intentions are only known to that person and are therefore completely subjective. Certainly, many people could share the same moral value but the value itself was entirely in the minds of the people and not in the object or act. Moore said the ethical properties in the act were independent of the human mind ascribing any moral value to it. To him, morality was external to human consciousness.

According to Moore, goodness is an experience. The concept of good is indefinable because it is "the ultimate simplest term," meaning the concept is at its smallest level and no one can reduce it further. A good act is an organic whole that we cannot divide into parts. Moore reasoned that a man, who rescues a child from drowning, results in something that is good. The result is good but not the act.

Goodness is real but it is also an organic unity with value found only in the whole. One can point out good things, but one cannot define goodness itself. According to Moore, trying to do so is committing a naturalistic fallacy, which is jumping the gap between the normative (*is*) and the objective (*ought*) theories. Just because something "is" does not logically mean that it "should be." Another parallel fallacy would be to give a blind person, such as Helen Keller, a scientific explanation of the color yellow and conclude that such an explanation enabled her to experience the color yellow. A scientific explanation is not the same thing as an experience and to think so is wrong (see chapter 8, "Tools for Critical Thinking").

The way intention is treated in the common law legal systems in English-speaking countries aids in understanding the practical implications of the Kant versus Moore disagreement. Matters of which laws shall be applied in a particular case is for the judge to decide. Matters of contested facts in almost all cases are for the jury to decide and often the intent of the defendant regarding the crime is the most important fact in dispute given to the jury. The judge tells the jury which laws apply in a case and what standard applies in matters of contested intent.

In criminal cases, the element of criminal intent is critical. If there is little doubt about the criminal intent of the defendant, the jury's verdict is guilty. If there is more than little doubt, their verdict is not guilty. In other words, the legal system takes a practical middle position between Kant and Moore. In court, the jury determines intent and thus sides with Kant; however, the courts realize that determining the intent can be difficult and thus they side with Moore. The judge's instruction to the jury on determining doubt concerning intent is the means for finding the middle ground between Kant's and Moore's positions.

POSITIVISM

The more evolved modernism is called positivism. Auguste Comte (1798–1857) took the empiricism of Francis Bacon (1561–1626), Thomas Hobbes (1588–1674), and John Locke (1632–1704) to a new level. Empiricism accepts experience instead of logical reasoning as the source of knowledge. To the British Empiricists, a person but especially a community of scholars must derive all knowledge or truth from experience rather than from logical techniques. Comte reasoned that human knowledge had moved through two stages—theological and metaphysical—and had reached the positive stage. The theological stage was the earliest and most primitive as it focused on explaining natural phenomena in terms of personal forces, spirits, or gods. The metaphysical stage was when man attributed natural phenomena to scientific laws or laws of nature.

In the positive stage, careful observation of events must made and be verified by the senses, such as sight, sound, and taste. Only experience can establish credible judgments about natural phenomena when keen and repeated observations confirm them. Comte's humanism postulated *love* as its principle, *order* as its basis, and *progress* as its aim. His concept is similar to religion but without a theology and rituals. Comte regarded altruism as humankind's highest duty and blessedness. Later positivists denied the objective existence of God, soul, moral value, truth, beauty, goodness, justice, and ethics. Typically, positivists restricted their philosophy to the realm of science and did not apply it to value areas they called emotive, but that changed with the movement toward "logical positivism."

Thomas Hobbes

Auguste Comte

Logical Positivism

In 1924, Moritz Schlick (1882–1936) created an intellectual seminar in Austria known as the Vienna Circle. This renowned group of scholars, which tangentially included Ludwig Wittgenstein (1889–1951), Alfred Jules Ayer (1910–1989), and Bertrand Russell (1872–1970), developed a philosophic theory built upon the ideas of Auguste Comte, George Edward Moore, and David Hume (1711–1776). The Vienna Circle became the foremost promoters of logical positivism. Comte's belief that an acceptable understanding of natural phenomena had to be based upon careful observation of events that was verifiable by the senses found a comfortable home with this group of thinkers. David Hume's contribution to logical positivism was the rejection of a metaphysical reality and the acceptance of valid empirical data only from those things experienced as sense impressions. In other words, human knowledge could only be built upon observable phenomena, which are objects of experience, not of reason.

During the nineteenth and twentieth centuries, the philosophic admiration for science grew to remarkable proportions for some. For example, British logical positivists regarded physics as the only meaningful language with all other language dismissed as irrelevant. They viewed physical evidence alone as verifiable and the only real source of knowledge. Thus, they argued that ethics, humanities, and the social sciences did not deal with credible knowledge unless they exclusively used the scientific method to research and make observations.

Bertrand Russell asserted "that which science cannot know, humankind cannot know." Thus, logical positivism precludes knowledge about all value judgments, including ethics. Logical positivists said that carefully reasoning people cannot prove goodness, beauty, truth, and morality, and therefore we cannot say that such attributes even exist. Values are merely emotions and consequently are subject to frequent change and they are unverifiable. Thus, values and ethics are foolish because humankind cannot base knowledge on *nonsense*. Therefore, one cannot reasonably argue about what is morally good or bad. The result of this argument is what we have come to know as moral relativity; that is, who is to say something is right or wrong and when it is right or wrong?

The Analytical School and the Principle of Verification

Bertrand Russell

Ludwig Wittgenstein's (1889–1951) and Alfred Jules Ayer's (1910–1989) contributions to logical positivism were particularly important. Wittgenstein argued that a great deal of confusion in philosophy arose from language. Vague references, misuse of terms, and semantic limitations create a dysfunctional level of confusion in the transmission of ideas and knowledge among people. For example, is a stool a chair? Can it not also be a step up to reach a high shelf or function as a seat or also as a small table? How is the listener supposed to interpret what the speaker means when the word "stool" is mentioned?

Thus, Wittgenstein and others such as Bertrand Russell considered the possibility of developing an ideal language free of defects. They felt

Ludwig Wittgenstein

that careful analysis of the language was possible and they focused not on the meaning of words and phrases but rather on their use. To them, the philosopher's task was essentially remedial and needed to focus on linguistic clarity as that was the only proper function of philosophy. Their language would possess a one-to-one ratio with facts of observations to mirror the structure of the world. To them linguistic analysis reduced ideas to the lowest logical components possible. The result was to enhance illumination on the central problems of inquiry.

Ayers addressed the subject of ethics directly, especially with the logical positivists' creation of the Principle of Verification. It noted that statements and judgments can be accepted as meaningful and valid only to the extent that sensory experience verifies them. Ayers denied the validity of any ethical theories. To him, right and wrong behavior is not a reality that can be evaluated because value judgments fail the Principle of Verification. Moral judgment is therefore merely an emotive self-expression. This philosophic theory is referred to as emotivism. Moral actions are evidence of the individual's feelings, as are events wholly outside the domain of valid knowledge. Emotivism is the doctrine that all evaluative judgments, including moral judgments, are nothing but expressions of personal preferences.

However, there is a problem with Ayer's reasoning. His Principle of Verification says that careful reasoning leads to accepting statements and judgments as meaningful and valid only to the extent that sense experience verifies them and that this principle is universally applicable. However, the very criterion he uses to determine verification is a sense experience that cannot be verified because it is just an emotional expression of preference. By his own definition, this principle is illogical.

Moral Relativism

Wittgenstein argued our individual and group values place us within logical sets of beliefs in what we now understand as a "paradigm." Thomas Kuhn (1922–1996) first used the term and its meaning in *The Structure of Scientific Revolutions* in 1962, but we can see it as practical application in the Wittgenstein argument. Paraphrasing Wittgenstein, people can logically exist and argue right and wrong behavior within their group, which shares specific values (their paradigm), but cannot logically argue across other groups with differing specific values (paradigms).

In other words, you can determine right and wrong within your own culture, profession, government, organization value set (paradigm) because others in that set share those same beliefs, values, and language with you, but you cannot say another person or group is wrong if they adhere to the values of a different group's paradigm with an alternative set of beliefs, values, and language. Thus, Wittgenstein's exception says yes, moral relativism exists but theorizing about a universal right conduct and good life, as Kant would have us do, is logically possible within the paradigm. To Wittgenstein, a political state can logically prosecute someone who has violated a law of that state because the defen-

A. J. Ayer

dant's existence in the state defines the paradigm that applies to everyone in that state. With Ayer, who took a more extreme logical position than Wittgenstein, laws and ethics cannot ever logically exist.

KOHLBERG AND MOTIVATIONS FOR NORMATIVE THEORIES

Reflecting on the moral development topology of Kohlberg (discussed in chapter 2) helps place the various normative theories of ethics into a philosophical perspective. Philosophers always build normative theory on their assumptions and then use logic to argue their normative theory. Thus, if someone successfully challenges their basic assumptions or even one of the key assumptions in their theory, the challenger successfully discredits the normative theory. If we agree with Descartes, all assumptions, except our existence, are subject to challenge as being a true representation of reality. Thus, all theories—normative or descriptive—are subject to doubt, uncertainty, possible successful challenge, and eventual change.

If we are to have and use a descriptive ethical theory, then we have to make a leap of faith in terms of that theory's key assumptions. As risky as making assumptions can be in theory building, we can narrow the distance of that faith leap by basing those assumptions on the rigorous thinking of knowledge from the community of scholars. One such rigorous tested set of assumptions can be found in Kohlberg's moral development theory (see chapter 2).

Kohlberg's key assumption in his theory of moral development is that people act morally based on a sense of fairness and justice that grows within some but not all people over a lifetime. Kohlberg's theory has relevance to normative ethical theory. What follows is an examination of the previous normative ethical theories placing each theory along the continuum of Kohlberg's stages of moral development. Exhibit 4.3 summarizes the stages of moral development as they relate to the philosophies discussed in this chapter.

Exhibit 4.3. Philosophers and the Stages of Moral Development

LEVEL	STAGE	KEY CHARACTERISTICS	PHILOSOPHER
One	Stage one	Seeking reward and avoiding punishment	Epicurus / Aristippus / Hobbes / Nietzsche / Epictetus
	Stage two	Reciprocity centered	
Two	Stage three	Achieving conforming relationships	Bentham / Mill / Royce
	Stage four	Fulfill a duty to the system	Kant
Three	Stage five	Fulfill social contract	Locke Plato
	Stage six	Seeking to follow de-fined principles or value assumptions	

Source: Adapted from Kohlberg by Thomas and Cynthia Lynch, 2018.

STAGE ONE

The key characteristic of stage one thinking is centered on the person being rewarded or avoiding punishment in order to perform what others call a moral act. In other words, a stage one person will not act morally by any inner motivation or knowledge of ethical theory but will act morally due to their perception of being rewarded or avoiding punishment for a particular deed that others would call a moral act. Thus, people in this stage do what is right by following rules and laws that are backed by the threat of punishment or offering rewards as a result of following those rules.

Certainly, many of the hedonists were stage one thinkers as they emphasized maximizing pleasure. One extreme of the hedonist group was the egoistic school, which strived for the utmost self-gratification without regard for others or even the long-term effect on themselves. As noted earlier, Aristippus argued that a person should enjoy every momentary pleasure to the fullest, lest the opportunity for such an experience be lost forever. Hence, there is the well-known expression: "Eat, drink, and be merry, for tomorrow we may die" (Ecclesiastes 8:15, Isaiah 22:22).

Epicurus's views were closer to stage two moral thinking as it represented a movement along the moral development scale from the views of Aristippus. Epicurus argued that many immediate pleasures are eventually detrimental and a person should avoid those pleasures. Further up the scale beyond stage one was ideal utilitarianism, which argued that the only pleasures a person is rightfully entitled to are those that advocate a goal of the greatest possible benefits for all humankind. In each case, the philosophers stress reward as the primary reason for acting with or without morals.

Thomas Hobbes, Arthur Schopenhauer, and Epictetus were pain avoiders rather than pleasure seekers. Their stress was upon using punishment or self-denial to achieve a morality within a society. Hobbes felt humans were untrustworthy and only a strong state could keep the public order. Thus, the ruler needed to threaten pain to establish order. Arthur Schopenhauer thought the only thing that a person could do is deny oneself all external gratification. Epictetus shared Schopenhauer's pessimistic view of humanity and his solution was also to achieve morality through denying oneself pleasure. Friedrich Nietzsche also saw desires as the problem of life but his solution was quite different—have a ruling class of supermen elite, with their higher ethical self-realization, govern the rest of society.

Stage Two

The key characteristic of stage two thinking is reciprocity. People in stage two consider right to be what is *fair* in the exchange process between the person or group and another person or group. Thus, the first person or group acts to meet their own interests (pleasures and rewards) and limitedly accept the interest (pleasure and rewards) of others within the context of the reciprocal agreement. Stage two thinkers are comfortable with contracts and they respect legal agreements.

Stage two thinkers are still oriented to their pleasure and avoiding punishments—in other words they are "me, my, mine" oriented and thus selfish thinkers, but they are open to the possibility that they can work with others they assume have the same value perspective. If they can find a person or group in which both can prosper or avoid punishment together through an agreement, they will sign on to that agreement as long as it is reciprocal and in their interest.

Some economists adopt this perspective but it is not one that our identified philosophers talk about in their normative ethical theories. Not surprisingly, this concept is at the heart of economic theory that dominates the world's major societies. In the paraphrased words of Adam Smith, somehow, an invisible hand, reconciles selfish acts, in the larger picture, when the market system works correctly.

Stage Three

Stage three thinkers move beyond using reciprocal agreements by instead using the maxim "the greatest good for the greatest number" as the key assumption of their theory. That maxim is a step short of the Golden Rule (do unto others has you would have them do unto you) value assumption but goes beyond the reciprocal maxim of stage two thinkers. With the reciprocal value assumption, a person is primarily selfish but is less selfish than the stage one thinker who is entirely "me, my, mine" oriented. Stage three thinkers remain selfish but assume they can identify a person or group with which they might be able to reach a useful bi- or multilateral mutually beneficial agreement.

With the acceptance of "the greatest good for the greatest number" fundamental assumption, the sphere of inclusiveness moves beyond being selfish but not entirely toward the very inclusive value assumption of altruism. Nevertheless, stage three thinkers are much more inclusive than stage two thinkers. They have moved their fundamental assumption to one of the greatest number in society. They have, however, identified their limit of inclusiveness to a minority that has received less than the greatest good for the greatest number.

The various consequential philosophers, such as Jeremy Bentham and John Steward Mill, fall into this stage because of their value of deciding correctness using the greatest good for the greatest number. With this ethical theory, slavery can exist if slaves are considered property rather humans. However, it should be noted that advocates of this ethical theory did consider slaves as human beings and did oppose slavery. Nonetheless, under this normative ethical theory, minorities of various kinds can be politically, economically, or socially ignored or even oppressed.

STAGE FOUR

Stage four thinkers move beyond stage three moral development by using the fundamental assumption of inclusiveness is being a member of a "system." These thinkers are social system oriented, which means they follow the system's (e.g., government) rules and laws. Of course, when their system ceases to exist or is nearly broken, their inclusiveness may also cease to exist. Stage four thinkers are more inclusive than stage three thinkers as they can easily embrace minorities of various kinds if they see those minorities as being a part of the larger system. However, if the system leaders define groups as outside the system, then those declared outside groups can be rightfully politically, economically, or socially ignored or oppressed. Of the philosophers discussed, Josiah Royce could be a stage four thinker primarily because of his stress on loyalty. Stage four thinkers embrace the system and "duty, honor, and country" are fundamentally important to them. Thus, loyalty to a system is a paramount assumption in their ethical thinking.

STAGE FIVE AND SIX

Stages five and six move much closer to altruism. Stage five thinkers move beyond stage four moral development by reasoning in terms of a larger social contract, as did the American founders who signed the Declaration of Independence. In that document, the American patriots argued that the King of England broke the essential social contract with the American colonies. This type of moral thinking moves much closer to embracing altruism by being oriented to a larger population with defined moral values such as freedom of speech. Kohlberg's stage six is the final step toward the universal but in doing so stage six makes a turn away from being holistic. This stage is about the universal but it is acceptance of a principle or theory that can be in conflict with other principles or theories. Of note is that later versions of the Theory of Moral Development (Rest et al. 1999) actually combined stages five and six.

CAROL GILLIGAN AND REVISING THE THEORY OF MORAL DEVELOPMENT

Reflecting on the moral development stages in terms of the great philosophers, as presented in Exhibit 4.3, is useful as it helps us reconsider Kohlberg's theory. As explained earlier, the key assumption of his theory of moral development is that people act morally based on a sense of fairness and justice that grows within a person as they mature. Given this assumption, this theory becomes problematical at stages four and five but even disappears in stage six. In stage four, the purpose of morality is to maintain the social order of society. In stage five, the key is the notion of a social contract, which is the value set associated with some social orders, such as used in the United

States and other nations. This raises the question of whether within a nation marginalizing and discriminating against sets of people based on their nationality, ethnic background, race, or gender is fair and just. For example, at the beginning of the American republic, the U.S. Constitution marginalized and discriminated against most African Americans by declaring them less than equal citizens. Certainly, many people would conclude that such acts of discrimination were not an advanced sense of fairness and justice and therefore should not be considered a more mature ethical act. Fortunately, there is another way to view moral development.

Empirical observations tended to confirm Kohlberg's descriptive theory that humans fall into moral stages and some advance as they move

Carol Gilligan

through life. However, Carol Gilligan (1936–) took issue with Kohlberg's theory. She said the assumption of fairness and justice as a motivation for moral action was male thinking. Kohlberg failed to consider caring and compassion as a motivator, which was more typical female thinking (Gilligan 1982). Gilligan raises an important question about the Kohlberg theory that relates to our discussion in chapter 1. The first determinant of a person's consciousness involving moral thinking—self-identity—corresponds nicely to the early stages of Kohlberg's theory, which shows an expansion of the self-identify from stages one, two, and three. Empirical testing does verify this assumption but it also allows us to consider an alternative assumption proposed by Carol Gilligan.

If we modify Kohlberg's theory to reflect the thinking of Carol Gilligan, then a sense for caring for others becomes critical and fits the ever-increasing movement away from an egocentric assumption within the theory to a more altruistic assumption as a person moves up the stages of moral development. As a person becomes less selfish and more selfless, they develop caring and compassion for others. That caring and compassion expands from themselves to an increasingly larger circle from family, to tribe, to nation, to others in the world, and eventually to the environment and the universe.

Therefore, if stages four, five, and even six are modified to reflect an ever-increasing caring and compassion, the revised Gilligan /Kohlberg theory becomes more parsimonious. In stages one and two there is little to no caring for others. In stages three and four there is caring for others but it is limited by the utilitarian maxim and the question of loyalty. The new stage five is more altruistic as it is fully caring for a large population with shared higher values. In the new stage six, caring and compassion expands to everything, including the environment, all creatures, and the universe.

Unfortunately, Gilligan framed her challenge to Kohlberg in terms of male versus female thinking reducing it to an issue of gender to many scholars. Certainly, many do consider caring and compassion to be female traits but framing her argument in that manner diminishes the significance of her remarkable contribution to moral development theory. The fact is her contribution builds on and improves on Kohlberg's theory. That alone is a substantial theoretical contribution to the descriptive theory of ethics.

DEVELOPING A MORE COMPLEX THEORY

The history of ethics gives us a mixed and often confused picture of what ethics is, and even its usefulness to a profession such as public administration. The Gilligan/Kohlberg descriptive theory is a major breakthrough in ethical theories because with it we can identify training that can help people enhance an individual's moral development. However, much more is needed to significantly improve the moral development within a profession. Fortunately, this can be done by looking at the public administration literature discussed in chapter 2 and using it to develop an even more robust practical ethical theory.

The Gilligan revision of Kohlberg's theory focuses on caring and compassion that can be restated as one determinant—the identification of a person as being selfish (egocentric) or selfless (altruistic). For purposes of building a more practical theory for public administration, there is a need to understand the limits of the three ethical approaches, especially in terms of that one determinant. For example, by knowing that Kantian ethics does not work with egocentric people, then one knows to always couple Kantian ethics with motivational rewards or penalties that result in egocentric persons acting morally even if the true motivator was not ethics.

Clearly, that one determinant is particularly important in understanding the limitations of normative ethics. What other determinants limit the effective use of one or more of the three approaches to ethics? Some likely determinants to achieving ethics are analytical ability (discussed in chapter 5), will power and self-control (discussed in chapter 7), ability to learn (discussed in chapter 8), and satisfaction motivators (discussed in chapter 6). For example, consequential ethics often requires strong mathematical abilities, but not everyone has such skills. Rule-based ethics requires a person to know the rules and possess the will power to follow those rules.

Virtue ethics requires self or organizational training to learn the necessary virtues, how to apply them in specific situations and practice to form good habits and responses . Thus, to be effective, two things must be present: (1) individuals with extensive knowledge of virtue ethics and how to apply it in practical situations and (2) excellent trainers to help employees create the needed habitual responses that flow out of applying virtue ethics to specific situations. For example, egocentrics and altruistic individuals require different satisfaction motivations. Egocentric people are motivated by pleasure or pain. Altruistic people are motivated by inner satisfaction, such as knowing what they do will benefit others.

CONCLUSION

As usual, Leon had some merit in saying: "Honestly, aren't these just old dead white guys not relevant to what real people are doing today?" Certainly, the modernists' and the postmodernists' negativism is cause for feelings of hopelessness about the relevance of ethics, as noted by Leon. However, we should be positive about the evolution of ethics. Clearly, the works of old dead guys like Aristotle, Kant, Bentham, and others did create ethical theories that are, to some degree, useful to real people today. In addition, people like Wittgenstein, Kohlberg, and Gillian in the last and present century made important advances in our collective thinking about ethics. Even the negativism of the modernist and postmodern great thinkers has been useful, as their work challenged more contemporary ethical thinkers to redouble their positive efforts, as will become clearer in chapters 6 and 12. Ethics can be more than just useful in public organizations. It can be significantly important in creating radically better places to work and accomplish wonderful public outcomes in the present and future.

REVIEW QUESTIONS

1. What is hedonism and are its implications the dominant value in the public service? Argue that it should be the fundamental value that defines what public servants do in the public services. Now, argue against this fundamental value. Which is the better argument and why is it better?

2. Compare and contrast Maslow's and Aristotle's approaches to self-realization.

3. In what way does a deep faith in God reinforce rule-based ethics? If that faith does not exist, what are the implications to rule-based ethics?

4. What is the importance of the rational thinking to virtue ethics relationship?

5. Compare stoic thinking to hedonism. What are the implications of stoic thinking in terms of ethics in public administration?

6. In what way is utilitarianism a sophisticated version of hedonism?

7. Compare and contrast Kant with Bentham in terms of ethics. Which is more altruistic? Why?

8. In what way is benefit-cost analysis used in budgeting a version of the hedonist calculus?

9. What is the similarity, if any, between the thinking of Schopenhauer and Buddha?

10. If Nietzsche's view of ethics were adopted in public administration, what would be the likely outcome?

11. What is the essential assumption of modernism? How did it compensate for that assumption in the quest for acceptable knowledge? In what way is positivism an extreme of modernist thinking? Compare and contrast modernism and logical positivism.

12. In what ways are doubt, faith, and the concept of intersubjectivity important to ethics?

13. Why is Locke's concept of a "blank tablet" important to ethics? In what way does DNA challenge Locke's concept and affirm Plato's and Aristotle's alternative concept?

14. What is the allegory of the cave? Why is this relevant to the acceptance of ethics reform?

15. In what way were George Edward Moore's ideas in conflict with Kant? How is this difference of thought important to ethics?

16. What is the implication of moral relativism to ethics in public administration? Why is it important?

17. Relate the various ethical philosophies discussed in this chapter to stage one moral development as explained by Kohlberg.

REFERENCES

Aristotle. 1980. *The Nicomachean Ethics*. Oxford, UK: Oxford University Press.

Denhardt, Kathryn G. 1988. *The Ethics of Public Service: Resolving Moral Dilemmas in Public Organizations*. Westport, CT: Greenwood Press.

"Epictetus." 2004. *Internet Encyclopedia of Philosophy*. www.iep.utm.edu/e/epictetu.htm.

"Epicurus." 2004. *Internet Encyclopedia of Philosophy*. ww.utm.edu/research/iep/e/epicur.htm.

Gabris, Gerald T. 1991. "Beyond Conventional Management Practices: Shifting Organizational Values." In *Ethical Frontiers in Public Management*, edited by James S. Bowman, 205–24. San Francisco: Jossey-Bass.

Garofalo, Charles, and Dean Geuras. 1999. *Ethics in the Public Service: The Moral Mind at Work*. Washington, DC: Georgetown University Press.

Gilligan, Carol. 1982. *In a Different Voice: Psychological Theory and Women's Development*. Cambridge, MA: Harvard University Press.

Gilligan, Carol, and J. Attanucci. 1996. "The Moral Principle of Care." In *Introducing Psychological Research*. London: Palgrave.

"Heraclitus." *Stanford Encyclopedia of Philosophy*. http://plato.standford.edu/entries/heraclitus/. Accessed May 30, 2010.

Hobbes, Thomas (1651). Leviathan. Revised Edition, eds. A. P. Martinich and Brian Battiste. Peterborough, ON: Broadview Press, 2010.

Jackson, Julius. 1993. *A Guided Tour of John Stuart Mill's Utilitarianism*. Mountain View, CA: Mayfield Publishing.

Kant, Immanuel. 1997. *Groundwork of the Metaphysics of Morals*. Cambridge, UK: Cambridge University Press.

Keller, Helen. Quoted in Dennett, Daniel C. 1991. *Consciousness Explained*. New York: Bay Back Books/Little, Brown & Co.

Kuhn, Thomas S. 1996. *The Structure of the Scientific Revolution*. Chicago: University of Chicago Press.

Mackie, J. L. 1977. *Ethics: Inventing Right and Wrong*. London: Penguin.

Newton, Lisa H. 1989. *Ethics in America*. Englewood Cliffs, NJ: Prentice Hall.

Nietzsche, Friedrich. 1989. *Beyond Good and Evil*. New York: Random House.

Roach, Geshe Michael. 2003. *Diamond Cutter: The Buddha on Managing Your Business and Your Life*. New York: Doubleday.

Sahakian, William S., and Mabel Lewis Sahakian. 1993. *Ideas of the Great Philosophers*. New York: Barnes and Noble.

Sherman, Nancy. 1997. *Making a Necessity of Virtue*. Cambridge, UK: Cambridge University Press.

Smith, Adam. 1776. *An Inquiry into the Nature and Causes of the Wealth of Nations*. London: W. Strahan.

5 Contemporary Ethics

PROFESSOR: *Yes, Leon, you have a question?*

LEON: *Well, it looks to me like Nietzsche, the modernists, and the postmodernists were correct. Like God, ethics is dead and aren't you just wasting our time in this class?*

In the twenty-first century, the two ethical normative theories that inform and influence public affairs and administration are deontological (rule-based) and consequential ethics (called also teleological), with deontological being the most influential. This chapter describes both types of ethics and the functionality of the two theories.

DEONTOLOGICAL ETHICS

KANT

Deontological ethics in public affairs and public administration focuses on the actions people perform and consequential ethics focuses on the expected outcome of actions. The classical source of contemporary deontological theories is Immanuel Kant. The seminal pillar of deontological ethics is the *obligation* that arises from moral laws or principles that were no longer based on God. Although a devout Christian, Kant insisted that moral law does not come from God but from ourselves. Using what he called pure practical reason, Kant argued that society should use the categorical imperative to generate maxims that tell people what they ought and ought not to do. The categorical imperative says that anything determined to be a rule must be unconditionally obeyed in all circumstances. The maxims consist of our duties and moral obligations. The use of this ethical theory permits reasoned people to judge what actions are ethical and what actions are unethical, regardless of the agent's (the person doing the action) intentions and the situational circumstances.

Modern thinking on ethics has impressively developed Kantian (rule-based) ethics, but doubts continue as to why we ought to carry out the duties prescribed by the maxims and principles that logically flow from the categorical imperative. Kant certainly believed in immortality and God, but he used neither as the key assumptions of his theory. Nevertheless, the unstated assumption of the moral theory are important. Like fellow Christians of his time, Kant believed that after death we would be judged, and a just God would provide happiness for those worthy of it and punish those who were not worthy. Thus, an unstated motivation for being ethical for him existed beyond the categorical imperative.

Today, however, many Kantian philosophers do not retain Kant's unstated assumptions. If a person is egocentric and reasons at Kohlberg's stage one or two, then the categorical imperative would mean Kantian ethics alone is not motivational to him unless the society enacted the categorical imperative with an enforceable law that has a considerable penalty. In other words, the questions raised by Leon at the beginning of chapters 2 and 3 tell us that there is little intrinsic motivation for an egocentric Leon to be moral without a pain avoidance or reward motivator.

CODE OF ETHICS

Exhibit 5.1 states the key duties or terms of the professional social conduct as defined and approved by the 2013 American Society for Public Administration Code of Ethics. It is a living document that continues to be improved and is periodically updated.

Exhibit 5.1. ASPA Code of Ethics

The American Society for Public Administration (ASPA) advances the science, art, and practice of public administration. The Society affirms its responsibility to develop the spirit of responsible professionalism within its membership and to increase awareness and commitment to ethical principles and standards among all those who work in public service in all sectors. To this end, we, the members of the Society, commit ourselves to uphold the following principles:

1. Advance the Public Interest. Promote the interests of the public and put service to the public above service to oneself.
2. Uphold the Constitution and the Law. Respect and support government constitutions and laws, while seeking to improve laws and policies to promote the public good.
3. Promote democratic participation. Inform the public and encourage active engagement in governance. Be open, transparent and responsive, and respect and assist all persons in their dealings with public organizations.
4. Strengthen social equity. Treat all persons with fairness, justice, and equality and respect individual differences, rights, and freedoms. Promote affirmative action and other initiatives to reduce unfairness, injustice, and inequality in society.
5. Fully Inform and Advise. Provide accurate, honest, comprehensive, and timely information and advice to elected and appointed officials and governing board members, and to staff members in your organization.
6. Demonstrate personal integrity. Adhere to the highest standards of conduct to inspire public confidence and trust in public service.
7. Promote Ethical Organizations: Strive to attain the highest standards of ethics, stewardship, and public service in organizations that serve the public.
8. Advance Professional Excellence: Strengthen personal capabilities to act competently and ethically and encourage the professional development of others.

Source: American Society for Public Administration Code of Ethics. http://www.aspanet.org/ASPA/Code-of-Ethics/ASPA/Code-of-Ethics/Code-of-Ethics.aspx?hkey=5b8f046b-dcbd-416d-87cd-0b8fcfacb5e7.

Codes of ethics, like the Ten Commandments, are often deontological and not aspirational. Organizations and professional associations have deontological codes of ethics, meaning they are maxims that flow from the reasoning of the categorical imperative and are not aspirational in nature. Leon asks a reasonable question but only in circumstances where the person making the ethical decision is egocentric and there are no rewards or punishments associated with the rule.

However, if such an egocentric person did firmly believe in God's heaven and hell, then Leon would be wrong. Just posting a deontological code of ethics on a wall without assigning consequences is not likely to be an ethical motivator for a significant number of people in a society, especially if they ignore the teachings of their faith tradition. In an increasingly secular society, there are many codes of ethics without enforced punishments or rewards. Thus, they are largely ineffective for many in organizational settings. For example, a College Sex Abuse Code of Ethics is effective when offenders, regardless of their stature in the school, are publicly punished but have little to no effect without such punishments. The public exposure and humiliation motivates those egocentric persons to not violate the codes.

Interestingly, moral thinkers at stages three and four also need to be aware that violators will be punished, but that need is not as overwhelming as for those in stages one and two. For them, the categorical imperative behind the code can be enough to motivate them because their concern is focused on conforming to what others expect of them, fulfilling a duty, or fulfilling a social contract. Negative exceptions for stage three and four thinkers occur normally due to the social pressure of public humiliation. For example, if a university fraternity, hall, or sports group has a group tradition or norm that to belong to the group a new member must violate the Sex Abuse Code as a test of group loyalty, then they are more likely to violate the code than abandoned the desire to join the group. Social pressure and loyalty to the group have a strong and often strange effect on stage three and four thinkers.

If rewards motivate stage two moral thinkers, what could motivate a large group of stage two thinkers beyond bribes? Aristotle argued that attaining the good life was a sufficient reward, but his argument fails for many people because the attainment of the good life requires a conscious awareness beyond egocentric thinking that might not exist. In addition, Bentham and Mill successfully redefined "good" life to be an external materialistic value rather than Aristotle's intent of an intrinsic value.

In other words, many people think only in terms of the short term and rarely in terms of a more sophisticated understanding of "the good life," as defined by Plato or Aristotle. However, when one reaches the higher stages of moral thinking, Kant and the meaning of "the good life" start to make sense as an ethical motivator. The Kantian categorical imperative is an essential inclusive concept that is in harmony with Aristotle's understanding of attaining the good life. The middle stages of moral development mark the beginnings of becoming altruistic.

Significantly for public organizations, moral development is cognitive. Thus, if a systematic education and training program existed to develop conscious, moral, and ethical development in employees at the lower stages of moral development, they can attained higher stages of moral development. The codes of ethics would be more motivational. If that occurred, the need for elaborate and expensive systems of punishments and rewards that are essential for the lower stages of moral development would not be as important.

DIFFICULT TO APPLY

Another limitation of deontological and especially consequential ethical theories (discussed later) is that they require a well-developed thinking, meaning a person who is highly rational and has some quantitative reasoning capabilities. Ethical theory, based on following the rules, requires people to think constantly in a logical manner. For example, using principle number 6 of the ASPA code—demonstrate personal integrity—as a rule rather than an aspiration, the public administrator has the duty to "demonstrate the highest standards in all activities to inspire public confidence and trust in public service." In the course of a normal week, a public administrator faces many situations that may require significant discretion and involve moral choices. Thus, that person must know the required duty, be able to recognize and understand when a situation arises that requires following that particular duty, and know all the possible options for action. Such a person must have a good memory using the two most used forms of ethics, be aware of all variables involved, and have the analytical capacity to think quickly in a highly complex political, social, and economic environment.

Applying abstract principles is difficult for a public servant to consider in the complex and fast moving environment of public administration. For example, how is a public administrator to know what actions on his or her part would inspire perfect or maximum public confidence and trust in public service? Believing all civil servants have such innate rational abilities is simply not realistic and is an unfair expectation of an employee who has not received adequate training.

Another difficulty is that the code itself can actually be dysfunctional in certain circumstances. For example, the code's call for public administrators to inspire public confidence and trust initially sounds wonderful. However, if the means to inspire public confidence requires them to obfuscate details, lie, kill, or allow harm to come to the innocent, then is the code really creating the type of professionalism that a democratic society needs? For example, if an environmental policy is put forward that the public administrators know will harm the water supply, do they stand fast in publicly supporting it? Of note, when elected officials attempt to cover up a past mistake with a lie and they are caught, their persona as a moral person normally suffers.

Another predicament is when a newly adopted policy benefits some constituents but harms others. In this situation, should the public administrator follow the code by telling those it harms to "trust" the new policy all the while knowing it will harm them? A public administrator knows that getting caught in a lie normally degrades his or her public trust and almost always the public will eventually know they lied. Thus, not telling some constituents that an adopted policy will harm them will eventually reduce the level of trust that they would normally have for an administrator. In some cases, remaining silent is as much a lie as telling one.

This situation places the public administrator in a dilemma. (An ethical dilemma occurs when there is no possible option in the circumstance that will not harm at last one party.) The official must weigh the options: (1) Should I lie to make the policy look and sound better than it is to instill public confidence in our new policy? or (2) Should I tell the truth and thus eventually increase public disrepute for myself and my agency? If I speak the truth, am I considered disloyal and a whistle blower? Such situations do occur in government and this reality calls into question a code that creates a moral dilemma for public administrators.

LEGALIZING ETHICS

Reformers often legalize ethics by creating rules and even laws based on Kantian ethical thinking. In addition, they also often create government units to enforce those rules. For example, the U.S. Office of Government Ethics produces many rules applicable to government workers. To illustrate, one rule says that a federal worker cannot accept a gift from a vendor, contractor, or grantor worth more than $25. In the domestic context within the United States, that is a reasonable rule, but outside the United States, where gift giving is considered polite and proper in society, this rule becomes a social problem. Normally, the public official resolves the problem by accepting the gift and then passing it on to the government so that the individual does not benefit from the gift but the country does.

Many state governments also have codes of governmental ethics and an office to enforce them. For example, the State of Louisiana has the Louisiana Ethics Administration Program with an eleven-member board appointed for staggered terms. The board administers the state's code of ethics with the stated purpose of ensuring:

- public confidence in the integrity of government,

- the independence and impartiality of elected officials and public employees,

- that governmental decisions and policies are made in the proper channel of the government structure, and

- that public office and employment are not used for private gain.

The Louisiana Board of Ethics' mission is based on deontological rules. When someone asks how the rules might apply to them, the board issues advisory opinions. When a possible rule violation exists, it conducts investigations. In addition, it conducts public hearings and training activities on its rules. If there is a violation, it is likely due to one of the reasons mentioned in Exhibit 5.2.

The Louisiana board focuses on complaints, investigations, and public hearings. By a decision of a 2/3 vote, the board can self-initiate an investigation. If they do so, they must notify the complainant and the respondent. They must consider any signed sworn complaints and they must send a copy of any complaint to the respondent. The board can consider information from a confidential investigation. It can subpoena witnesses, compel the production of documents, and do cross examinations. If a person is found to be in violation of the ethics code, the board can impose a fine and other penalties. The use of rules makes this approach to ethics more quantifiable, easier to enforce, and can bring a greater ethical awareness to public office.

The use of deontological rule-based ethics does not always produce the desired results. It can even create serious problems such as eroding trust within the organization, lowering morale, and creating inflexibility in government administration. Governments deal with complex public policy problems in society and rules are often just not flexible enough for the variety of common situational challenges of government. This approach to ethics is useful in many situations but it cannot resolve the full range of ethical problems faced by government because no volume of laws, codes of conduct, and threats regardless of their size can force all public employees to behave ethically in all situations.

Exhibit 5.2. Louisiana Ethics Rules

Conduct not allowed for a public servant includes the following
- Receipt of anything with an economic value by a public servant for services rendered to or for the following:
  - o Receipt of a thing of economic value from a source other than the governmental entity for the performance of official duties and responsibilities.
  - o Receipt of a thing of economic value for the performance of a service substantially related to public duties or which draws on non-public information.
  - o Receipt of a thing of economic value for assisting someone with a transaction with the agency of the public servant.
  - o Solicitation or acceptance of a thing of economic value as a gift.

- Elected officials and other public servants are not allowed to solicit or accept anything of economic value from paid lobbyist or their employers. This includes:
  - o Persons who have or are seeking to obtain a contractual or other business or financial relationship with the public servant's agency;
  - o Persons who are regulated by the public employee's agency; and
  - o Persons who have substantial economic interest which may be substantially affected by the performance or nonperformance of the public employee's official duties.

- Participation by a public servant in a transaction involving the governmental entity in which any of the following persons have a substantial economic interest:
  - o The public servant;
  - o Any member of his immediate family;
  - o Any person in which he has an ownership interest that is greater than the interest of a general class;
  - o Any person of which he is an officer, director, trustee, partner, or employee;
  - o Any person with whom he is negotiating or has an arrangement concerning prospective employment; and
  - o Any person who is indebted to him or is a party to an existing contract with him and by reason thereof is in a position to affect directly is economic interests.

- Bidding on, entering into, or being in any way interested in any contract subcontract or other transaction under the supervision or jurisdiction of the public servant's agency. This restriction also applies to the immediate family members of the public servant and to legal entities in which the public servant and /or his family embers own an interest in excess of 25 percent.
- A public servant's use of the authority of his office to compel or coerce a person to provide himself or someone else with a thing of economic value that they are not entitled to by law or the use of the authority of his office to compile or coerce a person to engage in political activity.
- A public servant or other person man not make a payment, give, loan, transfer, or deliver or offer to give, loan transfer or deliver a thing of economic value to a public servant when the public servant is prohibited by the Ethics Code from receiving such a thing of economic value.

Rules prohibit nepotism, which is when:
- Members of the immediate family of an agency head may not be employed in the agency.
- Members of the immediate family of a member of a governing authority or the chief executive of a governmental entity may not be employed in the governmental entity.
- Note that such family members are simply ineligible for employment.

Exceptions of nepotism are when:
- Persons employed in violation of this rule continuously since April 1, 1980;
- A person employed for one year prior to their family member becoming an agency head;
- A certified family member, who is a teacher, but disclosure is required;
- A licensed physician or registered nurse employed by a less than 100,000 service area health care provider; and
- During the two-year period following the termination of public service as an agency head or elected official, these individuals may not assist another for compensation, in a transaction, or in the appearance of a connection with any transaction involving their former agency nor may they render any service on a contractual basis to or for their former agency.
- During the two-year period following the termination of public service as a board or commission member, these individuals may not contract with, be employed in any capacity by, or be appointed to any position by that board or commission. However, during this same period, these individuals may not assist another for compensation in a transaction, or in an appearance in connection with a transaction involving the agency in which the former public employee participated while employed by the agency nor may the former public employee provide on a contractual basis to his former public employer, any service he provided while employed there.

Source: State of Louisiana. http://ethics.la.gov/Pub/Laws/ethsum.pdf. Accessed July 12, 2018.

Every rule is bound to have exceptions and often those exceptions are so numerous that the rule becomes moot. Also, no matter how clever the mind of the person writing the rule or law, there are always equally clever people looking for loopholes to circumvent the rules. Often when there are no loopholes present, public interest groups lobby to change regulations or the laws that supersede them to negate the effectiveness of the original codes.

Rules are undoubtedly useful in setting the ethical floor for the minimum acceptable behavior in an organized society and to motivate stage one thinkers if their failure to follow the regulations have consequences. However, rules come at a cost because they can also create red tape within a government agency and for the public the agency serves. Beyond creating frustration, red tape can lower the efficiency and effectiveness of public organizations. If government rules exist in the context of a mostly corrupt society, bribes to ignore the rules become commonplace and higher order reasoning and good character are significantly discouraged. Thus, rules have a much better chance of being useful in a society where corruption is unusual and when the necessity for rulemaking is limited.

CONSEQUENTIAL ETHICS

SOPHISTICATED HEDONISM

A major limitation of consequentialism or utilitarianism is its analytical challenge for determining the "greatest good for the greatest number." Such calculations are often made with a cost-benefit analysis, which is not easily done especially where benefits do not easily lend themselves to monetary quantification. For example, how does one determine the value of a human life lost in an automobile accident in the computation of "benefits and costs." Is a life worth less if lost in a car accident on a road and worth more if lost in an airplane accident? Insurance actuaries and economists use such logic to calculate the persons flying have a greater lifetime wealth than persons that drive on a road. Why? Because the average person flying has a larger income than the average person driving. Even more significantly, the maxim of the "greatest good for the greatest number" is often not sensitive to political minorities in society and thus racial and ethnic discrimination is possible under utilitarianism.

This ethical approach to decision making is based on the assumption of the hedonist (rational economic man) rather than on the more altruistic consciousness assumed by Kant. The "rational economic man" concept assumes that a market solution is needed for every action or policy. Users of this concept do not consider the viability of social solutions such as negotiation, compromise, and generosity. Their approach considers ethics in terms of political economics. For the utilitarian hedonist, corruption is normally considered something that is dysfunctional to the economy in general but not necessarily for a person or group in a particular situation. They look for how much monetary dysfunctionality exists for the person involved in particular situation but not the larger public. For example, a hedonist can consider bribes are a fact of life that they must calculate into the cost-of-doing business in the market price of items or services. Given their selfish orientation, hedonists ignore the larger cost to the society (often called externalities) that arises when bribes add to the total cost of making the product or performing a service and thus distort the cost of goods or services for a society. Thus, corruption at the society level almost always distorts the market and encourages increased criminal activity that further disturbs the social harmony of the society.

Because time is money, especially in the modern economy, private citizens and corporations learn that paying bribes to low- and even sometimes high-level public officials can expedite the service of government bureaus, such as passport agencies and driver's license bureaus. This reality can encourage low-level bureaucrats to deliberately provide slower service unless the "customer" pays a bribe for expedited service. This bribery provides an illegal money stream to often underpaid low-level bureaucrats who intentionally provide poor service to the public as a means to supplement their poor salaries.

A commonly used utilitarian reform answer to this ethical problem in government is to simply legalize the payoff. The reform transforms the bribe and makes it into fees-for-service to expedite the process (for example, getting a license or permit) and the additional revenue stream goes to the government rather than to the individual lower-level bureaucrat. For example, China and the United States process travel visas and passports at one regular (slow) speed but will process visas and passports more quickly if a traveler pays an extra "expedited" surcharge. Thus, they legalize the extra payment practice and divert the payment from the pockets of the clerks to the government's treasury. This does work but it also means that wealthy travelers get preferred treatment over their less wealthy counterparts, and the low-level bureaucrat is still poorly paid and looking for another way to supplement their income.

CALCULATIONS

In both the private and public sectors, utilitarian thinking can and does create dysfunctional social behavior. For example, a club owner might be faced with the problem that a local city fire marshal refuses to give him a permit to run his business because his venue has a fire hazard infraction. The owner is faced with an expensive decision, either pay to fix the building for $800,000 or pay the fire marshal a $20,000 bribe to overlook the infraction. He knows the fire marshal is known for often taking bribes and this fact adds weight to his decision to pay the bribe and not do the renovation.

In this case, the fire marshal is also a hedonistic thinker. He takes the bribe thinking that the extra money helps increase his compensation and the chances are fairly minimal that the fire hazard he cited would actually burn down the venue. But, within a week after taking the bribe, the club does burn down, killing forty people. Given consequential ethics, the club owner and the fire marshal were correct except for one important point: Neither thought to include in their ethical analysis the cost of a prison sentence and civil damages for killing forty people. Of note to realize is that such calculations can never accommodate for all possible scenarios because the future is not always predicable.

From an analytical perspective that calculation is often difficult because the analysts must know the *probability* of the club burning down and the cost to the club owner and fire marshal of long prison sentences plus any awards for civil damages for wrongful death and injuries because of the fire. Frankly and not surprisingly, both the club owner and the fire marshal would most likely just skip those calculations because those consequential analyses are difficult and probably beyond their educated ability to make. Nevertheless, their poor-or-none calculation resulted in the death of forty people, two prison sentences, and large civil damages that took all the assets that they both had before the fire. In this case, the hedonist prevailing attitude is that you are only unethical if you get caught.

In this type of ethical thinking, notice the importance of quantitative analysis and its impact on hedonistic thinking. When making their calculations using cost-benefit or other related analyses, the club owner would have to consider paying the big expense for fire proofing his establishment and the fire marshal would have to consider the loss of his illegal revenue and the need to live on his low government salary as well as the cost to his family if he lost his job, pension, or went to jail. Beyond the challenge of calculation, reflect on applying a different ethical approach (e.g., virtue ethics) to these ethical decisions. Would the use of virtue ethics have saved forty lives? Yes. Because both the club owner and the fire marshal would simply say that, "The building must be fixed because there is no other real option."

Too often in more complex situations, consequential ethical thinking is impractical. Even using the most advanced computers, how can someone even imagine all of the possible branches to those decision tree calculations? Complex situations require calculating an unfathomable number of benefits and cost consequences of a person's ethical decisions but also the policy decisions of a legislature acting for a society. Even if analysts could make such calculations, how can heart-felt analysts using reason attach a nondisputed numeric value, such as money, to a benefit involving intrinsic worth such as peace, tranquility, love, harmony, beauty, and life itself for those who might be harmed in a fire?

Clearly, someone can arbitrarily select a value but selecting a value that is nondisputable is simply impossible. For example, in making reparations to the families of 9/11 victims, awards were made based on economic determinations of the *potential* worth of the victim. However, is a person really worth less because he is a waiter in a restaurant rather than a financial analyst in New York? What if the busboy in the restaurant was working on a master's degree? How can someone calculate his potential worth if his future success of receiving the degree is still unknown? Yet, without a value such as "economic determination of potential worth" one cannot apply consequential thinking to do the necessary calculations. Thus, the notion of consequential thinking for individuals with a developed conscious becomes foolish, impractical, and sometimes even abusive to the notion of rational critical thought.

PRIVATIZATION

Another example of the utilitarian ethical perspective involves privatization. Hedonists think corruption is merely a cost factor that needs to be considered in the calculus of their decision making. Hedonists think that all people are egocentric even if they fool themselves by using altruistic language. One means to discourage public corruption is by shifting the decision maker's calculations or circumstances to force the potential corrupting persons to make the "correct" decision from a purely economic position based on hedonistic values. For example, politically some people advocate for the privatization of many government activities to remove government functions from state control and place them in the hands of private markets.

Part of their argument for privatization is not only that it takes the activity out of the government budget but that it also makes giving bribes to lower government officials impossible because there are no longer government officials in that activity. Of course, this approach would eliminate low-level government corruption but it would not necessarily stop the same corruption from happening in the private corporations and the awarding of contracts. Therefore, low-level corruption would continue but merely shift from the public to the private sector. For example, when government leaders privatize a state enterprise such as water treatment plants or air traffic controllers, top government officials can either give sweetheart deals to their favorite private sector leaders for a favorable price or they rig the bidding process for under-the-table large bribes. The result is that those top government officials become very rich and the new private monopolistic companies have little regard for the public's interest as they raise their prices, lower the quality of service, and sometimes even allow the now street-level corruption to continue unabated in their company.

For a utilitarian, the phenomenon of corruption produces market inefficiencies and unfairness in the distribution of public benefits and costs. To them, corruption distorts the channeling of private interests effectively, and their privatization efforts normally involve changing the political and economic context so that rational persons will function ethically out of their sense of maximizing their happiness from a hedonist's perspective. However, this requires top-level political support that often comes at the cost of high-level corruption even in advanced wealthy nations.

LEGALIZING CORRUPTION

Cozy Politics

Peter Kobrak's 2002 book *Cozy Politics* points to a political science version of the utilitarian analysis. Kobrak's thesis is that interest group politics of the corporate rich in the United States has corrupted American government at the highest levels. He argued that the "greatest good for the greatest number" is only a pretense and it actually does not apply in the United States because the richest 40 percent have an essential de facto monopoly on defining public policy for everyone. The situation in the United States has changed dramatically since Kobrak's book was published and since the Occupy Wall Street Movement (September 7, 2011). His 40 percent has been revised to the astonishing 1 percent, who are now the richest.

Kobrak postulates that the rich use their money and knowledge to *legally* corrupt American society through political means. This possibility was anticipated by the founders of the United States and is one of the reasons for the unique checks and balances approach in the U.S. Constitution. Kobrak says the relative political bargaining power of the rich benefits them disproportionately and hurts society as a whole. Thus, the result is not only an unfair distribution of public benefits and costs but more significantly a radical shift in national wealth to the already rich. Although this type of corruption exists on a massive scale in America, Kobrak makes the mind-jarring point that it is all quite legal.

Some examples illustrate this legal version of corruption. Until 2018, the stated American tax rate for corporations and rich individuals was high compared to other industrial nations but the tax code significantly skewed deductions, exemptions, and depreciations resulting in actual tax collection to benefit the rich and the very rich. As a result, there was a de facto zero to small tax rate for the rich, who played the political system, due to mostly massive legal tax loopholes provided for them. After 2018, the legal tax rate for all the rich is significantly. Thus, the system facilitates the so-called Matthew effect (Matthew 25:29) in which the rich get richer whereas the middle and lower classes get poorer and the poor remain poor.

After the presidential election of 2016, civic duty to vote and speak out on public issues increased due to the strong opinions within both political parties. Before 2016, there was a weaker sense of civic duty within the poor and middle class electorate. As a result, they did not wish to vote or the false promises of politicians easily fooled them to not bother to vote. This voter compounded the problem of legalized corruption because many poor and middle class Americans abandoned their only truly effective tool—the ballot box—to stop cozy politics. This type of situation is especially true in years when there is not a presidential election and the primary contests are at stake. Often in such elections, only 20 percent or less of the electorate successfully elect politicians who profit from cozy politics and in turn harm the poor and middle classes. In contrast, the interest groups that represent wealthy corporations and the rich parlay their influence using money and lobbying know-how into strong political power. In the 2016 election, the electorate voted in larger numbers against both of the established political parties and elected a populist president and congress that then compounded the negative impact of cozy politics.

In 2010, the Supreme Court ruling in Citizens United v. the Federal Election Commission that spending for political purposes is protected under the First Amendment as free speech (Duignan 2010). Thus, corporations and unions are not limited in the amount of their money they can contribute to a candidate. This ruling gave rise to the expression "dark money" referring to extremely large sums of money that is available to politicians without clear understanding as to the monies' sources from private interest group.

SIGNIFICANT INTEREST GROUPS

According to Kobrak, the rich minority corrupt the political process because political parties are increasingly less significant in American politics and interest groups are growing more significant. The rich can finance the interest groups that push their narrow agendas with great success in influencing Congress. Their success is partly due to the reality that running for public office at the national and sometimes state and local levels has become incredibly expensive. Political candidates need to raise millions of dollars for election campaigns in their continuing bids to gain and keep power by using direct but mostly indirect contributions.

Interest groups and their political action committees (PACs) made up of wealthy supporters supply much of the money for politicians to run for office. Kobrak (2002) notes that during *every week* of a senator's six-year term, the average senator must raise at least $10,000 for his or her re-election campaign expenses. In the years since 2002, the cost of television advertising and other media outlets has increased dramatically. Obviously, the need to raise massive amounts of campaign money drives the political views of the congressional candidates and discourages challengers, especially those who do not wish to be influenced by interest groups. For example, the Georgia Sixth District special election in June 2017 for a House of Representative seat shattered all other races for costs at roughly $60 million (Beckel 2017).

Legislation created what Kobrak called the "second constituency," which consists of wealthy individuals, corporations, and interest groups to whom a candidate must pledge at least access. The Citizens United case ruling made the "second constituency" remarkably powerful, as it permitted unlimited spending by special interest groups. For example, the Koch brothers' super PAC spent $889 million in the 2016 presidential primary election on behalf of a Republican candidate (Confessore 2015). These court rulings opened the door to unlimited spending, primarily in negative ad campaigns by interest groups, who often engage in "false news." Today, interest groups operate committees that are both connected and unconnected to the political candidate. Connected committees are somewhat limited in their spending but there are no limits on the amount unconnected committees can spend on the candidate's behalf. Governments in other countries are not legally allowed to interfere in American elections but have done so with some success, as was the case with Russia in the 2016 presidential campaign.

In the political jargon, "rent seeking" refers to individuals' or interest group's use of widespread and often growing political or institutional power to extract money from public assets with no stated quid pro quo. "Rents" create unavoidable costs to the public treasury that provide no or inappropriately little benefit to society. An example of "rent" is legislation that requires the

U. S. Bureau of Land Management to rent public lands to cattle ranchers for grazing their herds at less than 20 percent of the normal market value. The so-called non quid pro quo is largely done through campaign contributions by various cattle ranchers' associations to members of Congress who are on the committees that write the legislation for the Bureau of Land Management.

Kobrak calls the Washington lobbyists "porkophiles" and tells us they have raised rent seeking to a new level by making the practice legal. Members of Congress squeeze money from rich special interest groups, including the second constituency, by granting them access, which really means legislative favoritism that pays them the "rent" in the form of favorable decisions. Members of Congress find policy niches in their committee assignments that rich interest groups consider important because congressional committees can write legislation that creates favorable "rent." Sometimes "access" can mean the interest groups are actually invited into the process of writing the language of the legislation to create loopholes in laws when congressional committees meet to draft legislation. This practice provides a continuous source of financial support for the ever more demanding costs of political election campaigns. Essentially, campaign laws and practices have legalized political corruption. Without a massive electorate demand for reform, the prospects of changing the system are dim.

FUNCTIONALITY OF THE THEORIES

DEFINING THE FLOOR

As suggested earlier, deontological and consequential ethics provide an ethical "floor" in society that essentially defines a minimum level of acceptable ethical behavior. Realistically, the intelligent thinkers with a limited awareness of the public good will eventually find ways to circumvent ethical reforms. For governments to achieve a more stable ethical floor, a different approach to ethics is needed to augment the two dominant types of ethics presented in this chapter.

First, recognition of the inadequacies of deontological and consequential ethics by and of themselves is required. Clearly, these theories are necessary but insufficient for a sophisticated society that hires thousands of lawyers, accountants, and other highly educated people to subvert the purposes of ethics. In truth, the hired guns have largely obviated the positive impacts of ethical approaches.

Consequential ethics are insufficient but they can and do strengthen ethics in society in some limited situations. Therefore, governments are wise to take advantage of this type of ethics within their real limitations. This form of ethical decision making assumes that people think and act in their perceived best interest. Therefore, conditions within the system are manipulated so that persons actually act to benefit their own interests and also benefit the public good. An excellent example for the use of this approach was the passport system cited earlier. This use of consequential ethics works in that situation because most of the people who travel to other nations and need a quick turnaround for visa and passport applications are not poor.

There is a worth to both deontological (rule-based) and consequential-based ethical reasoning as they do make an important contribution to ethical thinking in the twenty-first century in certain limited situations but clearly not in all and maybe not even in most circumstances. Rule-based thinking gives us a baseline for ethical reasoning in a society, especially for the more ego-centered thinkers in levels one and two of Kohlberg's stages of moral development. Rules permit and help sustain a minimum level of civilization in society, especially when they are made into laws with appropriate punishment for noncompliance.

At its best, consequential thinking guides the essential selfish thinker to act not only in his own best interests but manipulates the system so that the actions of that person also serve the greater good. Thus, this results in steering even the more sophisticated thinkers into performing acts and services that are beneficial to society with a minimal need for a public enforcement mechanism. Both of these approaches are useful and probably necessary but they are also insufficient for creating the needed individual and group ethical behavior essential for the twenty-first century.

The fundamental nature of the market system is one reason the deontological and consequential approaches to ethics are typically insufficient. The market system has important strengths but it rarely exists in the idealized form that is taught in college economics classes. At its worst, capitalism perpetuates and harms the poor, disproportionately increases the wealth of the richest, harms the environment, harms the middle and poor classes, and often causes other social and economic ills beyond the scope of this text. Nevertheless, there is wisdom in the use of the market system as it encourages economic and industrial initiatives that positively impact the size of the economy, increases productivity, and makes it easier to discard less effective economic activities in society.

The market system does take advantage of the people who are stage three, four, and five Kohlberg thinkers by making it easier for them to direct their energy into actions that benefit all of society. Because the market system has both good and bad outcomes, the better economic reform is not to abandon the market system but to somehow mitigate its faults and stimulate the positive efforts to promote the common welfare as stated in the U.S. Constitution. What is needed is public recognition that the market system alone cannot produce the desired societal outcomes necessary for a whole society that also cares about the poor, the middle class, and the environment.

REDEFINING DEMOCRACY

A significant negative influence of consequential thinking is the redefinition of "democracy" to mean only "majority rule" that the wealthiest interest groups control. Consequential thinking at the macro level concerns the greatest good for the greatest number and this concept has helped redefined the American form of democracy. At the beginning of the republic, democratic participation was limited to males who owned property, but, even within that set of the population, there was a minority who used their minority rights to keep public focus on the public good as they defined it. Over time, the meaning of democracy was redefined to be the rule by the "majority," who are active private interest groups. They represent about 1 percent of the electorate and pay for the elections of their select politicians who are capable of winning a majority. That so-called majority is less than 30 percent of the voting population that go to the polls in most elections.

A review of the U.S. Constitution (see the Appendix) provides a quick examination of the intent of the American experiment in government. Although the electorate at the beginning of the republic was composed of white male landowners, the Constitution was written to protect everyone's right to speech, assembly, and fair trial. The preamble says the created form of government was for the whole society and the Declaration of Independence says that "all men are created equal, that they are endowed by their creator with certain unalienable rights, that among those are life, liberty and the pursuit of happiness." Over many years, the right to vote was extended to non-property owners, African Americans, women, and younger people, but political leaders in the last 150 years have sometimes misplaced their concern for the whole of American society to favor the richest in society over the larger public good.

The problem with this redefinition of democracy is that the theoretical benefit to "the greatest number in society" can easily mean harming the minority in society and by interpreting the majority to mean only those with the most wealth can buy politicians. Thus, a perpetual poor class and increasing poorer middle class becomes acceptable, issues like degrading education, limiting health care and harming the environment become reasonable. With this approach to thinking, placing Japanese Americans in internment camps during World War II was acceptable. In the twenty-first century, putting African Americans, Hispanic Americans, and possibly Muslim Americans in jails or de facto ghettos has become acceptable in the redefined meaning of "democracy."

With this redefinition, the constitutional guarantee of habeas corpus, which requires the government to bring an accused person in front of a judge to determine if there is a legal reason to incarcerate the person, can be ignored for selected minorities in order to protect the majority. That precedent, established in Nazi Germany during the 1930s and 1940s, shows how this approach can exist and how its use can be rationalized in laws to protect the majority from harm by the minority (Adams and Balfour 1998). These same procedures of holding people without due process occurred to Japanese Americans in World War II. Those who dispute using the term "Nazi" in relation to past actions that society now considers awful need to realize that those actions were always said to be done for the betterment of the majority in society without regard for minority rights. In fact, it is still used by America as a successful argument to hold combatants at Guantanamo Bay detention camp without any formal charges or trials and more recently to hold immigrants, who are also entitled to due process under American law.

CONCLUSION

To address Leon's comments at the beginning of this chapter, ethics is most definitely not dead. However, it is not functioning as well as it should in the twenty-first century, especially due to the almost exclusive use of deontological (rules) and consequential ethics. Both are limited in how they motivate positive human behavior. One inadequacy of ethical rules, which are converted into laws, is that those laws can be reinterpreted by interest groups in such a manner that the public good and interest of the society is either neglected or forgotten.

REVIEW QUESTIONS

1. Compare and contrast deontological and consequential ethics.

2. Give the pros and cons for a Kantian code of ethics.

3. Explain how one ethical motivation is associated with one's stage of moral development.

4. Why are deontological and consequential ethics difficult to apply?

5. Explain the Kantian logical connection between ethics and law.

6. Explain how something like paying a bribe relates to consequential ethics theory.

7. Explain Kobrak's utilitarian argument in Cozy Politics.

8. Make two arguments for and against Machiavelli's assertion that democracy is not a viable form of government over an extended time period.

REFERENCES

Adams, Guy D., and Danny Balfour. 1998. *Unmasking Administrative Evil.* Thousand Oaks, CA: Sage.

American Society for Public Administration Code of Ethics. http://www.aspanet.org/ASPA/Code-of-Ethics/ASPA/Code-of-Ethics/Code-of-Ethics.aspx?hkey=5b8f046b-dcbd-416d-87cd-0b8fcfacb5e7. Accessed July 12, 2018.

Beckel, Michael. 2017. "The Money Behind the Most Expensive U.S. House Race in History." *IssueOne*, June 16. http://www.issueone.org/money-behind-expensive-us-house-race-history/. Accessed July 13, 2018.

Citizens United v. Federal Election Commission. www.scotuslogcom/casefiles/cases. Accessed on July 17, 2018.

Confessore, Nicholas. 2015. "Koch Brothers' Budget of $889 Million for 2016 Is on Par with Both Parties Spending." *New York Times*, January 27. https://www.nytimes.com/2015/01/27/us/politics/kochs-plan-to-spend-900-million-on-2016-campaign.html?mcubz=0.

Cooper, Terry. 1982. *The Responsible Administrator.* Port Washington, NY: Kennikat Press.

Duggett, Michael, ed. 2001. *Ethics and Value in Public Administration.* Brussels, Belgium: International Institute of Administrative Sciences.

Duignan, Brian. 2010. "Citizens United v. Federal Election Commission." *Encyclopedia Britannica.* https://www.britannica.com/event/Citizens-United-v-Federal-Election-Commission.

Freeman, Stephen J. 2000. *Ethics: An Introduction to Philosophy and Practice.* Stamford, CT: Wadsworth.

Geuras, Dean, and Charles Garofalo. 2002. *Practical Ethics in Public Administration.* Vienna, VA: Management Concepts.

Jones, Clifford A. 1976. "Buckley v. Valeo." *Encyclopedia Britannica.* https://www.britannica.com/event/Buckley-v-Valeo.

Kobrak, Peter. 2002. *Cozy Politics: Political Parties, Campaign Finance, and Compromised Governance.* Boulder, CO: Lynne Reinner.

Lee Ye Hee, Michelle and Jeff Stein. 2018. "Dark Money Groups Don't Need to Disclose Donors to IRS, Treasury Says. *Washington Post.* https://wapo.st/2mn7?tid=ss_mail-amp. Accessed July 17, 2018.

Louisiana Board of Ethics. n.d. http://www.ethics.la.gov/Pub/Law/ethsum.pdf. Accessed July 12, 2018.

Lynch, Thomas D., and Todd J. Dicker. 1998. *Handbook of Organization Theory and Management: The Philosophical Approach.* New York: Marcel Dekker.

Lynch, Thomas D., and Cynthia E. Lynch. 1998. "Twenty-First Century Philosophy and Public Administration." In *Handbook of Organization Theory and Management: The Philosophical Approach*, edited by Thomas D. Lynch and Todd J. Dicker, 463–78. New York: Marcel Dekker.

Lynch, Thomas D., Richard Omdal, and Peter L. Cruise. 1997. "Secularization of Public Administration." *Journal of Public Administration Research and Theory* 7, no. 3: 473–488.

Madison, James. 1961. "Federalist No. 10." In *The Federalist Papers*, ed. Clinton Rossiter, 77–84. New York: New American Library.

Organization for Economic and Cooperative Development. 1996. "Ethics in the Public Service: Current Issues and Practice OECD." http://www.oecd.org/puma/gvrnance/ethics/pubs/eip96/execsum.htm.

Rose-Ackerman, Susan. 1999. *Corruption and Government: Causes, Consequences, and Reform.* New York: Cambridge University Press.

Selsam, Howard. 1965. *Ethics and Progress.* New York: International Publishers.

Sheeran, Patrick. J. *Ethics in Public Administration.* Westport, CT: Praeger.

Velasquez, Manuel G. 2002. *Business Ethics.* Upper Saddle River, NJ: Pearson Prentice Hall.

Windt, Peter V., Peter C. Appleby, Margaret P. Battin, Leslie P. Francis, and Bruce M. Landesman. 1989. *Ethical Issues in the Profession.* Englewood Cliffs, NJ: Prentice Hall.

Virtue Ethics

PROFESSOR: *Yes, Leon, what seems to be bothering you?*

LEON: *Why would anybody take the trouble to learn and apply virtue ethics? It's ancient! How can it possibly be relevant for anyone in the twenty-first century?*

Saying virtue ethics was developed early in the intellectual history of humankind is not a logical reason to say it is not relevant to us in our century. Before the advent of modernism and the need for observable evidence to accept something as true, virtue ethics was practiced in several cultures for thousands of years with some positive results. However, Leon's negativity toward virtue ethics is in good company because many contemporary influential philosophers considered ethics in general to be nonsense and virtue ethics, especially, to be foolish nonsense. Since the Enlightenment and until late in the twentieth century, notable philosophers firmly argued against this type of normative ethics largely because to them there was no end purpose (telos) to being human and without it virtue ethics made no sense. Only in the past half century has there been a resurgence in acceptance of virtue ethics.

PROLOGUE TO VIRTUE ETHICS

THE BOOK OF THOTH

The first Egyptian pyramids were built in 2850 BCE. Centuries earlier, the Egyptians produced a myth called the Book of Thoth, which was the basis for the normative ethics that served Egyptian civilization well for more than 3,000 years. Their ethics created a sense of internal accountability within the people of Egypt but also within the kingdom's leaders and its public administration. It guided their moral choices and served as an internal gyroscope to provide them with a sense of what comprised right and wrong behavior in their daily lives.

Like many civilizations, the Egyptians linked ethics to the religion of their society. Ancient Egyptians believed there was life after death. At death, each person was brought before the gods to determine if they had been good enough in life to have an afterlife. To the Egyptians, the heart recorded a person's spiritual deeds. Their heart was placed on the scale of justice. If a person's heart weighed more than an ostrich feather, then they failed the test and would not be allowed by the gods to proceed to the afterlife. To not being able to continue on to the heavenly life was the worst punishment that could occur to an ancient Egyptian. Even today in English-speaking countries, the expression "having a heavy heart" connotes sadness and regret (Budge, 1976).

EGYPTIAN CHARACTER VIRTUES

Although Egyptians did not believe the heart was the place of consciousness, they did believe it was the place that recorded the accumulated ethical decisions of a person's life. It was the seat of creative power, courage, and the affective life. Thus, it held the spiritual memory of an ethical being. Although not the place where the soul existed, the heart manifested the character of the soul. To the Egyptians, character or virtue was not only important, it was everything. Exhibit 6.1 is a set of guidelines for moral action based on virtues that create positive life habits as recorded in the Book of Thoth to provide advice on how to be a person of great virtue. The early Egyptians related the notion of heart and character as we sometimes do today. Essentially, moral conduct over a lifetime determined the weight of the heart. This same list appears on the walls of many of the discovered tombs in the Valley of the Kings in Luxor, Egypt. As one descends into a tunnel on the way to the tombs, the walls of the tunnel are painted with specific examples of what the Pharaoh did to satisfy each item on the list (Budge, 1976).

Religion provided the motivation for the public to adhere to their normative theory of ethics and that, in turn, was important to the Egyptian civilization. Although religions do not always motivate people, they do fortify and reinforce a culture's normative ethics, as noted by Nietzsche (see chapter 4). Thus, religion motivated many to adhere to their culture's ethical theory and it provided a source of spiritual wisdom literature that informed individuals. Religion helped them to understand virtue ethics and apply it to their daily lives.

THE JUDGMENT OF THE DEAD

The Egyptian tradition illustrates the importance virtues (Exhibit 6.1) tied to religion as a moral motivator. The Egyptians believed their possible afterlife was predicated on their moral conduct during their lifetime. The deceased was brought before forty-two divine beings who presided over the Hall of Truth and were judged by the great god Osiris who was the final judge.

Although Osiris presided over the judgment, the council represented the forty-two provinces of upper and lower Egypt. Nine of the judges are well known from the pantheon of Egyptian gods but others had names like Bone-Crusher, Shining-Tooth, Blood-Consumer, Flint-Eyes, and Entrail-Consumer (Bunson 1991). According to Joshua Mark (2012), "The soul of the deceased was called upon to render up a confession of deeds done while in life and to have the heart weighed in the balance of the Scales of Justice against the white feather of Ma'at of Thoth and Harmonious Balance."

Exhibit 6.1. Egyptian Character Virtues

➡ I have not done inequity.
➡ I have not been angry and wrathful except for a just cause.
➡ I have not polluted myself.
➡ I have not caused terror.
➡ I have not burned with rage.
➡ I have not worked grief.
➡ I have not worked and acted with insolence.
➡ I have not stirred up strife.
➡ I have not judged hastily.
➡ I have not been an eavesdropper.
➡ I have not multiplied words exceedingly.
➡ I have done neither harm nor ill.
➡ Every day, I labored more than was required of me.
➡ I have not spoken scornfully.
➡ I have not made any to suffer pain.
➡ I have told no lies.
➡ I have not done that which is abominable.
➡ I have not stopped my ears against the words of right and truth.
➡ I have never uttered fiery words.
➡ I have not avenged myself.
➡ I have not multiplied my speech overmuch.
➡ I have not behaved myself with arrogance.
➡ I have not been overwhelmingly proud.
➡ I have never magnified my condition beyond what was fitting.
➡ I have given bread unto the hungry and water unto those who thirst, clothing unto the naked, and a boat unto the shipwrecked mariner.

Source. Taken from a larger list in the *Egyptian Book of the Dead, The Negative Confession.* Translated by E.A. Wallace Budge, 1967, 346–351.

The god Anubis brought the deceased to the trial and Ma'at (Goddess of Justice, Truth, and Order) performed the weighing. If the heart was heavier than the feather, Ammut, the jackal, would devour it, and the person's soul would cease to exist. Rather than perpetual torment after death, nonexistence was the greatest fear of the ancient Egyptians. Thoth, God of Wisdom, would write down the decision of the test to record it for all time. If successful, Horus took the deceased to meet Osiris and also to meet the god Duat and his two sisters, Isis and Nepththys.

In Exhibit 6.2, the "Warning to the Living" shows how Egyptian society used religion to motivate the population to be ethical by applying the Egyptian character virtues.

Exhibit 6.2. Warning to the Living

You the Court that judges the wretch,
On the day of judging the miserable,
In the hour of doing their task.

It is painful when the accuser has knowledge,
Do not trust in length of years,
They view a lifetime in an hour.

Source: "The Judgment of the Dead." www.reshfim.org.il. Retrieved September 4, 2016.

ANCIENT GREEK VIRTUE ETHICS

ARISTOTLE

Aristotle argued that people should develop virtue and reach happiness through "practical wisdom." Aristotle and his associates argued that insights from practical wisdom helped people develop their virtues and character over their lifetimes. In ancient virtue ethics, prudence (in today's English, possibly the word "discernment" is a better translation) precedes all moral laws, principles, and rules. Therefore, prudence is the moral norm both for personal decision making and for internally processing correct behavior. Ancient philosophers felt that developing a virtuous character within one's self was necessary and possibly even sufficient to realize what was truly a good life; that is, a life worthy of being lived.

Aristotle

Plato

The ancient Greek meaning of a "good life" differs from our modern Western interpretation because of the more modern influence of utilitarianism, which equates pleasure with the "good" life. For Greeks' "a good life" did connote some level of comfort, pleasure, moderate consumption, and status, but the meaning was more complex than merely acquiring things and titles. For example, Socrates felt that only a person seeking wisdom could be considered to have a worthy life. To him, the ability to reflect and deliberate was essential because he felt that each person needs to go beyond their impulses and animal instincts. However, as we saw in Maslow's theory of human motivation (see chapter 2), in order to have time to self-reflect and seek wisdom, one must have certain physical needs taken care of first, such as food, clothing, and shelter.

For Socrates, Plato, and Aristotle, reasoning was critical for achieving a good life. Aristotle saw virtue as practical wisdom that reflected active thought and the development of character over a lifetime. Plato considered ignorance a vice and immoral behavior a cognitive mistake often caused by not thinking well. In their view, a person who engages in corruption must be stupid and not understand what is in their own best interest. Central to their virtue ethics was the soul, or the inner self. Aristotle believed that a person's true being was the soul and not the personality or physical body.

FUNCTIONALITY

Ancient Greek thought stressed the importance of functionality. For example, a good hammer and a good machine were those that functioned well in achieving the desired purposes of their users. Thus, the appropriate end for all things and beings, including humans, was to function well. Specifically, for humans, functioning well meant that the purpose of life, or the telos, was being happy. Thinkers such as Socrates, Plato, and Aristotle took the earlier understanding of human telos further by asking: Are the physical, psychological, interpersonal, social, political, and even spiritual aspects of the individual functioning well to achieve their deeper soul's meaning of happiness? For Aristotle, not all things we desire are truly good for us regardless of the strength of that desire or preference. For example, a person might desire the high experienced from illegal drug use but that experience does not contribute to achieving the good life, as defined by Aristotle.

Given his interest in biology and how systems worked, Aristotle thought in terms of causes. He identified four possibilities: material, efficient, formal, and final. He defined material causes as elements out of which people create objects. For example, the material cause of a marble statue is the marble itself. Efficient causes are the means by which the artist creates the object. In the sculpture example, it is the creative mind to imagine the finished product and skilled hands of the sculptor that are the efficient cause of his creation. The formal cause is the expression of the final product. In the case of the statue, the formal cause is the expression of the sculptor's finished statue but it can also be the viewers' idea of or reaction to the completed work.

The final cause is the purpose for which the item was created. Thus, the final cause is the end purpose, or telos. In some situations, the formal cause and the final cause are the same or almost the same. The telos is the perfection of the object in terms of the ideal purpose for which it was created. Thus, the final cause is intrinsic to the very nature of the object itself and is not something subjective within the artist or something anyone imposed on the artists. In other words, in a sentiment that is generally attributed to Michelangelo every block of stone has a statue inside it and it is the task of the sculptor to discover it.

To Aristotle, each person has a final purpose that he believed was the very essence of being human. That essence (telos) is the good life, or always living a life worthy of being lived in the context of the polis. A person needs to fully develop the soul in both the irrational and rational planes. That development occurs when a person evolves through three tiers, or levels, that are roughly similar to Kohlberg's stages (see chapter 4). The three tiers are vegetative, appetitive, and rational. In the first tier, humans share with animals an irrational element that Aristotle called the vegetative faculty, which he associated with nutrition and growth. The second tier is the appetitive faculty, which gives humans joy, grief, hope, and fear. In the third tier, emotions and desires are a mixture of irrational (pure animal behavior) and rational desires, which humans use to control themselves through reason. In the Kohlberg moral development stages, individuals have reasoned control over themselves, similar to the highest level in Aristotle's tiers.

He who exercises his reason and cultivates it seems to be both in the state of mind most dear to the gods. For if the gods have any care for human affairs, as they are thought to have, it would be reasonable both that they should delight in that which is best and most akin to them (that is reason).

Source: Elliot D. Cohen quotes Aristotle (Ethics, book 7, chapter 3).

The third tier is centered on the "rational calculative," which is the focus of morality that permits moral virtue to control desires based on contemplative reason and logic. The mastery of such reasoning is "intellectual virtue." With it, each person should decide what their *personal* objective, or telos is, using their thoughtful engagement of reason. To the ancient Greeks and certainly for Aristotle, this is the key point of virtue ethics that assumed that free choice involved rational thought beyond reacting to materialistic emotive seeking of pleasure. In the Kohlberg stages one and two moral thinkers, the individual telos is egocentric and hedonistic, which is parallel to the ancient Greek hedonists. More sophisticated Greek hedonists believed that the purpose of life was to live a life of pleasure, but they argued that occasionally rational thought was necessary to overcome desires for immediate pleasures that would eventually result in discomfort or harm.

Most ancient Greeks were polis centered, meaning Greek citizens strongly identified their personhood as being a part of a city-state, or polis. Thus, the culture of the ancient Greeks strongly encouraged citizens to be stage four and five moral thinkers. Aristotle argued that the good in humans lies in actualizing natural and acquired capabilities. Because human life is a goal-directed activity, a proper purpose for humans should be to actualize their potential for self-realization, including the development of their inner-self within the context of the polis. Aristotle disagreed with simple hedonism and even the complex hedonism of thinkers like Epicurus. Self-actualization meant the person needed to have an altruistic consciousness that included a selfless love for at least their polis.

How to Become Virtuous

To become virtuous requires the engagement of rational thought and instinctive thought. Rational thought considers abstract virtues and creates practical ways to form habits to support them.

When life requires a decision concerning right or wrong behavior, instinctive thought kicks in to make the correct decision based on developed habits without needing to return to rational thought to deliberate the correct course of action. Instinctive behavior is preprogrammed into instinctive thought. Therefore, unlike deontological and consequential ethics, which only require rational thought, virtue ethics requires both with training normally necessary to achieve instinctive behavior.

Aristotle was aware that some virtues are natural, meaning they are intuitively part of a person without that person needing any effort to rationally create them. However, other virtues he called authentic, meaning the individual must acquire them by education, training, and personal effort. For example, if an individual had the virtue of modesty, Aristotle would say that modesty was a natural virtue. But if the modesty virtue was instilled in a person through training, Aristotle would call it an authentic virtue. Aristotle discounted naturally acquired virtue because no personal effort was needed to acquire it, therefore there was no personal commitment or conscious awareness of it and it should be only slightly appreciated. However, he considered virtues, acquired due to conscious effort, as truly admirable and authentic. That effort demonstrated the value the individual placed on virtue as well as their determination and commitment to acquire it through hard work over time so it would be transformed into a habit governed by intuitive thought.

Aristotle believed that each virtue existed on a continuum between what he called the vice of deficiency and the vice of excess. Like the Buddha's (563–480 BCE) Middle Path, the virtuous person is one who practices the right moral conduct like courage. This concept takes the whole context of the situation into consideration, including the right time, reference to the right object, consideration of the right people, weighting the right motives associated with the situation, and finally selecting the right way to behave for the circumstance. Making moral decisions had to be contextual as one ethical decision does not fit all circumstances, but once the contextual situation is understood, intuitive thought could be employed instantly. Therefore, using a virtue as a continuum, there is always a correct decision that probably lies near the Golden Mean of that continuum. Exhibit 6.3 shows a continuum of courage.

Exhibit 6.3. Courage Virtue Continuum

Cowardly _____Courage _____Bravado
Deficiency vice   Golden Mean   Excess vice

Source: Thomas and Cynthia Lynch, 2018.

In Aristotle's published works, he limited himself to discussing only twelve virtues (see Exhibit 6.4). Some of the terms have fallen out of use in the popular lexicon, but they still are important qualities. Many more than twelve virtues can be identified and the ideal mix of virtues in any given situation depends on contextual circumstances, but Aristotle's twelve are a good start in illustrating his virtue thinking process.

Exhibit 6.4. Twelve Virtues and Related Vices

Deficiency Vice	Virtuous Mean	Excess Vice
Cowardice	Courage	Rashness
Insensitiveness	Moderation	Profligacy
Spiritlessness	Gentleness	Prodigality
Meanness	Liberality	Prodigality
Smallness of Spirit	Greatness of Spirit	Vanity
Shabbiness	Appropriateness	Extravagance
Malicious	Sympathy	Envy
Shamelessness	Modesty	Bashful
Animosity	Friendliness	Flattery
Self-Infatuated	Dignity	Subservience
Self-Deprecation	Sincerity	Boastfulness
Simpleness	Wisdom	Rascality

Most desired virtue decisions are at or near the continuum's mean, but each continuum exists within specific contextual situations (see Exhibit 6.5). In making an ethical decision, sometimes decisions must be made in an instant. For example, if a policeman comes upon an active crime situation, the hormone adrenaline kicks in. This can be good but it also could make the rational thinking process not function well for that given situation because the policeman needs time to contemplate his situation. He would be wiser to rely on virtue ethics because his training allows him to access his intuitive brain's established habit to deal with such a situation. However, taking time to think in this situation is not sensible because death or serious harm is immediately possible. Developed habits of virtue ethics provide instant access to the best moral decision on whether to use deadly force or not.

In a practical application of Aristotle's ideas, police organizations should add training units of ethicists that do rational thought exercises using scenarios which develop intuitive reactions using virtue ethics to address making quick ethical judgments. A police training group can take its findings from rational thought exercises and create training sessions for first responders to develop the best instinctive moral options for various quick action scenarios. The trainers can then provide the repetitive training that will produce the correct rational thought through instinctive habits. Finally, an analytical team of ethicists can confirm that the training provided was correct and adequate as well as assess whether that training accomplished the desired ends. That team assessment report can be transmitted back to the first analytical team so they can update the conceptual judgment on what virtue ethics are most appropriate for the likely first responders' scenarios.

Exhibit 6.5. Definitions of Aristotle's Twelve Virtues

Courage	when a person correctly understands his or her formidable challenge and then decides to confront that challenge
Moderation	desiring the pleasures from the sense of touch and taste in the appropriate amount for the person's well-being
Gentleness	exercising one's passion at the appropriate times and always in a controlled manner
Liberality	using wealth correctly
Greatness of Spirit	disposition toward one's accomplishment when greatness or some degree of greatness could be claimed
Appropriateness	spending at a level commensurate with a person's status and situation
Sympathy	feeling the appropriate pain or pleasure due to adversities and difficulties of others and themselves
Modesty	showing the proper regard of others regarding what the subject wears as well as their deportment around others
Friendliness	using the appropriate judgment in deciding what is proper and good in terms of accommodating his or her associates' desires
Dignity	using proper judgment in showing regard for people who are worthy of regard
Sincerity	being truthful about oneself
Wisdom	possessing three qualities: practical knowledge, ability to distinguish between good and bad, and depth of love toward self and others. Also, knowledge that one can learn and apply to life situations; truth, in that it allows a person to distinguish between good and bad; and goodness in that it is based on and flows from compassion and love for all

Beyond situations that require instant reactions, virtue ethics can be valuable where desired moral character qualities are important in job performance. For example, if dealing with the public is part of the job, then possible training in gentleness, modesty, friendliness, and sincerity is useful. The previously mentioned steps are appropriate. In addressing virtue ethics training, the following questions should be considered: 1) What likely confrontational situations might occur with the public on the job? 2) What training would help the employee deal with those situations? 3) Are the correct employees getting the necessary training? And 4) Is the training producing the desired moral outcomes?

Before moving on to why philosophers said virtue ethics failed as an ethical theory, the unique value of wisdom, as a virtue, must be stressed. All ethical training must include training on Aristotle's last, and arguably most important, virtue for ethics: wisdom. Wisdom is more than simple knowledge. It requires weaving multiple strands of knowledge and the ability to apply the collective "knowing" to lessons learned to arrive at the desired outcome in new situations and circumstances.

Wisdom, as a virtue, must be used in combination with all the other applicable virtues. To instantly apply wisdom in considering the context of each situation and how to react with the other appropriate virtues in varying circumstances is challenging but is also remarkably important in complex situations. Trainers should address the following questions: What wisdom is particularly important in situations where instinctive wisdom is needed? What training would help employees arrive at the correct wisdom decisions for the likely situations? Are our public organizations providing the necessary wisdom training? Again, the goal for the training is to successfully anticipate the likely situations that the employees are likely to face and select the correct virtue ethics to use with the wisdom virtue.

A CLOSER LOOK AT ARISTOTLE

A correct reading of Aristotle must emphasize that he did use a version of teleology in his thinking. For example, he did not advocate a teleology based on God's will as found in Christian, Muslim, and even Platonic thought. In addition, unlike other great ancient Greek thinkers, he viewed life more from a functional/systems perspective rather than a mechanistic one. His teleological assumption parallels what today is called the influence of DNA on all living things. Aristotle's teleological theory postulated that the essence of all living things not only shaped the living creature but also defined that living thing's telos, meaning its most fundamental purpose and value. For example, some plants naturally wish to grow and even turn to face the sun and most animals nurture their offspring that ensures the continuation of their species. Therefore, to him, plants and animals have a natural essence, which today we would say is built into its DNA.

An acorn has an inherent tendency to grow into an oak tree thus the tree exists not by chance but rather with some inherent essence that somehow defines it eventually as an oak tree. Aristotle made the argument that humans are social animals, which makes them politically well suited for life in the polis. Thus, political naturalism is a human essence and a foundation of his political philosophy.

To Aristotle, anything that inhibits the fulfillment of the complete attainment of the telos is bad or at least dysfunctional. To him, nature operates inherently for the sake of an end and therefore that functional end must be good. For human beings, the ultimate good or happiness is found in the perfect and full attainment of the human natural function, which he argued was the full realization of the soul (inner self) through reason. He recognized that his notion of the ideal essence of the soul was an inner urge and generally was not attainable, but he felt that the urge drives us to attain as much of it we possibly can. To Aristotle, that inherent urge was part of the human telos. If we accept that the appropriate telos of those working in American public affairs and public administration is found in the U.S. Constitution, then we can continue to use Aristotle's normative ethical theory today.

What is telos is found in the Constitution that could drive us make moral choices as public administrators in the United States? From the Constitution's preamble, there are several possibilities: (1) establish justice for all, (2) ensure domestic tranquility, (3) create and employ a successful common defense against those who would harm us, (4) promote a positive welfare for everyone, and (5) secure freedoms including the freedoms of speech and press. From the body of the text and its amendments, other possibilities include (1) selection of legislators and the chief executive office by election, (2) the right of habeas corpus, and (3) the full rights of citizenship regardless of gender or race.

THE FALL OF VIRTUE ETHICS

MODERNIST AND POSTMODERNIST PHILOSOPHERS

David Hume

The Ancient Greeks were not aware of the naturalistic fallacy or the so-called is/ought logic problem, which was first put forth by David Hume in *A Treatise of Human Nature* (book III, part 1, section 1) about 2,000 years after Aristotle. Hume questioned how a logical person can derive "ought" from an "is" statement. He logically argued that "is" (meaning descriptive statements of what exists) needed logically to be completely severed from "ought" (meaning normative or prescriptive statements). He argued this gap tends to render "ought" statements as having dubious validity at best and most likely having no validity, and therefore they cannot be considered moral knowledge.

Locke and other modernists challenged the basic assumptions of Aristotle's virtue ethics using Hume's arguments. Descartes, the father of modernism, tells us that any normative ethical theory is logically built on assumptions, and all assumptions, except for one's own existence, are subject to doubt. Locke focused on Aristotle's assumption that the concept of the essence of a thing determines its function. Ancient Greeks like Plato argued that all objects, including tables, chairs, pots, pans, and people, have an essence and the maximization of that essence is what determines the quality (i.e., poor, acceptable, good, and excellent) of the object.

To modernist philosophers, Aristotle's logical use, in his normative theory, of essence in humans was nonsense as there was no human essence just as tables or chairs did not have an essence. Locke said that having an essence was just a false assumption. Therefore, to Locke, Aristotle's belief in the human essence, meaning living a "good life" prompted humans to seek their attainment of human excellence, was foolishness. By extension, self-actualization, in more modern thought, is also foolishness.

Locke's rejection of Aristotle's virtue ethics was also predicated on rejecting the concept that humans had an essence at all by using what is called intersubjective knowledge. Locke said, "To return to general Words, it is plain, by what has been said, That General and Universal, belong not to the real existence of things, but are the Inventions and Creatures of the Understanding, made by it for its use, and concern only Signs, whether Words, or Ideas" (cited in Sahakian and Sahakian 1993). In less confusing English, Locke's argument against Aristotle says the so-called general and universal natures are mere concepts and not objective descriptive facts. Therefore, social constructs can and do change with the users of those constructs. Locke argues that it makes no sense to say that a social construct has an essence. We can identify an object by calling it a "chair," but the generalized concepts we use are not objects but merely shared or partially shared abstract ideas of a form. For example, a "chair" might be a stool, bench or a low table. The actual object has no essence. Therefore, like a chair, a human has no essence and therefore there they have no telos.

To modernists and later postmodernists, humans do not have a final purpose because there is no generalized purpose or meaning to life. With that logic, life just is an individual social construct that varies across humanity and is therefore without essence. There is no soul, as it is a merely a loosely defined social construct with no universal definition; and thus, there is no human essence that needs to be perfected. With their logic, beauty and love exist only subjectively and not objectively. With their reasoning, there is no final cause (as in the "cause" of cause and effect). Without an essence or telos, saying it should be internalized is foolishness, and therefore virtue ethics is foolishness.

A person can say something is beautiful or can love a piece of music, but such feelings are only emotive statements that are a subjective determination with no objective determination possible. Another more common why to say this is the common expression, "Beauty is in the eye of the beholder." A person can also say a particular decision was morally wrong, but such a feeling is merely emotive without the possibility of being objectively determined. Because of intersubjective thought, those concepts can exist among a set of people but they do not exist objectively for all people. For much of our intellectual history, almost all of society believed that not only God or gods existed but that God(s) created life for humankind and that it had some sort of deeper meaning or telos. Many modernists and almost all postmodernists rejected those assumptions entirely, and without those assumptions the concept of beauty, love, and a telos were rendered logical nonsense.

CUL-DE-SAC THINKING

In terms of fostering a useful ethical theory, modernists and postmodernists failed society by creating what some call "a philosophical moral cul-de-sac" that made normative theory useless. The very purpose of normative ethical theory is to create logical thought that can help humans make good rather than bad moral choices. If such aids to ethical thinking are useless, then humankind is left with no moral compass. Those making these arguments say that accepting that moral theories are merely subjective and emotive is not failing society but merely recognizing what is now obvious. They argue that believing in a falsehood is foolish even if it is practical way to achieve some desired end.

Despite modernist' and postmodernists' belief that ethics is just emotive and relativistic, people still had to continue to make ethical decisions in their daily lives and work. How should we weigh their options and make a logical defensible decision? Kantian philosophers argued that rule-based ethics helped create a more moral society. Consequential philosophers argued that pragmatic reasoning could, and did, help make useful moral decisions for the larger society. And eventually, a few philosophers reconsidered virtue ethics and argued that it was also a tool that could help improve morality within society.

THE CHALLENGE TO THE FALL

ERRORS IN LOGIC

The philosophers who disagreed with the modernists and postmodernists argued, with little success, there were two fallacies in those arguments. The first is a common logical error in modernist thought that not being able to prove something means it does not exist. The second is modernists built on René Descartes' "Cognito ergo sum"; that is, we know that a person's ability to think proves the person exists. Therefore, the first conclusion means that establishing facts to determine cause and effect is impossible. Modernists realized that second conclusion meant that humans had to accept the fact that no one could say anything about anything except their own existence. A pool of useful knowledge could not be built on extreme negativism. Some other standard had to be established. The standard they accepted was empiricism.

Empiricism says that some proposition can be considered as truth if there is empirical evidence of its existence and a community of scholars confirms the proposition with a laborious and meticulous empirical effort. Modernists accept that the presence of such observable evidence is sufficient for careful thinkers to accept a proposition and theory as truthful. They also accept the possibility that later evidence might lead other careful thinkers to update their conclusion about the truth of a theory. Alternatively, if there is observable evidence of careful thinkers that contradicts a theory, then they can conclude the theory is false. Thus, it is normally much easier to disprove a theory than confirm it. In their rigorous reasoning process, a theory can never be proven but only confirmed for the moment.

Another fault with the modernist logic is that if no observable or insufficient evidence regarding a proposition or theory exists, how can its truth be judged? To be logical, one can only say there is insufficient evidence to confirm or reject the theory, but cannot say the theory is false. The modernist test of observable evidence is associated with Thomas Kuhn. The details of that method are beyond the scope of this book, but we do note that the scientific method establishes that scientist can, with careful observable evidence, conclude a theory is false if their evidence is inconsistent with that theory. What the scientists cannot logically say is that if there is no observable proof of certain knowledge, the given proposition or theory is disproven. This logic may seem confusing but it is important. When not being able to confirm an asserted theory or fact is certain, some modernists will claim the knowledge is false when they in reality they just do not know if it is false or certain knowledge yet. Or, better said, they should simply admit that they do not know.

Now, let us apply this logic to the concept of telos. Just because modernists have not been able to prove, with observable evidence, that telos exists in all cases does not logically mean that a human telos does not exist and virtue ethics is emotive foolishness in all situations. The scientific method can affirm that there exists a subjective shared understanding of telos for some sets of humans that is within a paradigm. At least for that set of humans, a telos does exist and a limited use of virtue ethics is possible within that set of humans.

The second logical fallacy of the modernist arguments against virtue ethics involves consistency. This logical mistake can exist for even the most learned intellectuals. For example, Locke first argued that all natural things have a real constitution of their parts. However, he later took an intuitionist position and in doing so his full logical argument became inconsistent with his primary position. In discussing virtue ethics, some modernists argue that there are situations in which a telos does exist and therefore the use of virtue ethics is reasonable in those situations. However, other modernists argue that there are some situations where there is no telos and therefore all virtue ethics is foolish. The consistency mistake in the case of virtue ethics is in assuming that all situations are negated by one or more negative situations without accepting that exceptions are logically possible.

WITTGENSTEIN

The word "paradigm" was coined in the fifteenth century as a technical term that meant "an example exists of a conjugation or declension showing a word in all its inflectional forms" and evolved to mean "an outstanding clear or typical example or archetype" (Merriam-Webster online). Thomas Kuhn (1962) suggested that "paradigm" means "the practice that defines a scientific discipline at a certain point in time." Wittgenstein followers used "paradigm" to mean "shared and common fundamental subjective assumptions."

Although postmodern philosophers argued that ethics in general was emotive logical nonsense, Wittgenstein said there was an exception. He agreed that normative ethics are not objective, but if a paradigm of fundamental values exists, then those within the paradigm could use commonly accepted fundamental values to logically argue right and wrong. If, however, the people making right and wrong arguments were from different paradigms, then no logical correct conclusion about right and wrong was possible.

Given that the constitutional and other basic laws of a nation define common fundamental values, then a normative ethical theory such as virtue ethics can be applied and accepted by logical thinkers within that nation. Similarly, professions have announced values, goals, objectives, and a common practice. Therefore, they can also apply virtue ethics within their professions. In the context of public affairs and public administration in a country like the United States, there is at least one dominant fundamental subjective values set. It is articulated in the U.S. Constitution and reaffirmed each time a person takes the oath of office to uphold that document. Those values include using the vote to make public decisions, individual rights such as freedom of speech, and broad purposes as stated in the preamble (Exhibit 6.6; also, see the Appendix for the complete U.S. Constitution).

In virtue ethics theory, telos is not the all-inclusive human essence proposed by Aristotle, but rather a more limited telos that can be applied to professions like public administrators and within governments like the United States that have articulated a clear end purpose for their societies. The U.S. Constitution is the shared subjective moral paradigm for American public affairs and it is therefore a logical subjectively shared value set on which a normative ethical theory can be based. Because a set of fundamental shared values exists, an end purpose also exists. Therefore, Wittgenstein offers a solution to avoiding moral relativism for those in American public administration. His logic also holds true in other countries and even in international organizations if a common value set can be said to exist (see chapter 10 for a discussion of shared values).

Exhibit 6.6. Preamble to the U.S. Constitution

We, the People of the United States, in Order to form a more perfect Union, establish Justice, insure domestic Tranquility, provide for the common defense, promote the general Welfare, and secure the Blessings of Liberty to ourselves and our Posterity, do ordain and establish this Constitution for the United States of America.

CONTEMPORAY VIRTUE ETHICS

MacIntyre and the Concept of Practice

Alasdair MacIntyre revived virtue ethics in the 1980s with his book *After Virtue* (1984). He felt the intellectual community had lost the ability to seriously consider how normative ethics can be helpful to humanity. For example, his disdain for modernism and postmodernism is evident in his comments about G. E. Moore's *Principia Ethica*. Moore argued that moral precepts were mere preferences of an individual's emotions rather than absolute values. Thus, ethics and morals had to be considered individuated and relativistic because there was no common ground for moral reference using meaningful dialogue.

Emotive understanding of ethics gives us no established way of deciding among moral claims and thus moral debate is left dead. The emotive approach to ethics forces those in a moral debate to argue intuitively and their justifications must therefore hinge on their adopted moral system, which has no grounding beyond preferences. MacIntyre disagreed. He argued that Moore's attack on virtue ethics fails because it separates the individual's experience from his or her social and historical community. MacIntyre argued that to accept that separation was nonsensical and it directly resulted in a lack of twentieth-century moral dialogue.

MacIntyre rejected modernist and postmodernist conclusions concerning normative ethical theory. Like Aristotle, MacIntyre wanted to define "good" in such a way that reason can be used to determine its existence. In other words, he wanted a teleology that is similar to Aristotle's meaning of "good" that someone could define it without reference to a preferential concept that is only emotive in character. He wanted those who acted morally to do so as rational actors making decisions predicated upon factual determinations.

MacIntyre achieved his goal by using the functionality of a watch and the actions of a farmer. No one can define a watch without of the concept of a "good watch" because functionality was paramount to the understanding of the purpose of a watch. In parallel reasoning, a farmer cannot be defined independently of the concept of being a "good" farmer. In other words, like Aristotle, MacIntyre felt that functionality is key to rigorous moral reasoning. Therefore, if MacIntyre is correct, teleology can again become the basis for introducing rationality rather than emotive thinking in the moral debate.

MacIntyre's reasoning rests on the concept that practices exist that have an aim, an end purpose, or what can again reasonably be called a telos. When people engage in a practice such as public affairs, then rationality can inform them on what is good and bad behavior in terms of conduct-

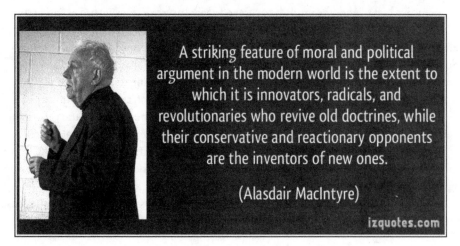

A striking feature of moral and political argument in the modern world is the extent to which it is innovators, radicals, and revolutionaries who revive old doctrines, while their conservative and reactionary opponents are the inventors of new ones.

(Alasdair MacIntyre)

izquotes.com

Alasdair MacIntyre

ing the public's affairs, meaning making public policy and demanding that public administrators follow policy as long as that policy is consistent with the end proposes of government as defined in the nation's constitution. Thus, by its very nature, such a practice has an end purpose and those engaged with that end purpose have a telos. Because that practice has a telos, one can use rational thought to define virtues important to achieving the telos that better enable public officials to achieve what Aristotle called *Eudaimonia*. Conversely, failing to apply those virtues defeats the optimal functionality of the practice's telos, which logically can be considered a wrong action using normative ethical theory.

THE IMPORTANCE OF PRACTICE

Practice is key to MacIntyre's version of virtue ethics. He defines practice as follows: "By a practice I'm going to mean any coherent and complex form of socially established cooperative human activity through which goods internal to the form of activity are realized in the course of trying to achieve those standards of excellence which are appropriate to, and practically definitive of, that form of activity, with the result that human powers to achieve excellence, and the human conceptions of the ends and goods involved, are systematically extended" (MacIntyre 1984, p. 187; emphasis added).

MacIntyre's use of the concept of "internal goods" is particularly important. He illustrated the use of that concept with an example from the game of chess. Although the end result of the game might appear to be to defeat the opponent, the true end purpose is mastering the moves, strategies, and intricacies of the game. If one cheats to win and is successful, the player only denies him- or herself the true benefit of engagement in the game and what can be learned from it.

MacIntyre (1984) notes that "a practice involves standards of excellence and obedience to rules as well as the achievement of goods. To enter into a practice is to accept the authority of those standards and the inadequacy of my own performance as judged by them" (190). To apply ethics and to be moral requires virtues consistent with "internal goods" and existing without them means that the individual's "good" cannot be achieved. MacIntyre defines virtue as "an acquired human quality the possession and exercise of which tends to enable us to achieve those goods which are internal to practice and the lack which effectively prevents us from achieving any such goods" (191).

So what is the link between virtue and practice? Virtues sustain a practice. They give individuals "internal goods" and thus serve as a motivation to overcome dangers, temptations, and distractions that are all too common in life. With external goods that characteristically result from competition, there are losers and winners as some gain or lose more than others in what the profession does and does not produce in the various institutions in which they serve. With internal goods, achievement is a good for the whole institution, the professional community, and the individual professional's inner self. There are no losers with internal goods. Internal goods are intangible positive feelings about the self. Virtues sustain the person's activity in practice and encourage the person to move toward the fundamental end purpose of that practice. Virtues are a means but they also become the ultimate end as they define a person's character or inner self.

LINKING PRACTICE AND PROFESSION

"Practice" includes the concept of what is commonly called a profession. To enter into a practice is to enter into a relationship with a community of contemporary practitioners, but also with those who preceded you and those who will follow you in that practice. In public affairs, there is a contemporary community of public administration, as there are for any other practices such as medicine or engineering. Practices are *not* institutions, which are necessarily concerned with creating goods and services for external groups.

Nevertheless, institutions are critical to practice as they sustain them and characteristically form a single causal order. For example, a doctor often works in the context of a hospital and a public servant works in the context of a government agency. In addition, the ideals and the creativity of the practice are always vulnerable to the realities of institutions; but the virtuous practice provides a counter to such realities as the corrupting power of institutions and the tendency to overwhelm the government processes with ever more complex Kantian rules and regulations.

MacIntyre takes the notion of teleology from Aristotle and redefines it as a social construct. Confronting modernism and postmodernism head on, MacIntyre makes Aristotle relevant again by stressing the social contextual nature of human existence. Morality again is brought back into the realm of the rational and moral debate is once again coherent. The importance of virtue ethics is reestablished, at least in the context of a practice such as arriving at a public policy or administrating one.

CONCLUSION

Leon is wrong about Aristotle's virtue ethics, as it is very relevant to the twenty-first century, but organizations and individuals need to fully understand it. In the past few decades, professions like public administration have begun to consider virtue ethics useful after the attacks on it by modernists and postmodernists have proven inappropriate. As Aristotle noted, virtue ethics is practically useful in public affairs. Given the thinking of Wittgenstein and MacIntyre, saying virtue ethics can and should be practiced in public affairs is obvious.

Virtue ethics is particularly useful to public officials where work requires almost instant moral decisions, such as police officers, first responders, firefighters, and the military. For example, governments should hire well-trained ethicists to develop common scenarios that are relevant to their agencies and what their employees will encounter in their work. In addition, training teams can teach how to respond to a well-developed set of situations using virtue ethics in each scenario.

Knowing that people are egocentric, altruistic, or a mix of both, the trainer can frame the rationale for the use of virtue ethics using the various perspectives of people operating at the various moral development. For example, to help egocentric trainees be motivated, trainers could also tell them if they follow their training that when issues arise that call their actions into question, they will have established criteria for explaining their action coherently. The key in training people at stages one, two, and three of moral development is to speak in terms of rewards and potential punishments rather than ethics statements, as the latter will not be motivational. Finally, an internal or contract evaluation group of ethicists needs to look at actual agency scenarios, the training exercises that employ virtue ethics, and the compliance of employees in using the training effectively. The evaluation group would be wise to accomplish their mission using critical thinking (see chapter 8).

The use of virtue ethics does not require people to have moral development over stage two or strong analytical skills required of consequential thinkers. However, it does require ethicists and trainers to have at least stage four moral development, knowledge of critical thinking, good analytical skills, the use of procedures and standards to help create an ethical work place, and normative ethical theories. For example, the trainers should develop scenarios that reflect knowledge of virtue ethics and the importance of building proper habits in employees that reflect desired virtue ethics so that, especially in emergency situations, they will react correctly. Regardless of the stage of moral development of the trainee, trainers can teach virtue ethics in such a way that the trainees can apply it to the situations they are likely to address.

Every elected or appointed official and all public employees can train in how to use the virtue of wisdom in their duties. In doing so, specialized units can develop decision-making scenarios for the various activities of government. Training units can be created to do the necessary training on the virtue of wisdom. And finally, a professional ethicist and organizational evaluation unit should determine if the training is accomplishing its purpose and make recommendations on how to improve the use of wisdom training.

REVIEW QUESTIONS

1. Explain the Book of Thoth and its implications to establishing ethics in a viable civilization such as existed in ancient Egypt for thousands of years.

2. Give practical examples of Aristotle's virtue ethics in public organizations.

3. Why did virtue ethics fall out of favor?

4. Explain the role of having a desired end result in virtue ethics.

5. Why is it more important to acquire an authentic virtue than to possess a natural virtue?

6. Explain the different meaning of "freedom" in virtue ethics as opposed to the definition commonly used in the Western world today.

7. Explain the roles of rational and intuitive brain thinking in virtue ethics.

8. What was Locke's dispute with virtue ethics?

9. In what ways does religion reinforce ethics? In what ways does religion diminish ethics in society?

10. What does recognizing the ego and inner self mean in terms of virtue ethics?

11. What links practice and profession?

12. In what way is practice key to MacIntyre's thinking?

REFERENCES

Aristotle, *The Nicomachean Ethics*. Translated by W.D. Ross. PBC Paperbacks Lt. Cambridge University Press: Great Britain, 1980.

"Aristotle." n.d. *Internet Encyclopedia of Philosophy*, edited by James Fieser and Bradley Dowden. Accessed December 4, 2001.

Budge, Wallace E. A. 1967. *The Egyptian Book of the Dead: The Papyrus of Ani Egyptian Text*. Transliteration and Translation. Dover Publication, NY. http://www.utm.edu/research/iep/a/aristotl.htm#Ethics.

Bunson, Margaret. 1991. *The Encyclopedia of Ancient Egypt*. New York: Random House.

Cohen, Elliot D. *What Would Aristotle Do?* 2003. Amherst: Prometheus Books.

Devettere, Raymond J. 2002. *Introduction to Virtue Ethics: Insights of the Ancient Greeks*. Washington, DC: Georgetown University Press.

Fox, Charles, and Hugh T. Miller. 1999. "The Promethean Spirit in Public Administration: Spirituality without Crutches." *International Journal of Organization Theory and Behavior* 2, nos. 3 and 5: 303–324.

Frederickson, H. George. 1997. *The Spirit of Public Administration*. San Francisco: Jossey-Bass.

Griffin, James. 1996. *Value Judgments: Improving Our Ethical Beliefs*. Oxford, UK: Oxford University Press.

Hume, David. 2016. *A Treatise of Human Nature*. Book III, Part 1.1. https://ebooks.adelaide.edu.au/h/hume/david/h92t/B3.1.1.html.

Johnson, Monte Ransome. *Aristotle on Teleology*. (Oxford Aristotle Series.) Oxford: Oxford University Press, 2005.

Josephson, Michael. 2002. *Making Ethical Decisions*. Marina del Rey, CA: Josephson Institute of Ethics.

"Judgement of the Dead." Accessed September 4, 2016. www.reshfim.org.il.

Kuhn, Thomas S. 1962. *The Structure of Scientific Revolutions*. Chicago, IL: University of Chicago Press.

MacIntyre, Alasdair. 1984. *After Virtue: A Study in Moral Theory*. Notre Dame, IN: Notre Dame University Press.

Mark, Joshua. 2012. "The Forty-Two Judges." *Ancient History Encyclopedia*. www.ancient.eu/amp/2-185.

McKay, Walter M. 2004. "A Modern Conception of Virtue Ethics." *Forum for Law Enforcement Ethics*. http://law-enforcement-ethics.com.

Miller, Fred. 2017. "Presuppositions of Aristotle's Politics." In *Stanford Encyclopedia of Philosophy*, edited by Edward N. Zalta. http://plato.stanford.edu/entries/aristotle-politics/supplement2.html.

Oakley, Justin, and Dean Cooking. 2001. *Virtue Ethics and Professional Roles*. Cambridge, UK: Cambridge University Press.

Organisation for Economic and Co-operative Development. 1996. "Ethics in the Public Service: Current Issues and Practice." http://www.oecd.org/puma/gvrnance/ethics/pubs/eip96/execsum.htm.

Richardson, Elliott, and the Council of Excellence in Government. 1992. "Ethical Principles for Public Servants." *Public Manager* 4.

Sahakian, William S., and Mabel Lewis Sahakian. 1993. *Ideas of the Great Philosophers*. New York: Barnes and Noble.

Stadler, Martin A. 2008. "Judgement After Death (Negative Confession)." In *UCLA Encyclopedia of Egyptology*, edited by Jacco Dieleman and Willeke Wendrich. http://www.aegyptologie.com/forum/attachments/Stadler_Procession_2008.pdf.

Thompson, Denis F. 1992. "Paradoxes of Government Ethics." *Public Administration Review* 52, no. 3: 254–259.

Zinaich, Samuel. 2003. "Returning to Virtue Theory: Some Problems and Challenges." *Global Virtue Ethics Review* 5, no. 4. http://www.spaef.com/GVER_PUB/index.html.

7 Ethics and Self-Control

PROFESSOR: *Yes, Leon?*

LEON: *Professor, you make such a fuss about thinking and ethics. Don't people just make knee-jerk decisions that we either label as a thoughtful ethical decision or a big mistake? Sometimes we get it right and sometimes we don't. You can't take the human out of the human being.*

Leon is quite correct in terms of describing the reality of how many ethical decisions are made but this textbook addresses how we *should* or *could* make better ethical decisions in a public affairs and public administrative context with the added assumption we can do so using our free will. There is an important difference between what we do and what we should do. Granted, many people, personally and professionally, do just make knee-jerk ethical decisions; and this is appropriate in some situations because an immediate decision is often critical and that is the best we can do in the moment. An alternative would be a non-decision, which is a de facto decision to not decide, or a late decision that could create even more problems than an in-the-moment decision. The term "non-decision" is a misnomer because it carries with it real and sometimes negative consequences. A non-decision is essentially saying either I don't know what to do, I need time to make my decision, or I just don't want to spend my time thinking about this.

The professional field of public administration is about being accountable to the public. Professionals expect and accept that if they make wrong decisions, especially ones that cause harm to others, they will be called upon to explain how and why they came to their decisions. In such cases, saying "I followed my gut," is not an acceptable justification for an action. In the public service, we are expected to use self-control and critical thinking to make rational, ethical decisions that we can clearly explain. If that expectation is not met, our professionalism may be questioned.

Too often, knee-jerk decisions are poorly reasoned and reflect the use of limited or poor information available to the decision maker. Thus, sometimes the circumstances of a non-decision might be better than those of a knee-jerk decision because it indicates a more reasoned and considered thought process. If persons or organizations can anticipate future ethical problems, they are almost always wiser to develop decision-making scenarios based on rational thought that can be used later to form strategies for action when the situation demands it. When those scenarios occur, the decisions of the moment appear to be hasty. However, because they are familiar from training an automatic response from the decision maker they have actually been well thought out and well-rehearsed.

The key to success in predicting potential ethical situations lies in employing rational thinking and training in the form of virtue ethics (see chapter 12). Complex ethical decisions can be best resolved if problems are properly anticipated and individuals are trained correctly on what to do. Often the development of alternative choices can help decision makers by minimizing surprises and making it significantly easier to face challenging ethical situations.

If ethical problems can only be anticipated in a general sense, then, as was suggested in the last chapter, the training can focus on creating within-the-moment decision-maker virtues and insights to help them make better quick decisions. In either type of situation, anticipation of the likely ethical problems and effective training is essential because it ultimately helps decision makers to quickly identify the nub of the situation and allows them to use self-control and willpower to act appropriately in tense situations.

Ethics, especially virtue ethics, assumes the decision maker's ability to use self-control. With ethics, you decide how you should respond in a particular situation, but actually behaving in that manner depends on self-control to overcome the high emotional stress context of the situation. The ability to do what you normatively wish to do is critical to moral action.

As we know from chapter 6, Aristotle was the first to create a systematic study of virtue ethics. He made self-control central to virtue ethical thinking. However, there are several emotional fallacies that in many cases make it difficult for professionals to exercise self-control and consider the inherent psychological questions of what it takes to apply rational self-control.

Exhibit 7.1. Importance of Reason

He who exercises his reason and cultivates it seems to be both in the state of mind most dear to the gods. For if the gods have any care for human affairs, as they are thought to have, it would be reasonable both that they should delight in that which is best and most akin to them (that is, reason).

Source: Elliot D. Cohen quotes Aristotle (Ethics, book 7, chapter 3).

SELF-CONTROL

WHAT CONTROLS YOU?

Who or what controls you? Do you easily get angry or upset? Are you too sensitive? Are circumstances such as a broken relationship, aging, falling in love, a loss of money, dealing with the

Exhibit 7.2. "Going Postal"

The term "going postal" was first used in the St. Petersburg Times on December 17, 1993. Reporter Karl Vick, in his article "The Year in Review, 1993," wrote "The symposium was sponsored by the U.S. Postal Service, which has seen so many outbursts that in some circles excessive stress is known as 'going postal.' " He went on to say that the stereotype was probably due to the combination of the following events:

- August 20, 1986, postman Patrick Sherrill walked into his workplace and killed 14 co-workers and injured six more before shooting himself.
- October 10, 1991, former postal worker Joseph Harris killed two postal employees in Ridgewood, New Jersey.
- November 14, 1991, the recently fired postal worker, Thomas Mcilvane, killed four people and himself at a Royal Oak, Michigan, post office.
- May 6, 1993, Lawrence Jasion killed one person, wounded three more, and killed himself in the Dearborn, Michigan, post office.
- May 6, 1993, Mark Richard Hilbun killed his mother and two postal workers in Dana Point, California.

In 1993, the postal service created eighty-five "Workplace Environment Analysts" positions and in 2000 the Postmaster General commissioned the National Center on Addiction and Substance Abuse to prepare a report. The commission's job was to make recommendations on how better to provide workers with the safest possible work environment. The center reported that, "Postal workers are no more likely to physically assault, sexually harass, or verbally abuse their coworkers than employees in the national workforce." And that "Postal employees are only a third as likely as those in the national workforce to be victims of homicide at work."

Source: "The Origin of the Term 'Going Postal.'" http://www.todayifoundout.com/index.php/2011/09/the-origin-of-the-term-going-postal/.

needs of parents or children controlling your thoughts and your decisions? Are feelings of intense loneliness, grief, guilt, or shame driving your decisions rather than a rational thinking process? If the answer is YES or even a sometimes YES to any of these questions, then you are not in control of your life. You are letting life's circumstances control your personal and professional life rather than making your choices through the power of your own critical reasoning processes.

External circumstances and egocentric understandings of the life around you often lead to self-destructive, happiness-defeating, and emotion-filled behavior that can result in dysfunction. At a minimum, you are permitting circumstances to trigger your emotions, which then control your reactions. To use ethics, including virtue ethics, professionals must be in rational control of their thinking and minimize the moments in which their emotions take control of their thinking process. Few people will *never* have a bad day, *never* make stupid emotional responses, or *never* get worked up over a little thing. However, unless there is some other underlying issue, we can successfully control our emotions so that there is only an occasional bad day, and we can feel and be better in our overall lives. More significantly, we can apply self-control to our lives through our innate reasoning power to make our workplace situations easier and even happier.

INSTRUCTION AND REPORT

Willpower is essential in ethics because the nature of our professional jobs requires us to not exhibit or engage in emotional outbursts. While self-control is critical, this does not mean that professionals should be indifferent and not have strong feelings about their work. Exercising willpower controls our strong feelings so that our self-control can exist. However, willpower is utterly useless unless we know how to use it. Public service professionals need awareness of their own largely unconscious thinking processes and how to consciously control them. This takes focused training, practice, and patience. When successful, we control our emotions and moral actions.

Our minds create an instruction that directs us to act or feel in a certain way in a certain situation. Instructions are groups of generalizations within the mind about what you should or should not do in a particular time and situation. Parents, families, peer groups, schools, teachers, religious organizations, institutions, social media, and others create and transmit overt, subtle, and sometimes subliminal instructions over our entire lifetimes. In addition, the mind creates a report that files all the situations we find ourselves in under an instruction. A report is sense data, which the mind interprets into useful information. With each instruction and report, reasoning occurs that results in an action or emotion. An emotion is a positive or negative feeling that is tied logically or illogically to the instruction or report. An action is movement or words that flow, often seemingly automatically from the instruction or report. (See Exhibit 7.3 for examples.)

When the instructions become either unrealistic for the current situations in our lives or have reached their expiration date for the larger society, such as attitudes on racism or sexism, or have become obsolete as we move from childhood to adulthood, the emotions or actions that were created in response to earlier instruction are probably destructive to either the subject or others.

Exhibit 7.3. Instructions, Reports, Emotions, and Actions

Parents and teachers often tell children to never talk to strangers because they may be dangerous and try to hurt them. That is an instruction. The report tells the child to move away from strangers as quickly as possible evoking the emotion of fear. Thus, every time the child sees a stranger in a store, on the street, in a playground, or any other place, they recall the earlier instruction and fearfully move away from the person as quickly as possible. This is the action.

But when the child grows up and becomes an adult, often the report stays filed in the brain, and whenever he or she bumps into a stranger on the subway, in the office cafeteria, or in a coffee shop, it triggers the same emotion and action response and they hurry away muttering something incomprehensible and divert their eyes to avoid making contact. Even though he or she is no longer a child, they are cold, fearful, and distant in their interpersonal exchanges.

In the workplace, public service jobs often require employees to come into contact with strangers, for example, during a job interviews, providing the service of the agency, or merely explaining how a process works to an interested member of the public. If we never change the original instruction, we will find we are unable to control our emotions, which makes our behavior dysfunctional and maybe even gives our boss reason to fire us.

Source: Thomas and Cynthia Lynch, based on Elliot D. Cohen. 2003.

(See the second paragraph in Exhibit 7.3.) Our willpower must overcome the problem. We need to inventory and reconsider our many instructions and reports. Public administrators are in service to the public good, and as such they are called to treat everyone with respect and dignity. The purpose of examining our instructions and reports is to help ourselves find our unconscious instructions or reports that are causing a destructive or harmful behavior.

Finding the offending instruction or report is not enough, as we must also repair the problem. This is accomplished by discovering the flaw in the earlier thinking and applying correct reasoning to replace the flawed instruction or report. Often, flawed reasoning leads to damning thoughts toward others such as discrimination or offensive behavior that turns into anger. Reprogramming our reasoning gives each person new grounds for hope and replaces the feelings of gloom and doom. It transforms a reassessment of the present and future by putting the instruction or report into a new perspective. It allows us to gain control of dysfunctional habits and move toward self-actualization.

Sustaining correct reasoning is quite difficult and requires focused practice. Most people easily lapse back into their old self-defeating flawed unconscious emotional thinking. A crisis of the moment, a bad day, unfair treatment by supervisor, a large loss of something or someone they value, or something else can easily trigger a reversion to the former flawed thinking. However, if we have done the inventory, we are at least aware of our irrational emotional thinking about the situation. Exercising ethics can help reorient our thinking to get us past the crisis and thus free us of the immediate emotional pain and act as a set of defenses to help avoid future pain and unhappiness. Flawed unconscious emotional thinking sometimes creates egocentric thinking that can result in psychological pain and dysfunctional social behavior.

Suppose that a young public administrator is emotionally down because his boss reprimanded him for something he did wrong. His reaction is to feel terrible, lose confidence in his ability to properly do the job, and be socially embarrassed in the office. He realizes that the boss was correct as the mistake was clearly his fault, but the result is he feels that he is a worthless failure in the job. In such a situation, he is in an emotional crisis with no rational defenses. Thus, he stews reliving the situation over and over again and suffers considerable pain. He has mentally filed this report under an earlier instruction from his school days that told him only the best in the class are worthy.

An antidote to this emotional crisis does not distort the realities of the situation, he is still responsible for his mistake, and it does change the mental instruction he uses to denounce himself and permits him to dispose of the original report that brought up his self-defeating instructions. One antidote he can apply is, "One failed workplace situation is unpleasant, but it is also an opportunity to learn valuable lessons for another day so that I can be the best that I can be in my next task. What can I learn from this?" This antidote focuses on learning lessons to help him get past the embarrassment and guilt of having made a mistake and turn a very negative situation into a more positive outcome for him.

By changing his instruction, the situation is no longer a horrific matter of abject failure but is now just an unfortunate situation that provides a valuable lesson for future professional growth. Left untreated, faulty thinking takes its toll on every person, as it is dysfunctional to their long-term happiness. Antidotes, meaning improved or updated instructions, are by no means excuses for mistakes nor are they a cure for bad behavior. However, they allow the person to rewire their thinking to overcome negative circumstances that occur in everyone's life.

In this simple case example, our young public administrator was challenged to change his internal self-programming to create new positive instructions rather than let his past instructions from his school days forever determine his inner self. Instead of an overly simple instruction to strive to be the best, in absolute terms, he could modify his instruction to view life as a process and strive to be the best professional he could be in the moment and be open to growth from each experience. A professional virtue is accepting mistakes as learning opportunities. By doing so, the professional takes charge of his or her life and makes the choices that permit growth and happiness.

To further illustrate this point, a little humor is appropriate. A new employee made an expensive mistake and was filled with remorse. When he was called into the office of the boss, he was terror struck expecting to be fired on the spot. He was surprised when his boss talked about a new project and he had trouble focusing on the words of his superior. The boss noticed him not being fully attentive and asked him if something was bothering him. He admitted that he thought she was going to fire him for his very big recent mistake. The boss replied, "That would be really a foolish thing to do! That mistake was a million-dollar investment in your training. We assume that it will help you become a valued employee in the future!"

FROM INSTRUCTION TO ACTION

INSTRUCTION, REPORT, AND ACTION

Human life is a growing process. As a person grows, circumstances program a large set of mental images and instructions into their mind. For example, one can have the instruction that "I must always be the best at whatever I do as defined by an outside authority such as a boss." However, if such an instruction is unrealistic, a poor or unethical action can result. For example, in some situations, a person might not challenge themselves to take a more demanding position in fear that they will not be the "best" at it. This discourages the employee from trying to grow into more demanding jobs. Or, such an instruction may encourage the individual to cheat in order to look good to get that "necessary" approval from others. To compound matters, if they fail at being the "best," the report to the instruction might require them to feel extreme failure and cause them to close down on ever trying again. Such an overstated narrow instruction leads to dysfunctional feelings and actions that result in negative ethical thinking.

As we have already discussed, mental images bombard us and form sets of mental instructions. As a person experiences life, perceptions constantly send reports to the mind with instructions on how to react and respond to a situation. Those reports interact with the already established instructions to tell us how to act, feel, or both. Because instructions are a group of generalizations about what you should or should not do, they are normative and often ethical in substance. They inform us about doing right and wrong or lead us to what we believe is a better way to live. Instructions can be rational or irrational as well as functional and dysfunctional.

Irrational instructions often have a "must" message in them and typically if verbalized use strong and sometimes crude language. The first set of statements in Exhibit 7.3 uses the imperative "never." If each of us perceives the facts of a situation, which serve as the reports about our responses to our instructions, these reports may or may not be accurate. They are statements of using "is" or "are" and are thus descriptive. The mind files these reports under a particular instruction and thus they are filed as a decision for our ultimate action or reaction. Individuals are rarely fully conscious of their own instructions when they engage in actions or feel emotions. Nevertheless, their instructions and the reports they receive drive them to act.

Self-defeating actions are normally due to unrealistic or irrational instructions and false or unfounded reports. Unrealistic instructions commonly lead to self-defeating actions. Reports are false when there is sufficient information to disprove them. Reports are unfounded when there is insufficient evidence to prove them. Thus, to avoid self-defeating actions a person needs to first train him or herself to avoid using either false or unfounded reports and be careful about what he or she believes are the facts. Second, one needs to occasionally audit one's standing instructions for validity. This is done by (a) knowing that instructions exist, (b) identifying the specific instruction to examine it, and (c) learning how to reprogram the unrealistic instructions. In other words, thinking through the "instructions" by considering multiple consequences—beyond the obvious first or second levels—is helpful in reframing instructions and reports. Thus, we should try to consider the full negative implications of the instructions and reports that we use.

Exhibit 7.4 is an example of a logic tree using the instruction that "I *must* always be the best." At the first branch, either I am successful or I fail. If I succeed, I go on to the second branch where I might be successful or fail after the second event. In fact, you might continue to be successful but with enough events you will eventually fail. Back to the first branch and the outcome that you fail at your first event and because you failed you decide to cheat.

If you were initially able to get by with cheating, two possibilities occur. Either you will be eventually caught cheating or you will get away with cheating. In that later situation, you have learned nothing from the experience except how to get away with cheating, but your cheating probably hurt the larger society in some manner. Because you get away with cheating, you cheat again but eventually you will be caught, as the odds are very much against repeating cheaters.

Let us say that after the second successful attempt that you failed on your third try. Two things might happen (1) you improve your next attempt and also change the "MUST" instruction and this time you are successful or (2) you fail again. However, with the second failure, you changed the MUST instruction and therefore you can approach your future work challenge in a more realistic and self-forgiving manner.

A more visible example of the negative consequences of poor instruction messages can be found in private and public organizations. Organizational units and employees are judged in terms of achieving desired outputs (produced work products and services) and outcomes (end results of a program such as profit in a private company and a better society for a public organization). Those outputs can be unrealistic. For example a bank can demand an unrealistic number of new accounts from its branches or a national guard can demand an unrealistic number of reenlistments. The former results in the staff generating fraudulent new accounts and subsequently bank clientele protests. The latter example results in giving out unapproved signing bonuses that later results in the government demanding the return of the bonuses from the soldiers. This eventually results in a very public embarrassing scandal.

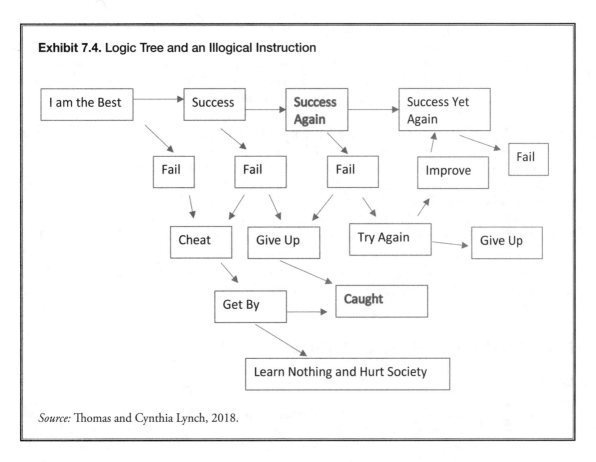

Exhibit 7.4. Logic Tree and an Illogical Instruction

Source: Thomas and Cynthia Lynch, 2018.

ANTIDOTAL REASONING

Once we conclude that our self-instructions are based on our own flawed reasoning, we can develop an antidote to the unrealistic instructions. An antidote to an instruction is replacement with a more reasonable instruction that corrects the earlier faulty one and hopefully provides a better basis for reaction or decision making. One or more antidotes always exist for an irrational instruction. For example, let us say that you were out with a friend who does business with your public agency. The meal ticket is expensive and your friend takes the bill while saying he knows that his expense account will cover the cost and your account will not.

Your instruction out of social politeness is "one should not argue over a bill when someone expresses an act of generosity." The report is your friend taking the bill and you letting him cover the total bill on his account. Your action is accepting his offer. At another time in your life, this might be a reasonable instruction, report, and action. However, now you are a public servant and your action is self-defeating because your friend paying the bill (if it is over $25) is an ethics violation under the law in the public sector and this will put your job and career at risk. An antidote could be "It's Okay, I will get it. I can't accept a gift over twenty-five dollars from someone who does business with my agency. Sorry about this but I really have no choice."

An effective antidote must prescribe how or how not to respond more rationally to situations that you might experience. Deciding on an effective antidote (a new instruction) requires some critical thinking. In the above situation using the antidote, your action could be to say, "Jack, we are good friends and I know you would not want to get me in trouble. I just can't accept your kind offer, but thanks for a very nice gesture." In this situation, the report would be the same, but the action is quite different.

An important precaution is to avoid dogmatically, absolutely, and inflexibly maintaining an antidote. There are always multiple possible refutations to any given instruction. No instruction is rational in all circumstances. So, in developing antidote instructions, one is wise to remain open to the possibility of updating the antidote later or developing a larger set of antidote instructions for use in varying situations.

To illustrate the need for updating an antidote, let us consider the same set of facts as before but add that the FBI placed a recording device on you because they believed your friend was involved in illegal activities. To make the contact with your friend as successful as possible, the FBI told you to let him pay the bill. Under those conditions, a different antidote instruction would be to cooperate with the FBI and hope your friend is not a criminal and will forgive you if he finds out that you recorded him.

EMOTIONALLY OUT OF CONTROL

EMOTIONS

Building on the section about emotional intelligence in chapter 2, when people are upset about something, such as being afraid, anxious, depressed, and so on, their emotions maybe controlling them. The something can be an actual, a possible, or an imaginary event, state of affairs, physical object, person, and even other emotions. When emotions erupt and a person is out of control, the body automatically reacts through surges in the body chemistry that effect the heart, lungs, gut, skin, muscles, and glands. This changes the person's brain function, blood vessels, and immune system.

Two subsystems (the sympathetic and parasympathetic nervous systems) react to emotions to provide a means of making energy available to the body in stressful situations and to conserve and restore energy. The sympathetic nervous system triggers a release of hormones that raise bodily activity levels in response to a perceived threat so that a person is hypervigilant and ready for the fight or flight response. Heart and lung rates increase. There is an increase in blood flow to the large muscles. The body secretes adrenaline and blood sugar levels rise. The parasympathetic nervous system counteracts some of the sympathetic systems to conserve energy and eventually return the body to normal levels.

In an emotional crisis, the autonomic nervous system transmits the crisis message to the internal organs and parts of the brain. Those neural signals generate physical feelings that give internal perceptions of the body's condition. Depending on the emotional state of the person, the feelings are pleasant or painful with varying intensity. Such emotional responses are part of the body's self-protection function. In our earlier illustration of the young public administrator being critiqued by his boss, his sympathetic nervous system sprang into action, which increased his blood flow to the larger muscles. He felt his heart pounding as he heard the critical words of his boss. He was ready for flight or fight, but mentally he took charge of his emotions and controlled his body's natural responses to a significant extent in order to carry on a civil conversation with his boss.

Minds work like a recording device with play, stop, rewind, replay, and fast forward functions. The brain's prefrontal cortices can replay a person's emotions and generate the same bodily physical feelings that are stored in the person's memory. Even though the experience that created that memory may not be exactly the same, the mental images replay and recall the same physical feelings. Those images are due to past experiences (see the discussion in chapter 3 on John Locke).

To continue building our illustration, let us say the young public administrator is home at night after that stressful conversation with his boss. He recalls his boss's words and re-experiences the same physical feelings of anger, embarrassment, failure, and incompetence he had during the interview. Like an old vinyl record, his emotions are stuck in a groove and he continually replays the same emotions. In the privacy of his own home, he does not feel the need to hold anything in check and now the repeated message gets stronger each time the experience is revisited.

If he can turn his thoughts toward searching for the positive lessons that can be learned from his earlier experience, then that can help him create an antidote that will help him learn from the experience so that he can better deal with the next similar experience and grow from it. Therefore, experience should help a person perform better than an inexperienced person in difficult situations. However, for some, the repeated recall of negative physical feelings can unfortunately amplify those feelings and create a dysfunctional emotion or even actions such as wanting to physically hurt a boss or coworker in order to exact revenge for the experienced pain.

CONTROL WITH REASONING

Aristotle noted that when people routinely allow feelings to well up inside and take control of them, then they are more likely to be unhappy in life. His alternative was for people to use reason to create antidotes that habitually direct thoughts, actions, and emotions toward living happily. In most animals, including humans, emotions automatically generate physical reactions. However, in most animals, the parasympathetic system quickly restores the body to its normal operating conditions.

Humans are different, in that they can and often do replay the memory tapes. Thus, they can spend their adult lives upset about things that went wrong long ago as children or even in their past generations. Fortunately, humans also have the capacity to use their cognitive ability to counteract the dysfunctional looping effect of continually replaying the mental tapes that cause their unhappiness. Unfortunately, that does not always occur.

Physical reactions accompany emotions. For example, the skeletal muscular nervous system gives visible responses such as changing the facial expression from a smile to a scowl or frown. These muscles usually function under conscious and voluntary control of the individual, but the ability to control them varies from person to person. In an emotional situation, some have little control. We say that we can read them "like a book," meaning everyone can clearly see what they are feeling. Others have what poker players call a tic—a small but noticeable reaction to a bad or good hand. A few people have an excellent "poker face," meaning nothing about them reveals what they are thinking or feeling.

Complete control of the sympathetic system is rarely possible as it is automatic, and some knee-jerk types of reactions such as blushing or breaking into a sweat cannot be helped. For the automatic reactions to continue beyond a few seconds though, a person must allow the specific mental instruction that replays the memory of a bad experience and thus brings up their uncomfortable emotions, which is then aggravated by the looping effect. If a person wishes to have better control over their sympathetic system, he or she must not let the mental replay command button be pushed. This again is accomplished with a new antidote instruction.

Physical feelings from emotions often influence and sustain the human ethical reasoning process. For example, we have seen this ethical reasoning process in several violent workplace situations. In fact, this behavior was dubbed "going postal" in 1993, after a series of such violent actions within the U.S. Postal Service resulted in many deaths. The very negative outcome of physically attacking the boss goes like this:

INSTRUCTION: No one should ever be ridiculed or publicly embarrassed, especially in the workplace.
REPORT: My boss just humiliated me.
ACTION: I need revenge for my pain, I will kill him.

This report plays and replays in the mind and creates the same physical feeling each time. The replay can go on for days, weeks, months, and even years before it is amplified enough to move the person to action. Note that the report can be accurate or not in terms of what really occurred. As the person moves further and further away from the event, the detail of the facts of the specific circumstance probably fade and only the amplified "feelings" from the continuous replay of the report will occupy the person's thinking process. Importantly, the dysfunctional instructions are framed as an absolute without exception. It is wiser to formulate instructions that are more balanced and reflect the realities of human nature. In addition, it is wise to focus the antidote on the deed and not at the doer in order for the direction of the subject's emotions to be less personal.

In the earlier illustration of the young public administrator, he was on an emotional roller-coaster, in the next minute he was in a rage wanting his boss to pay for his pain and humiliation, and in the following minute he was feeling guilt for making a stupid mistake in the first place. Such fluctuation reflects an irrational instruction. The guilt resulting from this irrational thinking uses the following type of flawed emotional reasoning:

INSTRUCTION: An employee, who made a mistake, draws the attention of his boss who becomes angry.
REPORT: I made my boss angry because of my work mistake.
EMOTION: Guilt for making the boss angry.

This self-defeating reasoning can set the stage for another and perhaps catastrophic chain of emotions that lead to an action, such as physically hurting the boss. The problem is accepting the unrealistic or easily disprovable premise behind the instruction. When this occurs, it creates an internal tug-of-war involving fear, guilt, disgust, and so on. Our internal battles are normally the result of irrational premises and poorly framed instructions that do not yet have an effective healthy antidote instruction.

In our scenario, the employee is in a repeating emotional loop and he becomes increasingly out of control of his actions. His responses intensify. He erupts and either quits his job or verbally or physically attacks his boss or both. Unrealistic instructions plus unfounded or false reports lead to self-defeat and unhappiness. In this illustration, the police arrested the young administrator, he went through a very public trial, and he spent serious time in jail for his crime.

Although the death of the boss and the drama of arrest and prison time are real tragedies, the underlying tragedy is that the young administrator and other persons like him remain clueless as to what happens to them in this type of situation. Even more tragic is that these unfortunate circumstances can usually be avoided. However, all too often the guilty person remains ignorant to how he could have avoided this chain of events and consequences. Although simple, the solution requires focused attention to expose the flawed instructions and reports, practice to refute them, and then replacement of them with more helpful antidote instructions and proper reports.

EXERCISING WILLPOWER

The success of exercising emotional control largely depends on a person's ability to employ willpower, which is like a mental muscle that is flexed to overcome self-destructive inclinations. Typically, a temptation is felt as a pressure of craving or desire for something. To counteract dysfunctional temptations, we exercise willpower to keep us from succumbing to those inclinations.

We need to practice our willpower over irrational premises and physical inclinations; and, while doing so, realizing that those feelings take constant effort to control. Willpower involves present and future thinking, feeling, and acting against one's irrational beliefs or carrying forward with one's rational beliefs. This requires using our internal or helpful external forces, such as a friend to remind us what to do. The exercise of willpower often is the first step in making a permanent change in our long-standing instruction.

A person uses willpower to control unreasonable actions, but willpower can also be a positive force that helps to push a person to rational actions and rational thoughts. When people begin to exercise their mental muscles to exert willpower, they feel awkward. The exertion is even painful at first as it is when we exercise any muscle. In time, and with more exercise, willpower can replace old habitual actions with new more rational ones.

One approach to assist in building the willpower "muscle" is to reframe the situation. Surprisingly, this is done simply by changing perspective and seeing the situation from a different point of view. Several philosophers, such as Schopenhauer, redefined evil from negative to positive by merely seeing evil as a learning opportunity. The renowned psychologist Viktor Frankl illustrated this in his book *Man's Search for Meaning*. Recounting his Nazi concentration camp experiences of marching in the dark to a worksite, traversing large puddles and stones while being prodded by shouting guards with the butts of their rifles, he observed that many belabored the pessimistic premise of torture and misery.

He instead chose to see his circumstances differently. He saw hope in small things like a flower blooming through the snow and mud and marveled at its persistence and beauty. He saw the salvation of man through love, and, for him, where there was life there was hope. This new instruction directed his emotions by giving him a new purpose even in a Nazi concentration camp. He did not deny his suffering but he reframed his perspective to bring good out of evil and that gave him a deeper understanding of the meaning of life. He exercised his limited physical freedom to choose a philosophic freedom to reframe the premise from which he viewed his reality with positive optimism.

COGNITIVE DISSONANCE

Cognitive dissonance is the tension between what you emotionally believe to be true and what you intellectually know is factually true. It references the level of mental discomfort of simultaneously holding two contradictory beliefs, ideas, or values. With cognitive dissonance, there is no match between knowledge and emotion. This commonly happens when our long-held belief systems of right and wrong that were taught to us at our grandmother's knee or in Sunday School are challenged by new real world facts. You know what you should do, but you do not feel like doing it. Often this contrasting situation leads to self-defeating behavior of inertia when the person should act promptly.

Confronting cognitive dissonance requires looking inside the inner self to recognize conflicted thinking, and, for many people, this is remarkably difficult. Inertia occurs when a person cannot tap into their inner strength to recognize and face up to the conflict and resolve it head-on. When persons overcome that inertia, the persons can then direct themselves outwardly against the currents of the status quo, temptations, and desires. This, in turn, builds a person's efficacy and power.

Willpower is a key factor in the human emotional fabric and emotional control. Without it, a person remains a slave to desires and their environmental, economic, historic, and social circumstances. Willpower is what defines a person as free because they can choose their own rational instructions and make those instructions a reality in their lives. By exerting willpower, people change the way they think, feel, and act. With it, they can stop self-defeating emotions, possibly unethical actions, and exercise their considered right behavior and actions that create the good life for them.

Willpower fights irrational thinking in two ways. If the antidote instructions say what we should not do, willpower enables us to follow those instructions. If the antidote instructions tell us what we should do, then our willpower pushes us to achieve those instructions. Thus, willpower helps us to both stop doing the irrational and it helps us to do the rational.

EMOTIONAL FALLACIES

VIRULENT EMOTIONAL FALLACIES

The assumption of this book is that knowledge can and normally will be a positive independent variable of life and that it will or can result in personal and social happiness. If a person knows what is "good," then that person will make the rational ethical choice for doing or being good. However, desires and appetites driven by poor instructions can lead people to make irrational decisions that are contrary to their own happiness even when they know better at some cognitive level of understanding. Thus, although the fundamental conclusions of Socrates and Aristotle are correct, their assertion needs modification to note that sometimes people get caught up in their own emotional fallacies that too often overcome their capacity for rational decision making.

The problem for ethics is to get past the emotional fallacies found in life. Only by doing so can ethics, especially virtue ethics, meaningfully guide a person. Realistically, floundering on emotional dysfunctional reasoning is a common occurrence. Fortunately, when that occurs and poor reasoning causes negative effects, pre- and post-reflections on those effects can help people to subsequently reconsider the instructions and reports that guided their unfortunate irrational decision making. For many, information feedback loops coupled with the genuine desire to live better lives can help them realize that they are thinking irrationally and lead them to search the necessary healthy antidote instructions.

Emotional fallacies are ways of thinking that have a proven track record of frustrating personal and interpersonal happiness. Those fallacies lead to dysfunctional instructions and reports that lead us to unfortunate actions and dysfunctional emotional loops. According to ethicist and political analyst Elliot D. Cohen, there are seven particularly virulent emotional fallacies. Exhibit 7.5 provides a brief explanation of each.

Exhibit 7.5. Virulent Emotional Fallacies

Virulent Emotional Fallacy	Description
Demanding Perfection	If the world fails to conform to some state of ideal, perfection, or near-perfection, then the world is not the way it absolutely, unconditionally must be, and this is unacceptable to the subject.
Awfulizing	If something bad happens regardless of how minor, then it is totally catastrophic, terrible, awful, and so on.
Terrificizing	If someone appears to have a desirable feature, then this person or thing is absolutely and totally terrific, perfect, and the best of its kind in the entire universe.
I-Can't-Stand-It	If something is difficult or challenging to deal with, then it is beyond the subject's capacity to tolerate and the subject cannot and must not ever hope to succeed at it.
Damnation	If there is something about the subject or about another person that they strongly dislike, then the subject or the other person is totally worthless.
I-Just-Can't-Help-This-Feeling	If the subject feels depressed, anxious, angry, guilty, or otherwise upset, then the subject might as well just accept and go with their feelings because it is not really in their control anyway.
Thou-Shat-Upset-Yourself	If the subject encounters a problem in their life that the they deem important, they have the moral duty to ruminate over it, never stop thinking about it, make themselves miserable and upset over it, and demand that others, for whom the subjects also deem it a problem, do the same.

Source: Thomas and Cynthia Lynch, based on Elliot D. Cohen. 2003.

When a person accepts an instruction that demands perfection, the person tells him or herself that the world must not fail in achieving their expectation of perfection. This emotional fallacy, commonly found in the political liberal left and conservative right, induces intense feelings of outrage, anger, and dismay when the world inevitably fails to conform to their personal expectations. This emotional fallacy is clearly irrational thinking as the person cannot accept that he lives in an imperfect world. Typically, this fallacy is manifested when one of the following occurs:

- A boss, someone special, or someone, who does not approve of you or what you say, criticizes you.

- As an employee, you make a mistake.

- You discover that everything does not work out as you planned.

- Someone, especially a boss or a fellow worker, treats you unfairly.

- Something bad happens to you or your significant other.

- You find that you can`t control everything, everyone, or something especially important to you.

- You determine that you can`t achieve what you want to.

- You discover that you failed or were less successful than you thought you were.

- You lose something or someone of substantial value to you.

The antidote is to change the irrational instruction that probably contains the words "must," "ought," and "should" to the less demanding word "prefer." Aristotle's middle path lies between "must" and "who cares." Both absolute extreme instructions direct a person to intense, self-defeating emotional responses often with negative emotional loops.

The "who cares" path creates a negative emotional response to situations of little or no social significance that gives rise to a cynical attitude. The "must" path creates frustration and sometimes negative depression or defeated emotional loops with very unfortunate consequences. The preferred middle path provides the person with direction and encourages him or her to strive for progress without the harsh consequence of failure. If he or she fails with the preferred path, they feel disappointed but not devastated and do not fall into the negative emotional feedback loop.

The *awfulizing emotional fallacy* tells us that when something we do not like happens, we think of it as totally devastating, catastrophic, and the worst thing imaginable. This instruction creates within us an extreme sense of anxiety or remorse when things happen that get in our way. The antidote is for us to remain humble about our misfortunes and focused on finding a lesson in the experience.

The *terrificizing emotional fallacy* tells us if someone or something appears to have some desirable feature, then to think of that person or thing as the most absolutely and totally terrific, perfect, and the best of its kind. This fallacy brings us to idolize the person or thing and to expect that no one else can possibility achieve that level of excellence. This unrealistic overly optimistic thinking can only lead to later frustration but more significantly it leads to avoiding confronting facts in evidence. For example, your elected boss is popular and wins a very significant election and praises you publicly. In your mind, she is the best leader in the world, but this assessment may lead you to overlook that she asked you to rig a contract for a favored political supporter.

The *I-can't-stand-it emotional fallacy* tells as that difficult or challenging situations are beyond our capacity to address. We feel that we cannot and must not even hope to succeed. Normally, such an instruction causes intense frustration when we are confronted with a difficult situation. Failure ensues because we do not adequately try. This low frustration threshold means even small frustrations defeat us easily and more importantly useful lessons from a series of trial and error experiences are lost.

This underassessment of a person's personal power removes the unique human trait of resilience that can result in eventual success. The antidote is to replace the instruction words "I can't" or "I can't stand it." Language of disempowerment reinforces the notion that something is beyond our control and efficacy and it is an affirmation of our unwillingness to try. Such language is a denial of our freedom. In terms of an antidote, the middle path of "I choose not to" or "I will do the best that I can" is wiser.

Being unduly humble tells us that we are unworthy and, in contrast, vanity is about a person who overrates themselves. The extreme form of vanity is the god complex. Again, the middle path is best. Typically, the two best antidotes are (1) to avoid rating the doer and focus on the deed and (2) reframe to appreciate the worth of some aspect of the person rather than using one or few attributes to pass judgment. In discussing this wisdom, Aristotle argued one should reserve the term "wicked" or "bad person" only to those who habitually voluntarily commit wicked acts.

The *damnation emotional fallacy* tells us that a particular person or group is totally worthless. This conclusion results in strong dislikes or aversions to a person or group. The reasons for these feelings are not as important as the existence of those strong feelings. Damnation can be of oneself or others. Any extreme of under- or overrating is irrational thinking.

Global damnation is about the worthlessness of a person or groups of people. Dehumanizing a target person or group gives permission to abuse them. This emotional fallacy is common among hate groups. Good indicators of the damnation emotional fallacy are the use of words such as "weirdo," "jerk," "doer," "retard," "pig," "schmuck," "nerd," "idiot," and "scumbag."

Often the use of dehumanizing words has no literal sense in the language composition or has an absurd literal sense. Derogatory terms are often gender, sexual, racial, nationality, and religion specific. Typically, such labels are loosely used but they also can be a part of one or more emotional loops that end with very negative actions such as beatings or killings. The healthier antidote is to stop the beginning of the loop and not use dehumanizing language.

The *I-just-can't-help-this-feeling emotional fallacy* tells us to respond with feelings of depression, anxiety, anger, guilt, or being upset. With accepting we have no ability to control our lives, we give ourselves permission to continue our self-defeating and irrational behavior. We become our own enablers and sustain our own misery by denying any responsibility for our emotions. Often, we shift the responsibility for control of our emotions to others or to some external events. We become a passive recipient of our own feelings and thus do not consider ourselves accountable for our feelings and actions.

Over the centuries, philosophers such as the stoic Epictetus noted that it is not events, people, or items that upset us but rather the way we think about those events, people, and items. Psychologist

Albert Ellis used that simple notion to create rational-emotive behavior therapy, which says that we feel what we think. We cognitively create our own happiness or unhappiness.

Certainly, we do not have complete control over all our thoughts and emotions all the time and past experiences do conjure up thoughts within us. However, often we can do better. For example, if we can recognize cognitive dissonance in our thinking, we know that our thoughts and feelings are contradictory or unreasonable but we nevertheless continue being governed by them. In such a situation, our goal should be to return to a posture in which we gain self-control and isolate the fallacy in our reasoning process. The antidote is flexing our willpower muscle but it must exist with a prior recognition that one or more fallacies are controlling our lives. Even without total control over our own thoughts and emotions, this combined antidote is how we create freedom in our lives.

With this deeper understanding of freedom, we have a way to manage our emotions. In doing so, we need to avoid freedom/responsibility disavowing language such as "aggravates me," "upsets me," "depresses me," "makes me anxious or nervous," or "lays a guilty trip on me." In those combinations of words, the verb acts on the subject rather than the subject being in control. Framing the language this way blames others for your emotions and ignores the likelihood that those emotions actually originated in you. Once we take responsibility for our own emotions, then the solution is within our grasp.

The *thou-shall-upset-yourself fallacy* assumes that we have a moral duty to confront problems in our lives by ruminating over them, thinking about them nonstop, making ourselves miserable over them, and demanding others react the same way. This is a common fallacy used by terrorists, but it also often happens in managerial situations. We keep ourselves in an unnecessary and prolonged state of irritability, anxiety, and malaise. Sometimes the problem is truly significant, but very often it is a real but involves relatively small issue. We react to a molehill problem by creating an emotional mountain for ourselves and possibly others.

The dysfunctionality of this fallacy is the disproportionate reaction of the people involved. The boss maybe acting inappropriately toward the employee, but the employee should not feel compelled to shoot him. Public administrators sometimes launch into this fallacy and emotionally drive themselves and others into explosive situations that are totally out of proportion to the original problem. People who engage in this fallacy seek absolute or ultimate certainty in the resolution of a problem. However, in the circumstances of public policy and management, such a standard is not always practical. The antidote to this fallacy is to simply not engage in it; instead, reason with probabilities and accept that nothing in life is ever certain. The healthy antidote, should include tolerance for ambiguity, especially for others who are also making their own moral choices.

INTERPERSONAL INSTRUCTION FALLACIES

In the context of public administration, people can easily succumb to interpersonal instruction fallacies that govern their actions. Often these fallacies invoke actions that create problems between and among people in the workplace. Exhibit 7.6 presents the fallacies with their descriptions.

Exhibit 7.6. Interpersonal Emotional Fallacies

Interpersonal Emotional Fallacies	Description
The-World-Revolves-Around-Me Thinking	Only the subject's preference is the true reality and therefore everybody else must share that preference.
Blackmailing	Emotionally withdrawing or threatening to withdraw something of value from a person or group if they refuse to do something the subject wants.
Making a Stink	Kicking, screaming, yelling, or otherwise throwing a temper tantrum, if the subject is not being respected, understood, heard, or heeded.
Pity Mongering	Crying, sobbing, weeping, pouting, moping, whining, and so on to look hurt, dejected, downtrodden, demoralized, dejected, rejected, or otherwise pitiful if the subject is in trouble or having difficulty getting what he or she wants.
Beating around the Bush	Verbally consenting while dropping hints of disapproval of a task, if they think someone has made an unreasonable request of them, but they feel intimidated about saying no.
Poisoning the Well	Using strong, negative language to intimidate and dissuade the person from doing or believing something, if the subject does not want someone to do or believe it.
Getting Even	Exacting revenge for something equally as wrong that was done to them.
Jumping on the Bandwagon	Acting, thinking, or feeling the same way as a person or group that the person admires.

Source: Thomas and Cynthia Lynch, based on Elliot D. Cohen. 2003.

The-world-revolves-around-me emotional fallacy is a belief that our preference is the only true reality and therefore everyone else must share that preference opinion. Thus, we expect reality to conform to our vision rather than adapting our behavior to reality. In this fallacy, we are the center of the universe and therefore the only genuine beacon of truth. There is no tolerance for other positions or ideas and we wonder how those who do not agree with us can be so wrong.

In public administration, often there is more than one reasonable way to approach policy and management challenges. However, rational discourse ends if one or more of the parties are stuck in the emotional fallacy that there is only one true way to solve the challenge. The antidote for this fallacy is to develop the human capacity to empathize with others and in this type of circumstance using the Golden Rule is particularly useful. This approach helps to create tolerance and the ability to hear and accept new ideas, and encourages understanding of another person's point of view.

This antidote strengthens the value of compromise and the wisdom of seeking out several mutually agreeable alternatives. Thus, tolerance, mutual respect, empathy, understanding, and willingness to compromise are productive antidotes. This is often only achieved after we carefully listen to and consider the relevant circumstances of others.

The *blackmailing fallacy* is characterized by withdrawing or threatening to withdraw something of value from the other party. In more distant interrelationships, the item of blackmail is often money such as a withdrawal of monetary support. In closer interrelationships, the object of blackmail is often emotional such as the withdrawal of friendship. This fallacy fails to work out differences with others and instead resorts to some form of physical or emotional threat. An antidote instruction is to treat others as rational, self-determined persons and not as objects of manipulation, even if others do not threat you that way.

The *making a stink fallacy* resorts to extreme emotional outbursts intended to be heard and heeded. This behavior is common among two-year-olds and spoiled children. Unfortunately, some people never quite outgrow this emotional behavior. Normally, this fallacy creates tremendous tension in public settings and promotes added disunity when the organization needs just the opposite. The senior author of this book witnessed such a screaming outburst by an assistant secretary of a federal department. The result was a continuous gap in communication at the highest levels in the department that only resolved itself with a change of administrations.

For those who fall victim to this fallacy, a good antidote is to admit this emotional behavior and accept the inappropriateness of it. We need to resist treating others as mere objects of our emotionalism. Typically, a person can recognize that they engage in this fallacy but they lack the willpower to meaningfully address it.

The *pity mongering fallacy* occurs when people, who are in trouble or are having difficulties getting what they want, use crying, pouting, moping, whining, looking hurt, acting dejected, depressed, and rejected, behaving in a demoralized manner, and so on as a manipulative tool on others to achieve their desired ends. In other words, this is a common behavior among teenagers and sadly some people never outgrow it. This fallacy may get others to abandon their relevant positions and give in to the drama; however, it does not create healthy human interrelationships.

Clearly, sometimes pity is appropriate but it should be freely given by others and not demanded. If this fallacy is used frequently and is successful, it erodes the purpose of an organization's standards and in time those standards are forgotten. For example, students typically seek to lower their teacher's grading standards using this fallacy. The students' argument is that life has dealt them a terrible blow, and they should be excused from the work of the course because of their duress. If successful from the perspective of the students, their grades may increase but they also fail to learn the material in the course. Thus, the purpose of education, which is to learn, is forgotten and the student is less able to perform on the job when they eventually graduate.

The antidote for this emotional fallacy is more complex than many of the others. Sometimes life really does deal people a really bad hand. The challenge is in how to deal with the exhibited emotions and how long such emotions are acceptable. Helping the person realize they are engaged in this fallacy and then telling them to give it up is *not* useful advice for most. Normally, the problem is the person's social network that they rely on heavily. Often that network is just a few individuals, who may not be able to support the person.

The antidote lies not in telling them to stop being emotional but rather in reaching out in a more understanding manner to help the person transition out of this thinking mode over time. The antidote goal is to build within the emotional person internal resilience and viable social friendships. Encouraging others in the workplace to reach out to them as friends is often useful. Essentially, the antidote is counterintuitive, as the normal reaction to people who complain is to avoid and even reject them. Instead, the solution is acceptance not of the whining but of the person's circumstance and to help them realize that they are a valued individual. This developed self-worth has a better chance to help them develop a desire to excel in the context of the organization.

The *beating around the bush fallacy* occurs when people perceive others as making unreasonable or wrongful requests of them and they feel too insecure or intimidated to say "no." They attempt to save face by verbally consenting while nonverbally dropping hints of disapproval. This happens often in authoritarian relationships where the subject feels that the only right answer is the answer that the boss wants to hear. The problem with the use of this fallacy is that important information is cut off from the boss. In addition, the person engaged in this fallacy is stuck in a cycle of self-perpetuating guilt.

There are, of course, many occasions in the workplace when we should just do what the boss demands. However, if there is added or updated information that can help the boss make more intelligent decisions or the employee does have strong negative feelings about the decision, then some frank discussion is in order. If that cannot happen because of this fallacy, then the situation is probably dysfunctional. There are diplomatic ways of communicating and we need to learn to use them. Therefore, the antidote is saying NO when there is a good reason to do so. However, finding an acceptable style of saying no for the situation is key. Normally, with respect to the bosses and the circumstances, you should communicate the reason for saying no clearly and without emotions creeping into your voice. In most cases, bosses respect people who act with integrity.

The *getting even fallacy* is when we think someone has wronged us and we feel we must do something equally wrong to them to even the score. Sometimes the Bible verse "an eye for an eye" (Exodus 21:24) is cited as a justification, but that justification takes the meaning of the words out of context because this quote is really referring to guidance for a judicial decision. This is not meant for individuals to take the action of retribution themselves. In addition, Matthew 5:38-48 says if hurt, we should "turn the other cheek." We often see this fallacy used in international decision making and among adolescents in their peer relationships.

This revenge-seeking behavior is rarely about justice; it is normally just about vengeance. The antidote is to not respond in kind, but instead respond with a sobering remark. For example, if a fellow employee treats you with sarcasm implying stupidity, the antidote is to help the offending person understand that you see their ploy. For example, "I think inferring that a fellow employee is stupid is inappropriate in the workplace." The goal of the antidote is to stop the crossfire but to also help the other party understand an interpersonal problem exists between them that cannot be ignored.

The *jumping on the bandwagon fallacy* is when people tell themselves that they must act, think, or feel exactly like others. Those others can be your peers, such as those who share your nationality, gender, or race, or some well-known person with a Twitter following. The result is that external forces define your life's values. Group thinking is not surprising as humans, by nature, are social animals and great imitators. However, group think in organizations is a real issue because only conformity exists for those with this fallacy and it precludes self-discernment and reflection that is important for a growing and aware employee.

The absurdity of this fallacy becomes apparent when the group makes a particularly irrational decision. For example, if the workplace group uses drugs socially, this means that you will also regardless of its irrationality or dysfunctional outcome for you. The antidote is to ask questions and seek answers. Is the group behavior rational or functional? Willpower becomes important to successfully employ this antidote. If you realize your group is making irrational decisions, willpower is critical to resisting climbing on their bandwagon.

CONFRONTING FAULTY EMOTIONAL THINKING

CHECKING FOR EMOTIONAL FALLACIES

In life, people make decisions, act, and experience emotions. However, they rarely consider the premises of their decisions, which we call the meta-stage in reasoning (discussed in detail in chapter 11). To confront and correct a pattern of faulty emotional thinking in which emotions control the person's life rather than reason, we must address the meta-stage of reasoning. As we noted at the beginning of this chapter, normally, people just do not think about what instructions they are following and what reports they file. The instructions are there but we tend to employ them as our default settings. Fortunately, we can use the meta-stage of reasoning and reprogram our automatic reasoning processes. To do so we need to work backwards by first identifying our conclusions and emotions. Exhibit 7.7 lists seven emotions plus the object of each emotion in emotional reasoning and a common dysfunctional related reaction.

In thinking backwards in the meta-stage of reasoning, the first steps in considering emotional fallacies are to (1) identify our emotions and (2) identify the related reports. In the first step we ask ourselves, "In any given situation, which one or more of the emotions did I experience?" In the second step we consider the reports associated with the instructions and emotions. As all emotions have an object, each report addresses an object, as suggested by Exhibit 7.7. Emotions are always about something and we need to identify what that something is. Thus, we need to recall the complete reports, especially the resulting emotions. It is essential to isolate whether and which emotional fallacy controls us. In doing so, we need to appreciate that perception is important and not what actually did or did not take place.

The third, fourth, and fifth steps are to find the offending instructions, refute the irrational premises, and, finally, to find antidotes for the refuted premises. The third step is to identify the instruction or instructions as summarized in Exhibits 7.3 and 7.4. We may think there is only one emotional fallacy, but there is a strong likelihood there are several at work simultaneously, as they tend to exists in groups. If more than one exist, we need to examine each one and identify the related irrational premises behind each instruction. Finally, the individual needs to arrive at a new antidote for each refuted premise and substitute the antidote in their reasoning processes. Knowing what is logically incorrect in the meta-stage and actually doing it in real life can be vastly different. Therefore, we must not only be aware of our emotional fallacies but also develop a plan and implement it to apply the necessary antidotes. If all of this seems like a lot of work, it is. However, the rewards for self-growth, work place harmony, and rewarding professional relationships are worth the investment of time and effort.

Exhibit 7.7. Emotions, Objects, and Reactions

EMOTIONS	OBJECT OF EMOTIONS	REACTIONS
Anger	For something that someone did.	Strongly, negatively rate the action itself or the person who did it.
Guilt	A moral principle, which we think we violated.	Strongly condemn the perceived violation or subject for the perceived violation.
Shame	An action or state of thinking, for which we perceive others to strongly, negatively judge us.	Strongly perceive this judgment as extremely undesirable and strongly feel negative judgment of self, action, or state of being.
Depression	Event or state of affairs.	Strongly, negatively rate one's own existence.
Grief	Loss of a person, animal, or thing that you are strongly, positively attached to.	Without the object of grief, the subject perceives their own existence as bleak.
Anxiety	Future event or possible future event.	You think you will or might experience serious negative consequences.
Fear	A present or possible event.	You perceive there is something dangerous and threatening to yourself or others.
Jealousy	The person or state of a person who has something you want but don't have.	Negatively rate this person having that which you think you lack.

Source: Thomas and Cynthia Lynch, based on Elliot D. Cohen. 2003.

REFUTING EMOTIONAL FALLACIES

There are at least four approaches in the meta-stage to reconsider the wisdom of the current instructions: (1) checking for counterexamples, (2) checking for evidence, (3) checking for self-defeating consequences, and (4) checking for double standards. Each approach helps to refute an irrational instruction and weaken its emotional appeal.

(1) Checking for counterexamples can happen automatically when we discover that an instruction's premise proves false. However, we can be more systematic by researching the existing literature or possibly even conducting rigorous inquiry on the subject. Regardless, we need to look for counterexamples to help us avoid tunnel vision or oversimplifications.

(2) Checking for evidence is very useful in refuting an irrational premise. We should ask: "Where is the evidence that the instruction's premise is correct?" "What does the evidence tell us about that possible false instruction or emotional fallacy?" Typically, the evidence determines the correctness of the premise behind the instruction but it can also suggest a powerful antidote to a fallacious instruction.

(3) Checking for self-defeating consequences is a good approach to reconsider the wisdom of an instruction because there are many irrational premises in fallacious instructions and they tend to occur when it is difficult to consistently apply a solution. Although no one can perfectly predict consequences, most people can isolate self-defeating consequences and thus avoid them. The challenge is to explore possible consequences, which helps us to realize the likely implications of our emotional reasoning.

(4) Checking for double standards often shows an irrational instruction about the treatment of others. Applying a variation of the Golden Rule test, such as "How would I like it if others did the same thing to me?" can be helpful in discovering this improper treatment. If the answer is not the same as applied to others, then a closer look is needed to understand why.

FINDING ANTIDOTES

Instructions sometimes use absolutistic uncompromising demands often using words such as should, shouldn't, must, or mustn't. Typically, they are irrational in their concreteness and the purpose of the antidote is to correct that language to say something more reasonable. Regardless of our chosen antidote, we are wise to not assume that any antidote is perfect or beyond improvement. Typically, life's experiences permit one to improve antidotes overtime by checking them periodically against counterexamples, more evidence, self-defeating consequences, and double standards.

Even highly useful antidotes many not work in every situation. One needs to be always mindful of exceptional circumstances but also guard against making up exceptions or phony excuses for not pushing oneself harder. Do not forget that smart people are really very good at rationalizing. Again Aristotle's middle path is more appropriate. Exhibit 7.8 points out the "emotional golden means" in each situation.

CONCLUSION

Leon is correct that many people allow their emotions to control their lives with false emotional fallacies. Many do live knee-jerk lives, as they make one decision after another with little regard for ethical or moral rational thinking. These are very human traits but being human also means that one can be rational in our efforts to transcend life's emotional fallacies. This is essential for being an ethical person in an ethical work environment.

Exhibit 7.8. Emotional Golden Means

One Extreme	The Other Extreme	The Golden Mean
Demanding perfection of yourself or others	Damnation of yourself or others	Accepting yourself as an imperfect person who is trying harder.
Perceiving an absolute duty to upset yourself over your problem.	Avoiding responsibility at all costs.	Doing what you reasonably can do about your problem and then accepting that you tried your best.
Using deceit, threats, pity, blackmail, and other manipulative devices to get your way.	Failing to assert yourself.	Treating yourself and others as rational, self-determining persons.
Magnifying risks of bad things happening in your life.	Underestimating dangerous situations.	Accurately assessing the probabilities.
Awfulizing about events in your life.	Denying that bad things happen.	Putting the bad things in your life into perspective relative to other aspects of your life.

Source: Thomas and Cynthia Lynch, based on Elliot D. Cohen. 2003.

This chapter explains how anyone can transcend their irrational emotional fallacies by identifying their life-governing instructions, key reports, and their predictable emotions and actions. This chapter also explains how the meta-stage of reasoning can help determine healthier antidotes. Emotions do not have to determine what people do and how they react. Individuals can govern their own lives with their own rational thoughts, but only if they improve their meta-stage reasoning and use willpower to achieve their own freedom.

REVIEW QUESTIONS

1. Explain the importance of self-control and reasoning in ethics.

2. Explain the connection of this chapter to the discussion of Locke in chapter 4.

3. In what way can the egocentric understandings of life lead to self-destruction, happiness destruction, and dysfunctional emotion-filled behavior?

4. Explain the importance of "instruction" and "report" in determining our emotional responses.

5. How can someone reprogram their "instructions"? Explain antidotal reasoning.

6. Compare and contrast sympathetic and parasympathetic reactions.

7. Explain the looping effect and its significance.

8. How does one increase the effectiveness of willpower?

9. What is cognitive dissonance and why is it important?

10. What are emotional fallacies? Explain the seven discussed in the chapter.

11. Why is the middle path significant?

12. Explain the significance of rational-emotive behavior therapy.

13. What are the eight interpersonal emotional fallacies?

14. What are the six emotions, the objects of each emotion, and the correspondent reactions?

15. Explain the steps necessary to counter the emotional fallacies.

16. What are the four approaches in the meta-stage to reconsidering current instructions?

REFERENCES

Cohen, Elliot D. 2003. *What Would Aristotle Do?* Amherst, NY: Prometheus Books.
Cooper, Belle Beth. 2016. "8 Common Thinking Mistakes Our Brains Make Every Day and How to Prevent Them."
    https://blog.bufferapp.com/thinking-mistakes-8-common-mistakes-in-how-we-think-and-how-to-avoid-them.
Ellis, Albert. 2001. *Overcoming Destructive Beliefs, Feelings and Behavior.* Amherst, NY: Prometheus.
Frankl, Viktor E. 1984. *Man's Search for Meaning: An Introduction to Legotherapy.* New York: Simon and Schuster.
Vick, Karl. "Violence at Work Tied to Loss of Esteem." 1993. *St. Petersburg Times,* December 17.

8 Tools for Critical Thinking

PROFESSOR: *Yes, Leon. You have another question?*

LEON: *Why don't we just speak our minds? This is an ethics course. Why are we talking about critical thinking?*

Much of this chapter builds on the notes and readings developed from the work of Richard Paul and Linda Elder. A list of their books is in the reference section of this chapter. Alarmed at the level of cognitive dissonance and lack of logic in her student's writing, one of the authors of this book spent the last fifteen years building "critical thinking" into the introduction course for the MPA program. She started with a series of small booklets developed for mastering high school subject areas created by that the Foundation for Critical Thinking in California. Eventually, Richard Paul and Linda Elder, authors of those booklets, published their first textbook, *Critical Thinking: Learn the Tools the Best Thinkers Use* (2005). In 2013, they published their second book, *Critical Thinking: Tools for Taking Charge of Your Learning and Your Life*. These publication are the resources for most of the material in this chapter.

BASICS

Since the inclusion of student learning outcomes in the university accreditation process, most undergraduate and graduate courses in social sciences use critical thinking as a student learning outcome in their syllabi. However, very few address how the student is expected to acquire that skill. In most cases, the assumption is that, with the completion of all the course assignments and exercises, critical thinking will occur as a by-product. Few social science courses confront this topic head on as a systematic topic of study as this chapter does.

Practicing critical thinking vastly improves our ability to communicate thoughts clearly in writing and common speech. This is particularly true for and important in ethics and certainly helps in answering Leon's question. As professionals and simply as people, we are constantly meeting and

"You must be the new hire.
Welcome aboard. Here is our
prepackaged curriculum.
If time permits, encourage
critical thinking."

Source: www.CartonStock.com.

interacting with others. In doing so, we are judging others and others are judging us on the quality of our thoughts and the use of words as we present them. What we say, the manner we say it in, and the means by which we present ourselves is how the world perceives us. In chapter 7, we learned that emotional outbursts are not functional in our communication and do not contribute to our ethical thinking process. In this chapter, we learn that clear critical thinking allows us to better guide and direct others by organizing our thoughts and articulating them well.

In fact, if our presentations do not reflect clear thinking, people start avoiding us or simply stop paying attention to us. For example, if you jump to conclusions without knowing all the facts and details of a situation, then eventually those who work with you will not trust your judgment. If you cannot finish a sentence or thought before jumping to another, listeners will be confused and may stop listening to you. Because they are lost by your remarks and they may take your thinking off in another direction and you thus lose what you were really trying to communicate to them. Alternatively, they may be so confused by your jumping from one fact to another that that they tune you out altogether. If you embellish or exaggerate details, eventually no one will believe you.

If you cannot understand the underlying concepts and connecting implications and consequences of your words and actions, you are doomed to keep repeating the same critical thinking mistakes. According to Paul and Elder, there are eight key structural elements in critical thought, which are salient for professionals in public affairs and administration. For example, whenever we engage in thinking, we should be aware of the purpose of our thoughts.

As much as we would like to believe we are open-minded and neutral on issues, our thinking begins from a *point of view*. Our thoughts are always based on our various *assumptions* that often were formed when we were very young. Thoughts inevitably *lead logically* to actions that will have *implications and consequences* when implemented, and sometimes even without being implemented. In the course of good critical thinking, we use *facts, experiences, and data* to support our thoughts and to refute the thoughts of others. If done well, this will lead us to make appropriate *inferences and judgments* from the facts articulated. Our thinking is almost always based on concepts and theories that we may not clearly realize or communicate well. And finally, thoughts *answer a question or solve a problem*.

Paul and Elder also posit nine universal intellectual standards that we can and should apply to each of the structural elements. The first five standards are clarity, accuracy, precision, relevance and depth. Clarity is considered the gateway standard because without it we cannot determine any of the other standards. Accuracy addresses the correctness of our statements. A statement can be clear but not necessarily accurate. For example, saying "The sky is green" is very clear but not particularly accurate. Precision is the degree of detail of the statement. Statements can be clear and accurate but not precise. For example, a more precise statement might be "The sky is azure blue." Relevance is the logical connection of the statement to the subject under consideration. If the subject under discussion is the government's financial statement, the color of the sky is not really an appropriate statement to interject into the discussion as it has nothing to do with the subject. So, a statement can be clear, accurate, and precise but not relevant. Depth refers to the detail of the statement. A statement can be clear, accurate, precise, and relevant, but be too superficial to add any significant meaning to the discussion. For example, the statement "This year's budget looks interesting" lacks depth because it adds nothing substantial to the discussion.

The other four standards are breadth, logic, significance, and fairness. Breadth also refers to detail but focuses on scope. A statement can be clear, accurate, precise, relevant, and have depth but only represent one of many perspectives on the issue. For example, "The budget increase in the police department was $1,000,000." That statement fails to communicate that the reason for the increase was a 20 percent increase in street crime. Logic relates to the rational organization and consistency in the statement. A statement can be clear, accurate, precise, relevant, deep, and have considerable depth and breadth, but be too disorganized and contradictory to be logical. Significance is the importance or the purpose of addressing the question or problem. A statement can be clear, accurate, precise, relevant, deep, and have considerable breadth, and be logical but also trivial and thus not be important to the question or problem.

Finally, fairness is critical to public affairs and administration because everything we do is supposed to represent our democratic values of the public good and thus fairness is a feature of not only what we do but how we do it. Fairness focuses the public's interest or at least is an attempt to not be biased in the statement toward some self-serving purpose. A statement can be clear, accurate, precise, relevant, deep, logical, significant, and have considerable breadth and depth but be too self-serving to be justified.

THE HUMAN MIND

NATURAL TO THINK

As humans, we naturally think. Untrained or undisciplined minds often base their thinking on biases, distortions, preferences, incomplete knowledge, ideology, or prejudice. Of course, there is more to being human and more to the human mind than just thinking. We also feel and desire things that can be remarkably powerful and can help or hinder our thinking depending on our emotional quotient and ability to critically think. The quality and depth of our thinking is what sets us apart from other animal species. Higher order animals such as elephants and dolphins, whales, and apes exhibit a whole range of emotions including affection, caring, and wanting. Like higher order animals, humans share those emotions; however, we can also use our thinking to inform, shape, and even determine how we feel and decide what we want in more complex ways.

When we think well, humans act in ways that help rather than harm themselves, others, and even their environment. Though thinking, feeling, and wanting are equally important in principle, it is only through thinking that we can take command of our minds. Through thinking, we figure out how to deal with destructive perspectives, emotions, and false logic and change or redirect our unproductive desires. Fair-minded reasonability empowers and frees us from careless and sloppy thinking. Exhibit 8.1 explains the mind's three distinctive functions of being human: thinking, feeling, and wanting.

Exhibit 8.1. The Mind's Distinctive Functions

THINKING	FEELINGS	WANTING
The part of the mind that: • Figures things out • Makes sense of life's events • Creates ideas • Defines situations, relationships, and problems	Are created by thinking that: • Assigns a positive or negative value to the events of our lives.	Desire allocates energy to action that determines both what is desirable and what is possible.
Makes sense of the world by: • Judging • Perceiving • Analyzing • Determining • Comparing • Synthesizing	Tells us how we are doing by being: • Happy • Sad • Depressed • Anxious • Stressed • Calm • Worried • Excited	Drives us to act with: • Goals • Desires • Purpose • Agendas • Values • Motives

Source: Paul and Elder, 2014, p. 56.

DYNAMIC INTERRELATIONSHIP

There is an intimate, dynamic interrelationship between these three functions. Each one continually influences the other two as noted in Exhibit 8.2.

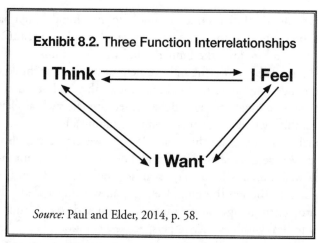

Exhibit 8.2. Three Function Interrelationships

I Think ⇄ I Feel

I Want

Source: Paul and Elder, 2014, p. 58.

To explain Exhibit 8.2, some examples are useful. When we are being verbally attacked by a coworker, we think we are being threatened. Thus, we feel fear and we want to run away from that person or fight back. When we feel depressed, we think that we are hopeless and there is nothing we can do to change the situation and thus we give up because we lack the motivation to do anything else. When we want to improve our eating habits, it maybe because we think that our diet is causing us harm and we feel frustrated with our body. Though we can look at these functions separately to better understand them, they can never be completely separated. Each depends on the others. Thoughts, feelings and desires constantly interact with each other to produce behavior as noted in Exhibit 8.3.

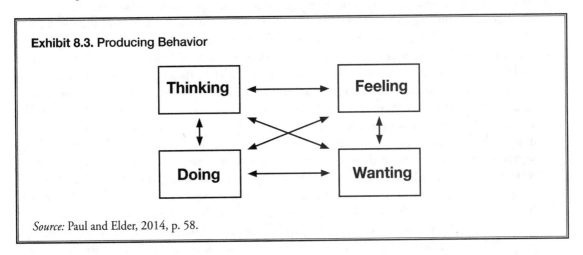

Exhibit 8.3. Producing Behavior

Source: Paul and Elder, 2014, p. 58.

Thoughts, feelings and desires play important roles in the mind as they constantly influence and are being influenced by each another. However, the process of thinking should be the key to producing rational behavior. To change a feeling, we must change how we think about what leads to that feeling. To change a desire, we must change the thinking that underlies the desire. Exhibit 8.4 explains this relationship. Rather than letting your emotional reaction to the circumstances control your actions, you should ensure that your thinking controls your behavior instead.

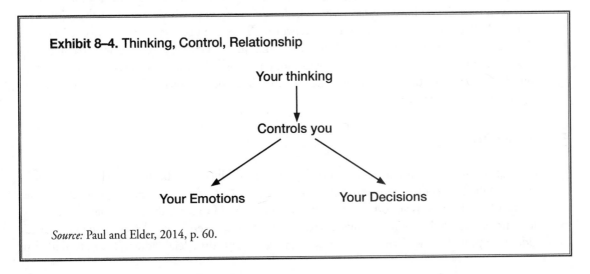

Exhibit 8–4. Thinking, Control, Relationship

Source: Paul and Elder, 2014, p. 60.

Two Different Mind-Sets

Egocentrism and our potential rational capacities guide and direct the three functions of the mind—thoughts, feelings and desires. Egocentric tendencies function automatically and unconsciously like the default settings on a computer. Rational tendencies arise only from active self-development and involve conscious and deliberate thinking. We have to intentionally override our original default settings. Most human beings do not naturally consider the rights and needs of others, nor naturally appreciate the point of view of others, or more importantly the limitations of their own point of view. As more evolved humans, we become explicitly aware of the degree of our own egocentric thinking only if we are educated or trained and make the effort to do so. As we will have learned from Nelson Mandela in chapter 11, we do learn to hate and we therefore can learn to love.

As humans, we too often live with the unrealistic but confident sense that we have fundamentally figured out the way things actually are in the world and that we have done so objectively. We adamantly believe in our intuitive perceptions to be absolutely correct—regardless of how inaccurate our perceptions of circumstances prove to be. Instead of using intellectual standards in thinking, we most often use self-centered psychological standards to determine what to believe and what to reject. Paul and Elder (2013) describe "innate egocentrism" as the assumption that what you believe is true, even though you have never bothered to question or examine the basis for your belief. In other words, "It is true because *I* believe it." They also describe "innate socio-centrism" as the assumption that the dominant beliefs within the group you belong to are true even though you have never bothered to question or challenge the basis for these beliefs. In other words, "It is true because *we* believe it."

Paul and Elder (2013) define four other types of innate thoughts that often drive our decision making. For example, "wish fulfillment" is the belief in whatever puts me (or my group) in a positive rather than a negative light even though I have not seriously considered the evidence for the negative account. In other words, "It is true because *I want* to believe it." I believe what makes me "feel good," supports my other beliefs, does not require me to change my thinking in any significant way, or what does not require me to admit I am wrong about anything.

"Self-validation" is the strong desire to maintain the beliefs that you have held for a very long time even though you have not seriously considered the extent to which those beliefs are justified, even in the face of strong evidence. In other words, "It is true because *I have always* believed it." Finally, "selfishness" is holding fast to the beliefs that justify getting your own way, having more power, money, or personal advantage even though those beliefs are not justified, grounded in sound reasoning, or supported by evidence in anyway. In other words, "It is true because *it is in my personal interest* to believe it."

Egocentric Thinking

Egocentric thinking exists in two forms: skilled and unskilled, but both pursue the same ends. Highly skilled egocentric people use their intelligence to effectively rationalize gaining their desired ends at the expense of others. They distort information to serve their personal interests and are quite articulate in arguing convincingly for their ends, often using altruistic language. They hide their prejudices well and often succeed in moving up the social ladder. They are skilled in

Exhibit 8.5. Nonegocentric versus Egocentric Thinking

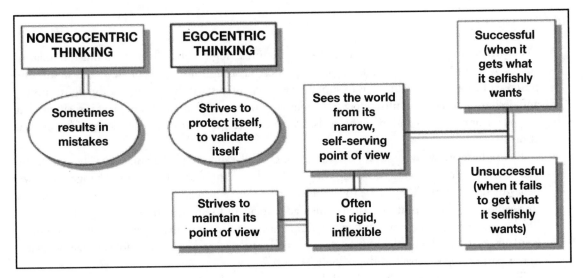

Source: Paul and Elder, 2014, p. 210.

telling others what they want to hear and either dominate or subordinate their behaviors to effectively manipulate others.

Another form of this type of thinking is called "gas lighting." The term is taken from the title of 1938 stage play *Gas Light* by British playwright Patrick Hamilton. In it, a husband systematically psychologically manipulates his wife into believing she is insane. She accurately notices things missing or rearranged in the house, but he insists that she is mistaken or imagining things. Over the course of the play, he successfully convinces her she is losing her mind. Since the 1960s, the term "gas lighting" has come to mean efforts to manipulate someone's perception of reality. Media and politicians, including some presidents, are often accused of gas lighting the public with obfuscations and double-speak to confuse an issue and make the public feel that they cannot believe their own ears, eyes, or instincts (Gibson 2017).

In contrast to intelligent egocentric thinkers, unskilled egocentric thinkers lack the intelligence or education to convincingly rationalize their actions. Thus, they are not usually trusted and their prejudices are more blatantly obvious. They are often trapped in negative emotions that they do not understand; and they are usually unsuccessful at both domination and submission as a means for achieving their ends.

The term "rationality" is often mistaken as self-serving. Literature on critical thinking often uses this term to refer to a systematically way of thinking that uses sound reasoning and logic to serve justice. A reasonable person uses the same standards to judge an enemy as well as a supporter. They do not need to rationalize their actions or create false facades. They respect the rights and needs of others to be heard and readily admit their own wrong thinking or opinions if there is evidence to support it. They are flexible and open-minded and try not to misuse language. They try to understand other points of view with empathy and display intellectual integrity, courage, humility, and perseverance.

THE NONLOGIC OF EGOCENTRISM

ILLUSION OF LOGIC

Egocentrism does have an appearance of self-contained "logic," but it is only an illusion. Clarity comes by focusing on its apparent logic, its purpose, assumptions, point of view, and so on. The purpose of egocentric reasoning is to support personal interests at the expense of the rights, needs, and desires of others, and ultimately to validate itself. Egocentrism's point of view is seeing self at the center of the world and everything else as a means to get what he or she wants with minimal effort.

By implication, what might follow self-serving is self-validating behavior. Typically, egocentric people use information and knowledge to get what they want without having to change their own behavior significantly. They come to conclusions that serve or seem to serve their own advantage, thus validating their opinions. Their selfish advantage and self-validation sets their direction in life toward getting what they want and avoiding having to compromise, negotiate, accommodate, bend, or change in any fundamental way to get it. They are remarkably predicable in their behavior, as this pattern repeats itself in their "logic."

To successfully develop as a rational thinker, we must be willing to identify these naturally occurring egocentric tendencies in our own lives and determine which of them are most prominent or problematic for us. For example, egocentric memory has a natural tendency to "forget" evidence and information that does not support our thinking and to only "remember" the evidence and information that does. Myopic thinking is absolutist, with an overly narrow point of view: "I'm right, and you're wrong. Period." Righteous thinking naturally tends to lead us to see ourselves in sole possession of "The Truth." Hypocrisy ignores flagrant inconsistencies (a) between what we profess to believe and the actual beliefs our behavior implies or (b) between the standards we apply to ourselves and those we apply to others. Oversimplification allows us to ignore real and important complexities in the world in favor of simplistic notions when consideration of those complexities would require us to modify our beliefs or values. Selective "blindness" permits us to not notice facts and evidence that contradict our beliefs or values. Immediacy is the overgeneralization of immediate feelings and experiences so that one, or only a few, events in our life seem highly favorable or unfavorable to us. Finally, egocentric absurdity is the natural tendency to fail to notice when our thinking has "absurd" implications that we refuse to see or even acknowledge as possible.

As mentioned, egocentric think is the natural default setting in our brains. We are genetically wired to want to preserve and sustain our bodies in hostile environment. Therefore, rational thinkers must take conscious steps to correct their thinking whenever they can. Just to abstractly recognize the pathology of the human mind is insufficient. It requires developing a habit of identifying these tendencies as they occur. As is the case with any habit, correction of these tendencies takes time and practice. For example, we can correct the natural tendency to "forget" evidence and information that does not support our thinking by routinely and deliberately seeking out evidence and information contrary to our thinking and directing our explicit attention to understanding it. We can correct the natural tendency to think in absolutes ways by routinely seeking points of view that modify conflict with or even contradict our own. Exploring other cultures, social strata, professions, literature, and the arts also helps to expose and identify our personal prejudices.

We can correct the natural tendency to feel superior because we are confident that we alone possess "The Truth" by regularly reminding ourselves of how little we actually do know. Knowledge is never complete. We can also try to explicitly state the unanswered questions that surround whatever knowledge we may think we already have. We can correct the natural tendency to ignore flagrant inconsistencies between what we profess to believe and the beliefs that our behavior demonstrates by regularly comparing the criteria and standards by which we judge others with those we use to judge ourselves. We can correct the natural tendency to ignore real and important complexities in the world by regularly focusing on those complexities, formulating them explicitly in words, and mapping them.

If we explicitly seek out as many facts and as much evidence as possible on an issue, we can correct the natural tendency to not notice facts and evidence that contradict our beliefs or values. By developing the habit of putting positive and negative events into much larger perspectives, we can correct the natural tendency to overgeneralize immediate feelings and experiences. We can find balance in tempering negative events with the acknowledgment of positive events with an awareness of others. Balance helps us avoid falling victim to our emotions and being immobilized by them. For example, when we fail to notice that our thinking has absurd consequences, we can correct the natural tendency by making the consequences of our thinking explicit and assessing them for their realism. This requires that we trace the implications of our beliefs and their consequences through multiple iterations in our behavior by asking ourselves, "If I really believed this, how would I act? Do I act that way?"

DEFENSIVE MECHANISMS OF THE MIND

The human mind routinely engages in unconscious processes that are egocentrically motivated and that have a strong influence on our behavior. We already mentioned that egocentrism is natural to the human condition. It is the natural default position that our brain operates in unless we choose to change or reset it. When we are thinking and acting egocentrically, we seek to get what we think we need but in reality, it is what we really want. We see the world from a narrow self-serving perspective. Yet we perceive ourselves to be purely driven by rational motives. The mind cleverly disguises our egocentric motives through an elaborate mechanism of self-deception.

Several defense mechanisms help us deceive ourselves and prevent us from making progress in our rational thinking. Defense mechanisms overlap and interrelate with the intellectual pathologies as well as the informal fallacies we discussed in the previous chapter. When we are in denial, we refuse to accept undisputable evidence or facts in order to maintain a favorable self-image or a favorite set of beliefs. For example, if individuals think of themselves as "patriots," they may deny clear-cut evidence that their country ever violated human rights or acted unjustly. Such evidence is contrary to the established self-image of their national identity.

With that type of identification, individuals adopt the qualities and ideals they admire most in other people and institutions, including patriotism. Through socio-centric identification, they elevate their sense of worth based on their group identity. For example, a football fan experiences a sense of personal triumph when his or her team wins and parents vicariously live the successes of their child. When we attribute to others what they feel or think in order to avoid unacceptable thoughts and feelings about ourselves, we are projecting. For example, a husband, who no longer loves his wife, may accuse her of not loving him to unconsciously deal with his own dishonesty in their relationship.

Thoughts, feelings, or memories that are unacceptable to the individual are prevented from reaching the consciousness level by repressing them. This often occurs when the memory is too painful to remember such as acts of violence, or "forgetting" things that are considered unpleasant such as a dentist appointment. We rationalize and give reasons for our behavior that are not the true reasons because the action came from unconscious motives that we do not recognize or understand and cannot consciously accept. For example, a father who beats his children may rationalize his behavior by saying that it is for their "own good" to become more disciplined and better behaved, when in reality he just lost his temper.

Lumping people together based on some common characteristic is stereotyping. This forms a rigid, biased perception of the group and individuals in that group. One common form of stereotyping is cultural bias that assumes the practices and beliefs of one's culture are superior to those in other cultures regardless of facts to the contrary. Another form is to assume the characteristic a few members of a culture are generalized to all in that culture.

Stereotyping can lead to scapegoating a group or individually blaming another person, group, or thing for one's own mistakes, faults, misfortunes, and problems. When we divert instinctive, primitive, or socially unacceptable desires into socially acceptable activities, we are sublimating our thinking. Finally, when we unconsciously misinterpret facts in order to maintain a belief, we are thinking wishfully. Wishful thinking leads to false expectations and usually involves seeing things more positively than is reasonable in the situation.

MISUNDERSTANDINGS

There are many misunderstandings about emotions and reasoning. Emotion and reason do not necessarily conflict, nor do emotion and reason have to function independently of each other. Just because a person is emotional, does not mean that he or she cannot reason well. A rational person can experience emotion and not necessarily be cold and mechanical. Emotional people are not necessarily lively, energetic, warm, and incapable of good reasoning.

If you believe otherwise, then you must give up the possibility of a rich emotional life if you decide to become a rational thinker, or you must abandon all hope of rationality if you are passionate about anything. These misunderstandings lead us to think of thought and emotion as dichotomous, like oil and water, rather than being a unity of opposites—that is, inseparable, discrete and opposite functions of the mind much like the two sides of a coin. They falsely lead us away from discovering the thinking that underlies our emotions and influences our critical thinking. They lead us to think that there is nothing we can do to control our emotional life, nor improve the quality of our thinking.

When our thinking is rationally based and of high quality, our emotions follow. Emotions become a state of consciousness having to do with the arousal of feelings. The emotional state we are in refers to any of the personal reactions, pleasant or unpleasant, that we may have in a situation. Intelligence is the ability to learn or understand from experience or respond successfully to new experiences. It is the ability to acquire and retain knowledge. Intelligence implies the use of reason in solving problems and directing conduct effectively. Emotional intelligence brings knowledge and wisdom to bear upon our emotions and it guides our emotions through a process of high-quality reasoning. It assumes such reasoning will lead to a more satisfactory emotional state. Critical thinking brings intelligence to bear upon our emotional life. It enables us to take command of our emotions to think through the situation in order to arrive at good judgments. It provides us with a much more satisfactory emotional life and it provides the positive link between intelligence and emotion.

Some Basic Definitions

The term "affect" is the dimension of the mind comprised of emotions and desires. When life situations affect us emotionally, they leave us with the emotional effect of happiness, sadness, joy, and so on. Affect is the counterpart of cognition, which is the dimension of the mind that thinks. Through cognition, we make sense of the world. We make assumptions, inferences, and judgments as well as interpret situations and experiences. We conceptualize and then formulate ideas or mental images.

The brain has cognition and affect—more specifically, thinking, feeling, and wanting—is often referred to as the human mind. These processes can be conscious or unconscious. Critical thinking is an intentional, disciplined, self-directed cognitive process leading to high-quality decisions and judgments through analysis, assessment, and reformulation of thinking. It presupposes an understanding of the parts of thinking or elements of reasoning, as well as the intellectual standards by which reasoning is assessed and intellectual traits that dispose us to think in deep and honest ways.

CRITICAL THINKING IN ETHICS

Critical Thinking Is Crucial

Developing our ethical reasoning abilities is crucial because human nature has a strong tendency toward egoism, prejudice, self-justification, and self-deception. Powerful sociocultural influences shape our lives and exacerbate these tendencies. We can actively combat these tendencies only through the systematic cultivation of fair-mindedness, honesty, integrity, self-knowledge, and a deep concern for the welfare of others. In other words, we can reprogram the default settings in our human tendencies through virtue ethics.

All human behavior has consequences for others. No one lives in sterile isolation, so every action we take has an influence or consequence on someone or something else. Often, we are capable of acting in ways that increase or decrease the welfare, well-being, or quality of others' lives. For example, just reacting with a smile changes the quality and perhaps the direction of an exchange between individuals. We are capable of helping or harming. For example, by not giving honest feedback to someone—even if we think it is an act of kindness—keeps that person ignorant of a problem that they might otherwise be able to fix.

Certain core ethical behaviors are nearly universally cited as bad behavior, such as cheating, deceiving, exploiting, abusing, harming, or stealing. Even very young children have a good grasp of what it means to help or harm others, to be fair, keep promises, and share well. Both Jean Piaget

Auguste Rodin's "The Thinker"

(Weiskopf n.d.) and Lawrence Kohlberg developed their theories of moral development based on the observations of children's cognitive moral development. The United Nations' Universal Declaration of Human Rights captures many of those core ethical behaviors.

Unfortunately, no universal agreement on moral principles or a universal normative ethical paradigm exists, but the Universal Declaration of Human Rights, promulgated in 1948 by the United Nations, comes surprisingly close. Another attempt at such a universal statement, which was largely developed by philosopher Hans Küng in 1996, is from the Parliament of World Religions. However, even such remarkable agreements on ethical principles cannot change the world for the better until the balance of altruistic versus egocentric thinking moves significantly toward the former and away from the latter.

Only individuals can be agents (the doers) of ethical actions. Just because institutions such as the United Nations adopt measures such as the Declaration of Human Rights does not mean society will become more moral. For moral principles to be effective, individuals must put those measures into action in their daily lives and that is unlikely if they remain egocentric thinkers. Even if they are altruistic, putting such principles into practice requires intellectual skills, ethical insights, and determined focus on compassion for others.

The world does not present itself to us in morally explicit terms. We live in a world of illusion in which propaganda and self-deception are rife. Public discourse and mass media are not neutral centers for open discussion and debate. We are bombarded with sensory messages that feed our insatiable appetites for superficial entertainment and conspicuous consumption of material goods. Private lobbying groups, political parties, and sometimes even foreign governments spend tremendous amounts of money manipulating public opinion. In a bifurcated society, those forces encourage the public to literally think in the extreme rigid terms of black or white. A bifurcated society assumes that our friends are good because they are like us and that those who disagree with us are evil. They spawn beliefs that even contextual situations can only be understood as right or wrong.

Often, advocates of political positions argue that the ethical thing to do is quite obvious and self-evident, in spite of the fact that there is an honest fundamental disagreement on the issue within the larger population. In contrast, when political advocates see that popular public opinion is likely to force action on an issue with which they disagree, they stall by using debate or delay as a means to postpone the discussion and reframe the issue to divert the public's interest and advance their own cause. Interestingly, this apparent counter position is often praised as ethical by one group and condemned by another as unethical. In fact, a common debate ploy is to call something unethical when often the issue has little to do with ethics and everything to do with a preference of opinion.

Through example, practice, and encouragement we can cultivate important intellectual and virtue traits. We can learn to respect the rights of others and not simply focus on fulfilling our personal wants and desires. The main issue is to not only be able to distinguish between helping and harming, but to also to be able to redirect our gaze to look outward to others rather than inward on ourselves. Judging from past and more recent behavior of nations, political leaders, religious institutions, and political groups, few appear to value the lives and welfare of others as much as they value their own.

Some people advocate that it is proper to value their (individual, group, corporation, or nation) interest first. Few think about the consequences for other groups as they pursue money, jobs, positions, power, prestige, and property for their group. The result is that few in society act consistently on ethical principles when dealing with what they consider to be "outsiders." A double standard in applying ethical principles is remarkably common and unfortunately dysfunctional to a harmonious society. We are doomed to remain unable to make good decisions if we systematically confuse our sense of what is ethically right with self-interest, personal desire, or social taboos. Ethically motivated people practice the art of self and social reflection and critique, while at the same time recognize the pervasive pitfalls (moral intolerance, self-deception, and uncritical conformity) in making ethical judgments.

Being an ethical person takes a developed consciousness that is concerned about others, engaged in deliberation, and can sustain mindful effort. Few spend the necessary time thinking deeply about their own judgments in an ethical context, or trying to tie their judgments together into a coherent perspective. Few invest the time and effort to get the ethically relevant facts about the world. Few invest the time to develop the skills to trace the implications of the facts they do have. Even fewer can identify their own moral contradictions, or clearly distinguish their self-interest and egocentric desires from what is genuinely ethical. As a result, with egocentric leaders and unenforceable Kantian ethics in ethical education and training, few will understand the value of ethics let alone master the complexities of moral reasoning. Ethical judgments end up a conflated mixture of genuine and pseudo morality, ethical and moral prejudice, and so-called ethical truth and self-serving hypocrisy.

THE PROBLEM OF PSEUDO-ETHICS

Skilled ethical thinkers routinely distinguish their field of study from other domains of thinking such as those from social conventions (conventional society thinking), religion (theological thinking), politics (ideological thinking), and law (legal thinking). However, too often the unskilled ethical thinker confuses these very different modes of thinking with ethics. For example, some professional groups treat highly variant and conflicting social values and taboos as if they were universal moral principles. For another example, some take religious ideologies, social "rules," and some laws to be inherently ethical in nature when they are not. Public administrators need to be able to differentiate between other modes of thinking commonly confused with ethics and real ethical behaviors. They must also remain free to critique commonly accepted conventions, political ideas, and laws using the ethical concepts described in this textbook.

ELEMENTS OF ETHICAL REASONING

Ethical reasoning has the same basic structure that underlies all critical thinking as discussed at the beginning of this chapter. Whenever we engage in thinking, we are thinking for a purpose. We are also thinking within a point of view and we base our thoughts on various assumptions. Our thoughts lead to actions that have implications and consequences and we use facts, experiences, and data to support or refute our thoughts. We make inferences and judgments based on concepts and theories. Finally, all ethical reasoning address a specific question or solve a particular problem.

Ethical reasoning in public administration must not only be logical but it must also focus on accomplishing the public good. Its purpose is to act to help rather than harm other persons and the environment. Its point of view is seeing the world holistically as a place where individuals and groups live in harmony and help rather than harm others. Its assumptions are (1) that only some humans are capable of distinguishing ethics from other modes of thinking, (2) that only some can grasp fundamental ethical principles, and (3) that few act consistently. Its implications are that if we create ethical outputs, then the resulting outcomes will benefit society. Information about our options for action is important. By inference, ethics concerns judgments about what helps or harms others and the environment. The concept of contributing to, rather than undermining, the well-being of others is central. Ethical actions and outcomes focus on addressing the theory motivating the golden rule: If you live a worthy life then you make a better world because you do unto others as you would have them do unto you.

Fundamental Ethical Concepts Embedded in Language

As we learned from Ludwig Wittgenstein in chapter 5, language is imprecise and sometimes creates confusion. Occasionally a word has multiple meanings, which makes communicating with clarity a problem. Beyond confusion and clarity, emotionally charged words are especially dangerous because they build upon emotionally centered positive and negative meanings. To identify and understand complex ethical concepts, we must also familiarize and sensitize ourselves to the impact of the language. Exhibits 8.6 and 8.7 explain the impact of language on ethical behavior.

Ethical Principles Emerge from Concepts

Each professional discipline comes with its own vocabulary and jargon. Before we proceed, we must recognize these terms and know how to use them. An ethics vocabulary that consistently uses words in the same manner is important. Some of the guiding words in ethical reasoning are "concepts" and "principles." Concepts are abstract or generic ideas conceived in the mind and principles are fundamental laws or assumptions. To become skilled in any domain of reasoning, it is wise to understand the principles of that domain. For example, to be skilled in mathematical reasoning, understanding fundamental mathematical principles is important. Similarly, to be skilled in ethical reasoning, we must first understand fundamental ethical principles. Ethical principles are implicit in ethical concepts and are the guiding force in ethical reasoning.

As in any discipline, the identification and application of ethical principles can be fairly simple, but in some cases it is remarkably complicated. For example, lying about, misrepresenting, or distorting information to gain a material advantage over others is clearly a violation of the basic principle implied in the concept of honesty. Likewise, treating others as if they are worthless or imagining ourselves to be more worthy than others is a violation of the principles implied in the concepts of justice and equality. However, life is not always that simple and often situations arise

Exhibit 8.6. Language Associated with Ethical Behavior or Motivation

Concept	Words		
Going beyond what is obligatory to improve the lives of others.	Generous Altruistic Philanthropic	Unselfish Charitable	Benevolent Humanitarian
Dealing with people objectively to be fair.	Impartial Unbiased	Equitable Objective	Understanding Dispassionate
Relating to people in ethically appropriate ways.	Polite Civil Tactful	Courteous Tolerant	Forbearing Respectful
Being forthright and honest.	Honest Loyal	Integrity Faithful	Trustworthy Truthful
Relating to people in commendable ways.	Kind Warm Tender	Friendly Cordial Gentle	Gracious Obliging Warm-hearted
Being willing to forgive to alleviate suffering.	Pardon Absolve	Forgive Merciful	Exonerate Compassionate
Acting out of a concern to behave ethically.	Upright Even-handed	Honorable Open-minded	Scrupulous
Acting out of a concern for the feelings of others.	Empathetic Sympathetic	Considerate Compassionate	Understanding

Source: Paul and Elder 2005.

where several ethical principles apply and may even be in conflict. On occasion, we will have to find a way to choose between or among competing principles, or rank them in some order of importance. In these cases, it is important to engage in dialogical reasoning with the utmost care and intellectual humility.

ASKING ETHICAL QUESTIONS

How we frame a question determines the response we get. For example, in scientific research, the way in which the researcher asks the research question determines the facts that they will consider germane to the study and those that they will omit because the researcher considers them too remote. In some cases, how the research question is phrased can even determine the kind of analysis that is performed on the data. For example, if the question is "Does X effect Y?", then the answer can only be yes or no. This then requires a follow-up question that contains a scale to measure the degree of effect. Alternatively, the first question could have said "What items effect Y?", then the researcher would receive new data on all possibilities.

Exhibit 8.7. Language Associated with Unethical Behavior or Motivation

Concept	Words		
Using intellectual skills to get others to act against their own best interests.	Cunning Sly Wily Betray Dupe Cheat	Trickery Defraud Swindle Deceive Mislead Betray	Duplicitous Misrepresent Subterfuge Double-deal Delude Beguile
Ignoring the rights and needs of others to get what you want.	Greedy Selfish Grasping	Egotistic Covetous Acquisitive	Self-conceit Avaricious Self-aggrandizement
Causing pain or suffering	Bully Hurt Cruel Brutal Vicious Unkind Pitiless	Tyrannize Oppress Dominate Ruthless Merciless Malicious	Inhuman Inconsiderate Malevolence Ill-willed Rancorous Malignant
Causing emotional discomfort	Rude Petty Unkind Uncivil Callous Hateful	Heartless Dishonorable Bellicose Insensitive Impatient Belligerent	Disrespectful Discourteous Quarrelsome Ill-mannered Contentious Pugnacious
Mental rigidity	Biased Bigoted Zealot Small-minded	Unfair Fanatic Jingoist	Intolerant Chauvinist Narrow-minded
Not telling the truth	Lying False Disloyal	Insincere Deceitful Dishonest	Hypocritical Disingenuous Untruthful
Behavior resulting from a perceived grievance.	Spiteful Vengeful	Vindictive Retaliation	Revengeful Holding a grudge

Source: Paul and Elder 2005.

Similarly, in ethical reasoning, how we ask the question can determine what comes into the conversation and what is left out, which in turn determines the range of information we can consider and the conclusions and inferences we can ultimately draw. For example, if we ask the question "Is it cruel to subject an innocent animal to unnecessary suffering?" we are likely to get the simple answer: "Of course it is." However, if we ask the question another way—"Can animals be used to help find a cure for human cancer?"—we are more likely to get a much more complex response that reflects on a much wider range of issues associated with the question.

When dealing with very simple ethical questions, there is usually a clear-cut answer. However, when faced with a more complex question, there are typically multiple viewpoints. Each stakeholder is likely to have his or her own unique perspective on the issue. That which seems to be a reasonable solution to one may be offensive to another. Openness to a range of insights from the various viewpoints as well as willingness to question one's own viewpoint is critical. To reason well through a complex or complicated ethical issue one must consider a wide range of relevant perspectives, obtain insights from all of them, identify weaknesses and partialities in each, and integrating what is learned into a more comprehensive, many-sided whole. Each viewpoint should serve to correct the exaggerations or distortions in the others and add facts that were missing, as demonstrated by Exhibit 8.8.

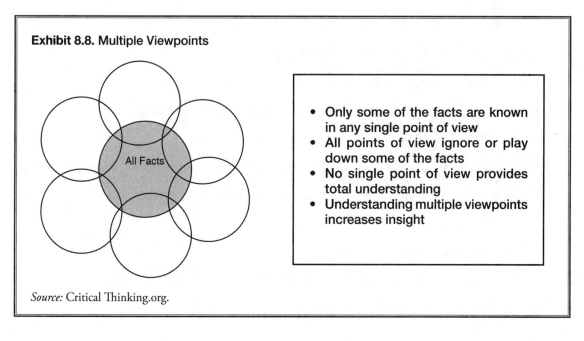

Exhibit 8.8. Multiple Viewpoints

All Facts

- Only some of the facts are known in any single point of view
- All points of view ignore or play down some of the facts
- No single point of view provides total understanding
- Understanding multiple viewpoints increases insight

Source: Critical Thinking.org.

Ethical Reasoning Competencies

There are five important practices associated with ethical reasoning. First, the exercise of independent ethical thought and judgment. Second, a developed insight into egocentrism and sociocentrism. Third, the exercise of ethical reciprocity. Fourth, the exploration of thoughts that underlie ethical reactions. Fifth, discipline to suspend ethical judgment until all the available information is reviewed.

In addition, there are several macro level ethical competencies:

- Avoidance of oversimplification of ethical issues.

- Development of an independent ethical perspective.

- The ability to clarify ethical issues and claims.

- The ability to clarify ethical ideas.

- Development of criteria for ethical evaluation.

- The ability to evaluate ethical authorities.

- The ability to raise and pursue root ethical questions.

- The ability to evaluate ethical arguments.

- The ability to generate and assess solutions to ethical problems.

- The ability to identify and clarify ethical points of view.

- The ability to engage in Socratic discussion on ethical issues.

- The ability to practice dialectical thinking on ethical issues.

Micro level ethical skills include the following:

- The ability to distinguish facts from ethical principles, values, and ideas.

- The ability to use critical vocabulary in discussing ethical issues.

- The ability to distinguish between ethical principles and ideas and examine ethical assumptions.

- The ability to distinguish ethically relevant from ethically irrelevant facts.

- The ability to make plausible ethical inferences.

- The ability to supply evidence for an ethical conclusion.

- The ability to recognize ethical contradictions, ethical implications, and consequences.

- The ability to refine ethical generalizations.

ESSENTIAL INTELLECTUAL ETHICAL TRAITS

The intellect is another critical component for ethical thinking. For example, intellectual humility is the conscious awareness of the limits of one's own knowledge and perhaps even one's capacity to know. This includes sensitivity to circumstances in which one's native egocentrism is likely to manifest as self-deception as well as sensitivity to bias, prejudice, and the limitations of one's own viewpoint. Intellectual humility depends on recognizing that one cannot claim to know more than what one actually knows. It does not suggest that one be submissive or weak. It does, however, require us to set aside intellectual pretentiousness, boastfulness, and conceit, and search for deeper insights into the logical foundations of our belief or strongly held opinions.

Intellectual courage is the conscious awareness for the need to face and fairly address ideas, beliefs, or viewpoints for which we have strong negative feelings and to which we have not given a serious hearing. This courage is connected to the recognition that ideas considered dangerous or absurd are sometimes rationally justified (in whole or in part) and that conclusions and beliefs inculcated in us from a young age are sometimes false or misleading. To determine for ourselves which is which, we cannot just passively and uncritically "accept" what we think we have "learned." Intellectual courage comes into play because our search for knowledge inevitably leads us into uncomfortable territory in our thinking, which can be quite unsettling. If we are true to the process, we may be forced to discard or challenge some strongly held ideas or beliefs in our social group. We need courage to be true to the veracity of our thinking in such circumstances, knowing that a consequence might be that our family or group might sever themselves from us because of our changed thinking.

Intellectual empathy is a conscious awareness to imaginatively put oneself in the place of others to genuinely understand them. It requires us to put aside our egocentric tendency to not question our long-standing thoughts and beliefs. This trait correlates with the ability to reconstruct accurately the viewpoints and reasoning of others and to reason from premises, assumptions, and ideas of others that go beyond our own egocentric perspective. This trait also correlates with the willingness to remember past occasions when we were wrong despite an intense conviction that we must always be right. We must be able to accept that there is the possibility that we might have been deceived or were simply mistaken.

Intellectual autonomy is exercising rational control of one's beliefs, values, and inferences. The goals of critical thinking are to learn to think for oneself and to gain command over one's thought processes by asking questions. This requires a commitment to analyze and evaluate beliefs based on reason and evidence, to question, to believe upon discovery, and to conform when it is appropriate.

Intellectual integrity is the need to be true to one's own thinking, to be consistent in the intellectual standards one applies, to hold oneself to the same rigorous standards of evidence and proof to which one holds one's antagonists, to practice what one advocates for others, and to honestly admit discrepancies and inconsistencies in one's own thoughts and actions.

Intellectual perseverance is a conscious awareness of the need to use intellectual insights and truths in spite of difficulties, obstacles, and frustrations. It is firmly adhering to rational principles despite the irrational opposition of others. It is the need to struggle with confusion, uncertainty, and unsettled questions over an extended period to achieve a deeper understanding or insight.

Confidence in reason is the belief that, in the long run, one's own interests and those of humankind will be best served by giving reason free play. People must be encouraged to come to their own conclusions by developing their own rational faculties. It is our faith in that belief, that with proper encouragement and cultivation people can learn to think for themselves, to form well-reasoned viewpoints, draw reasonable conclusions, think coherently, and logically persuade each other through reason. It is a faith in people to become reasonable, despite the deep-seated obstacles in the native character of the human mind and society.

Intellectual fair-mindedness is the conscious need to consider all viewpoints alike, without reference to one's own feelings or vested interests, or the feelings or vested interests of one's friends, community, or nation. This implies adherence to intellectual standards without reference to one's own advantage or to the advantage of one's group.

FALLACIES OF REASONING

Our everyday common communication has flawed and deceptive ways of reasoning. Those flaws are elusive so that unless a person is a practiced critical thinker they remain difficult to detect and can easily lead to a false conclusion. This discussion focuses on material fallacies in which the error lies in the factual content of the argument rather than its structure. This discussion is concentrated on linguistic fallacies, irrelevant evidence, and miscellaneous fallacies. Sometimes the fallacies overlap and a given argument can contain several errors, some of which are more central to the validity of the argument than others. The challenge for the critical thinker is to detect the decisive error, distinguish it from the rest of the argument, and be alert to the possibility of additional fallacies present in the whole argument. As an experiment, try to relate these fallacies to the everyday media stories in your life such as political speeches, advertisements, Facebook or Twitter posts, news reporting, and so on.

LINGUISTIC FALLACIES

Linguistic issues include emotive language, ambiguity, equivocation, amphibology, speech, composition, division, and vicious abstraction. Here are some quick definitions for each. When words in an argument lack definite meaning or their sole purpose is to arouse unreasoned feelings, we call it the *emotive language fallacy*. Such arguments focus on the stimulating emotions rather than conveying logical information. For example, calling someone a terrorist without facts to support such a label is such a fallacy. Lobbying advocates often use this fallacy to incite negative group behavior toward targeted individuals or groups of people. The ambiguity fallacy similarly uses unclear language to hide their precise meaning by using language tricks such as ill-defined terms, vagueness in meaning, and a variety of imprecise ideas.

Using a term for more than one thing to create the impression that the term expresses only one consistent meaning throughout the argument is an example of the *equivocation fallacy*. It leaves an incorrect assumption that the key word is consistent throughout the argument. For example, "there is evil in the world today and it must be confronted." The key terms are "evil" and "confronted." Both terms can be interpreted differently by various people. Each of them has multiple meanings and thus suggests there are equivocal and a fallacy exists in the argument.

The *amphibology fallacy* uses a statement that permits two interpretations. It differs from equivocation in that amphibology pertains to the entire argument whereas equivocation limits itself to single terms. In addition, with amphibology the entire argument has a dual interpretation due to its structure and not to any misuse of the advocate. Normally, they hinge on a misplaced modifier. For example: "The economy of our nation, with a flawed premise, carries us into the next decade." In this example, which has a flawed premise, the economy or the nation?

The *speech or figure of speech fallacy* is the failure to distinguish between variant meanings of sentence elements, such as suffixes. William S. Sahakian and Mabel Lewis Sahakian (1993) cite an example of this fallacy by quoting John Stuart Mill: "The only proof capable of being given that an object is visible, is that people actually see it. The only proof that a sound is audible, is that people hear it; and so of the other sources of our experience. In like manner, I apprehend, the sole evidence it is possible to produce that anything is desirable, is that people do actually desire it." Note the "ble" suffix connotes "can be seen" "is visible" and "can be heard" "is audible," but it does not mean, "can be desired" "is desired." Instead, it means merely "it should be desired."

The *composition fallacy* is the false assumption that a statement about an integral part of something necessarily holds true for the larger composite whole. This fallacy applies to statements about things considered as parts of a whole but not to statements about things considered as separate entities. This fallacy reasons incorrectly from facts about the members of a group to draw conclusions about the entire group. It is remarkably successful in misdirecting the reader. For example: "A White House composed of a few top senior talented individuals explains why the White House staff is outstanding." The error lies in diverting our consideration from the whole White House staff that consists of many hundreds of people, all of whom have talent to offer and can make very important contributions to a few senior talented individuals, regardless of the number of senior staff. Another example is, "A White House of the world's best staff persons would be the best White House possible." For the White House to be successful, the staff must work as a team, with each person properly supporting the efforts of the president. Individual prima donnas acting independently could result in disaster for the president.

The *division fallacy* is the converse of the composition fallacy. What holds true for the composite does not necessarily hold true for each component part considered separately. One cannot divide an organic whole. In many situations with groups of people, the whole gains a gestalt, and the whole is greater than the sum of its parts. For example: "The Franklin D. Roosevelt White House was the best and therefore they must have had the best White House press secretary." The fallacy is not that the press secretary may or may not have been the best, but in attributing the high quality of service of the team to a particular White House staffer.

The *vicious abstraction fallacy* is the removal of a statement from its context, which changes the meaning of the argument. This is done by dropping context to emasculate the statement and distort its meaning. Typically, this is easy to accomplish. For example, "St. Paul said, 'Money is the root of all evil'" when in fact he said, "The *love of* money is the root of all evil." Notice the significance of the fallacy because with the fallacy one should ban money altogether, but with the actual words persons seeking to do away with evil should focus on their attitude toward money. Another example of this fallacy is "Ralph Waldo Emerson said: 'Consistency is the hobgoblin of little minds.'" The proper quote is "Foolish consistency is the hobgoblin of little minds." Again, the fallacy leads us to take a very unforgiving attitude toward people who are consistent in their reasoning processes. We are led to think that they are too stupid to even have a new thought. Whereas, the correct quote focuses us on the term "foolish." This stress is important for an overriding judgment when applying consistency. Now, we can understand the full context to mean that people with small minds are doomed to perform rote tasks without question or complaint.

IRRELEVANT EVIDENT FALLACIES

Another set of fallacies use arguments that are irrelevant to the central issue to "win" an argument, not by proper logic but by creating a diversion, much as a magician's sleight of hand hides the truth from his audience. The Latin names say it all: *Argumentum Ad Ignorantiam, Argumentum Ad Misericordiam, Argumentum Ad Verecundiam, Argumentum Ad Baculum, Argumentum Ad Hominem,* and *Argumentum Ad Populum.* Loosely translated into English they are: an Appeal to Ignorance, an Appeal to Pity or Misery, an Appeal to Prestige, an Argument to Force, an Argument Against the Person, and finally an Appeal to the Popular.

Collectively, the irrelevance fallacies attempt to prove or disprove the wrong point, thus fooling the audience into believing a logical case was argued and proven. The argument presentation may seem very cogent but it obscures the fact that the point being made is not essential or even relevant to the real issue under consideration. Another version is to disprove an irrelevant point rather than the point of the question. Typically, these fallacies come up in complex arguments often proving something that no one denies or even questions.

An example of this would be the President of the United States arguing that an enemy nation has inhumane policies toward its own people as a justification for our invasion, occupation, and installation of a new government to replace the old regime. Although it is quite true that the old regime did conduct inhumane policies against its own people, that is rarely considered adequate justification for invading and occupying a sovereign nation unless the entire world community concurs that such action is necessary to avoid radical loss of life.

Argumentum Ad Ignorantiam is an appeal to ignorance of others. It assumes that (1) what might possibly be true is actually true, (2) a given thesis is correct merely because no one can prove it to be incorrect, or (3) by disproving a nonessential part of the argument an advocate can destroy an opponent's entire argument. For example, a philosopher argues that a particular methodology is the only way to define acceptable truth and certain knowledge because no one can prove that assertion as incorrect. Just because one cannot find something does not mean that it does not exist. It simply means that you cannot find that something at the moment. Or we may not have a good enough instrument to find it at the moment or we may be looking in the wrong place for it. Of course, the option that it does not exist remains open too.

Argumentum Ad Misericordiam is the appeal to pity. This fallacy advocates evading the pertinent issues and make an emotional appeal for pity or empathy. It is particularly powerful if the appeal to emotions is strong. For example, "Professor please change my grade from a B to an A because if you don't, my grade point will drop and I will lose my assistantship. I will not be able to support myself and I will have to drop out of school." Occasionally, if the parameters of the original argument are narrow, this could be an acceptable argument. For example, "Professor, I did not do my homework because my father died last night." When stating acceptable excuses for late homework, a professor is not likely to anticipate such an unusual request and would not likely communicate such a thought in his or her syllabus. Nevertheless, the professor could consider such an excuse as logical and acceptable.

Argumentum Ad Verecundiam appeals to prestige, where the advocate equates prestige with evidence. Advocates gain support by associating their argument with highly respected individuals or hallowed institutions. For example, "This is exactly the same approach used by Harvard and Oxford and you should apply it here." Another example is "Look, I am the professor and you are the student, believe me."

Argumentum Ad Baculum uses overt force or disguised coercion to make the point. Essentially, the advocate says, "might makes right." For example, "The United States is the most powerful nation in the world and the other nations of the world should respect that reality and support the United States in all United Nations votes." Another example is "This agency only employs intelligent people who support the mayor's political campaign."

Argumentum Ad Hominem appeals to personal ridicule and shifts an argument from the points of the argument to the personality of the opponent. In politics, and especially in American politics, this is common in elections. Certainly, the character of leaders is an important consideration when voting, but often political opponents frame the arguments about policy differences in terms of personalities and not issues. Typically, the use of this fallacy focuses on the opponent's reputation, lack of moral character, low intelligence levels, inferior social position, lack of education, shortness in stature, low energy, or other personal shortcomings. For example, "Governor Romney is easy going and is therefore obviously low energy. The position of president requires high energy and he is simply and clearly unqualified." Easy going does not mean low energy. Easy going people can and often do a great deal of work. Thus, the argument fails.

Argumentum Ad Populum is an appeal to the masses and it happens when the advocate departs from the question under discussion by appealing to the feelings and prejudices of the multitude. Typically, this is an appeal to patriotism or a negative appeal to prejudice. Patriotic appeals are powerful when the country is under attack. Prejudicial appeals are powerful when there is a deep-seated hatred or jointly held distain of others due to race, religion, nationality, or the status of being an immigrant. Some high level politicians use this fallacy. Extreme examples are Hitler, Mussolini, and Stalin in the middle of the twentieth century. In the twenty-first century, noted politicians are again using the this appeal to prejudice to get voter support in elections.

Miscellaneous Material Fallacies

Finally, a third set of fallacies has interesting names, including *the accident, the converse, the post hoc, the non sequitur, compound questions, begging the question, tu quoque, misplaced authority, genetic error, false analogy, insufficient evidence, pathetic and contradictory premises*. Here are some brief definitions.

When we attempt to apply a general rule to special cases that are acknowledged exceptions to that rule we have an *accident fallacy*. In other words, we used a universal statement or rule about a matter for which the rule does not apply. A more complex version of this fallacy is to ignore key prevailing conditions or differing conditions that make the rule inapplicable to the specific case. For example, in most Western governments, there is a universal rule against nepotism. Nevertheless, there can be exceptions to that so-called universal rule. For example, in sparsely populated areas , nepotism laws logically make no sense because most people in the community are related to each other and the needed expertise is simply not available unless the nepotism rule is waived.

The *converse fallacy* is called the fallacy of selected instances or the fallacy of hasty generalizations. It attempts to establish a generalization as a rule or scientific law by offering an example of single instance without the requisite representative number of instances. We best understand this in statistics as over-generalizing a small sample size to the larger population. This happens often when polling is done incorrectly and the sample size is not adequate to generalize to the whole city, state, or country. An example is "I talked to thirty people and they all answered 'no' to the question." If there are 30,000 people in the population of a town and only thirty were canvassed, the sample is inadequate to make the assertion that everyone in the town said no. In this situation, the thirty people interviewed might belong to the same church or political club and therefore it would be a biased sample.

The *post hoc or false cause fallacy* is reasoning from a sequence of events to the total consequence. Causality is based on a sequence of events not just one. The fact that a person moves a switch to the up position and the light goes on does not by itself mean that flipping the wall switch up turns on the ceiling light. A person can be tempted to assume that after the switch is flipped up and down several times, that the switch alone has caused the consequence that follows. The switch is likely the cause but there might be another unknown cause that just happens to occur at the same time as the movement of the switch, like the completion of an electrical circuit that has an even more direct consequence for the outcome. Clearly, if such switch flipping occurs many times and there is a theory that explains how the flipping of a switch turns on the light, then the statement is less likely to be a fallacy. Ideally, the theory in this situation would have to account for all the mediating and possible intervening variables that could account for the light going on or off at the flip of the switch.

The *non sequitur*, or "it does not follow," *fallacy* is the presentation of a conclusion that does not logically flow from given premises or statements. In this fallacy, the statements may all be relevant unlike the irrelevant inference fallacy, but the relationships are logically disconnected. For example, more ice cream is sold in the summertime and there are more deaths by drowning in the summertime. Therefore, ice cream causes people to drown. Another example is that most basketball players are tall and therefore all tall people are basketball players.

The *compound questions* or multiple questions, or "poisoning the well," *fallacy* combines several questions in such a manner that all opposing arguments are precluded. It places one's opponent in a self-incriminating position. The wording of the argument falsely implies that the advocate raised the prior questions and correctly answered them as a basis for the question under consideration. For example, "Answer yes or no. Did you stop beating your wife?" The question already assumes that you beat your wife when that fact has not yet been established. Some lawyers and investigators use this fallacy deliberately when questioning suspects. If the suspect answers the question with a simple yes or no, the investigators claim the suspect has incriminated himself.

The *begging the question fallacy* has several forms, including circular reasoning, failing to prove the initial thesis, and using the original thesis as proof of itself. Typically, this fallacy is used in complicated arguments that have many steps resulting in that which must be proven ultimately becomes the defense of itself. For example: "Books on capitalism are better than books on socialism." "How do you know?" "Economic experts all concur that capitalism books are better than socialism books." "Who are the experts?" "They are the economists who maintain that books on capitalism are better than books on socialism."

The *tu quoque fallacy* claims the person's critics are doing the same things as the advocate. This argument is typically used on parents by their children. It is a common defensive argument but usually fails because the conditions and context may not be the same in all situations for all people. If the conditions are identical, it can be a good defense. If the situations are not identical or if the actions of all parties are indefensible, then the argument fails. Teenagers typically use this fallacy in appealing to parents to extend their curfew. They often say, "You stayed out till midnight when you were my age." The "not identical situation" is that you had to work till one in the morning at a part-time job as a teenager to contribute to the family and your child does not have to work at night. He or she just wants to go to a party.

The *misplaced authority fallacy* cites an authority in matters not related to his or her field or specialization. In such cases, the opinion of the expert falls outside the scope of the expert's competence. Newton and Einstein were remarkable scientists but neither were expert in the arts. To use their opinion in that area of knowledge might be interesting but it would not be compelling. Fund raisers sometimes deliberately use this fallacy as a marketing device to draw the public to an event. For example, the XYZ organization might have a chocolate tasting competition among area chocolate retail stores and the organization invites the public to buy tickets to their event and eat to their heart's content. The Local NBA basketball team are the taste test judges. They will draw the crowd but have little to no expertise on high quality chocolate.

The *genetic error fallacy* confuses the validity of a statement with the cause of origins of a thesis. An argument is not necessarily false because the advocate can trace it back to its beginning in human history. Conversely, the source of an argument maybe historically interesting but it is not relevant as a logical proof to the issue at hand. Saying that the statement is false because its source was an insane man is also an error in logic. An insane man can be correct on occasion, especially when one understands that there are many types of insanity that may or may not have anything to do with making a particular logical argument. Also, saying that a statement is false just because its source was an evil person is an error in logic. Just because a person is evil does not mean that he did not occasionally make correct statements.

The *false analogy fallacy* misuses the valid analogy argument. If an analogous argument in reasoning exists, then the argument is valid. But, any major difference destroys the analogy and the validity of the argument. For example, "Joe Candidate is a very successful movie actor and good businessman who has always made a profit in business. Therefore, he would be a great governor." Some skills and knowledge acquired in business and making movies are relevant to government but many are not. There is nothing logical in this argument unless the person making the argument clarifies where and how the analogy is parallel.

The *insufficient evidence fallacy* accepts inadequate data as a basis for a conclusion. A prosecutor may argue to the jury that a defendant had a gun but that fact alone does not establish the person used the weapons to kill the victim. Certainly, it is part of a circumstantial case against the defendant but it alone is not proof for the case. The prosecutor needs to establish that the defendant used the gun to attack the victim or there is a strong likelihood that the defendant not only had it in his possession at the time of the crime, but that he used the gun to attack the victim in order to establish a valid argument.

The *pathetic or anthropomorphism fallacy* ascribes human feelings, body parts, and qualities to nonhuman animals or to inanimate objects. "The trees looked sadly at the ever-nearing fire" might be good poetry but trees cannot see nor can they emote sadness. Some philosophers argue that objects and events have no intrinsic value but people attribute value to them. Trees maybe beautiful but it is those who see the trees that attribute the quality of beauty to them. Similarly, organizations do not really live and breathe. The humans who work in the organizations live and breathe.

The *contrary to fact conditional error fallacy* alters facts and then draws conclusions from them. Thus, any conclusions derived from the false premise cannot be accepted as valid. One can draw logical conclusions from accepted true facts. For example, "If Germany had won World War I, Americans would speak German today." The first so-called fact that Germany won World War I is false and only the actual historical fact could determine the outcome. Any speculation on what might have happened if another event had occurred is simply fiction or speculation. It is not a valid logical argument.

The *contradictory premises fallacy* is simply that self-contradictions are necessarily false. Thus, when an argument contains two or more premises that contradict each other, then no conclusion is possible because any conclusion would be a contradiction to the other and one premise therefore, cancels out the other. One premise maybe true, but both or all cannot be simultaneously true. For example, "Can God create a stone so heavy that he cannot lift it?" Implicit in the argument is a self-contradiction and thus it is a logical fallacy.

CONCLUSION

Leon asked two questions: (1) Why don't we just speak our minds? (2) Why are we talking about critical thinking in an ethics course? Thinking critically is not easily done and probably not being done when someone merely speaks their mind. The adage, "Think before you open your mouth," is sage advice and this chapter explained how that thinking can and should be done. When it comes to communicating with others about important ethical issues and ideas, the quality and clarity of thinking and the arguments put forward make a huge difference in a person's ability to think ethically. Career public servants are always expected by elected officials or appointed officials to be able to explain how they arrived at their conclusions or decisions. Critical thinking is essential in making those presentations. Critical thinking is helpful in all three normative approaches to ethics but it is particularly important in rule-based ethics.

REVIEW QUESTIONS

1. Why is critical thinking important in ethics?

2. What are the eight elements to the critical thought structure and the nine universal intellectual standards?

3. Explain the duality in the paradox of thinking. Explain the three interrelationships functions of "I think," "I feel," and "I want."

4. Explain the two different mind-sets and their implications to critical thought.

5. Explain the illusion of logic in egocentrism.

6. Explain the defensive mechanisms of the mind.

7. There is a wide array of interrelated pathological dispositions that are inherent in egocentric thought. We saw many of them play out in the presidential election cycle of 2016–2017 in the United States. From the primary season to the national election, there were signs of these dispositions in all political camps. Cite three examples of those signs.

8. What is emotional intelligence and what does it have to do with critical thinking?

9. What is a pseudo-ethics and why is it important?

10. Why should ethical thinking be logical? In what way must virtue ethics also be rational?

11. Explain the impact of language on ethical behavior.

12. Explain the interrelationship of ethical principles and concepts.

13. What are the essential ethical traits?

14. What are the linguistic fallacies? Define each and cite an example from history or current items in the news.

15. What are the irrelevant evidence fallacies? Define each and cite an example from history or current items in the news.

16. What are the miscellaneous material fallacies? Define each and cite an example from history or current items in the news.

17. What are the three speculations on the general nature of truth? Which do you prefer and why?

REFERENCES

"Aristotle." *Internet Encyclopedia of Philosophy*, edited by James Fieser and Bradley Dowden. http://www.utm.edu/research/iep/a/aristotl.htm#Ethics. Accessed on July 14, 2018.

Barnet, Sylvan, and Hugo Bedau. 1993. *Critical Thinking, Reading and Writing: A Brief Guide to Argument*. Boston: St. Martins.

Ennis, Robert. 1996. *Critical Thinking*. Upper Saddle River, NJ: Prentice Hall.

Foundation for Critical Thinking. www.criticalthinking.org. Retrieved on December 4, 2001.

Gibson, Caitlin. 2017. "What We Talk about When We Talk about Donald Trump and 'Gaslighting.'" *Washington Post*, January 27. https://www.washingtonpost.com/lifestyle/style/what-we-talk-about-when-we-talk-about-donald-trump-and-gaslighting/2017/01/27/b02e6de4-e330-11e6-ba11-63c4b4fb5a63_story.html?utm_term=.b8f299008339. Accessed July 14, 2018.

"Georg Wilhelm Friedrich Hegel." In *The Basics of Philosophy*. Accessed October 11, 2017. http://www.philosophybasics.com/philosophers_hegel.html.

"Gorgias of Leontiom." *Internet Encyclopedia of Philosophy*. Accessed October 11, 2017. www.iep.utm.edu/gorias.

Joyce, James. 2003. "Bayes' Theorem." In *The Stanford Encyclopedia of Philosophy*, edited by Edward N. Zalta. http://plato.standford.edu/archives/win2003.entries/bayes-theorem/.

Kant, Immanuel. 1997. *Groundwork of the Metaphysics of Morals*. Cambridge, UK: Cambridge University Press.

Kohlberg, L. 1976. "Moral Stages and Moralization: The Cognitive-Developmental Approach." In *Moral Development and Behavior: Theory, Research and Social Issues*, edited by T. Lickona, 31–53). New York: Holt, Rinehart and Winston.

Küng, Hans, ed. 1996. *Yes to a Global Ethic*. New York, NY: Continuum.

Lohmar, Dieter. 1997. "Truth" In *Encyclopedia of Phenomenology*, edited by Lester Embree et al., 711–712. Dordrecht, the Netherlands: Kluwer.

McKeon, Matthew. n.d. "Logical Consequence." *Internet Encyclopedia of Philosophy*. Accessed October 11, 2017. http://www.iep.utm.edu/logcon/.

Paul, Richard. 2012. *Critical Thinking: What Every Person Needs to Survive in a Rapidly Changing World*. Tomales, CA: Foundation for Critical Thinking.

Paul, Richard, and Linda Elder. 2005. *Critical Thinking: Learn the Tools the Best Thinkers Use*. Concise Edition. Upper Saddle River, NJ.: Pearson/Prentice Hall.

Paul, Richard, and Linda Elder. 2008. *How to Detect Media Bias and Propaganda*. Tomales, CA: Foundation for Critical Thinking.

Paul, Richard, and Linda Elder. 2012. *Fallacies: The Art of Mental Trickery*. Tomales, CA: Foundation for Critical Thinking.

Paul, Richard, and Linda Elder. 2013. *Critical Thinking: Tools for Taking Charge of Your Learning and Your Life*. 2nd ed. Upper Saddle River, NJ. Pearson/Prentice Hall.

Paul, Richard, and Linda Elder. 2014. *Critical Thinking: Tools for Taking Charge of Your Learning and Your Life*. 3rd ed. Upper Saddle River, NJ: Pearson Education.

Paul, Richard and Linda Elder. 2013. *Ethical Reasoning*. Tomales, CA: Foundation for Critical Thinking.

Pomerleau, Wayne P. n.d. "William James." In *Internet Encyclopedia of Philosophy*. Accessed October 11, 2017. http://www.iep.utm.edu/james-0/#SH3b.

Poster, Carol. n.d. "Protagoras." In *Internet Encyclopedia of Philosophy*. Accessed October 11, 2017. http://www.iep.utm.edu/protagor/.

Preston, Arron. n.d. "George Edward Moore." In *Internet Encyclopedia of Philosophy*. Accessed October 11, 2017. http://www.iep.utm.edu/moore/.

Sahakian, William S., and Mabel Lewis Sahakian. 1993. *Ideas of the Great Philosophers*. New York: Barnes and Noble.

Weiskopf, Daniel A. n.d. "The Theory—Theory of Concepts." In *Internet Encyclopedia of Philosophy*. Accessed October 11, 2017. http://www.iep.utm.edu/th-th-co/.

9 Moral Leadership

PROFESSOR: *Leon, you look confused. What's wrong?*

LEON: *What's the big deal about "moral" leadership? We all know the bosses just do what they want to do, and we just do what the boss tells us to do.*

That may be Leon's perspective as a follower, but research tells us a different story about leadership (see Exhibit 9.1). Leaders actually do set the example for their subordinates to emulate and research shows that the more morally mature the leader is, the more followers will engage in higher moral reasoning (Bass and Steidlmeier 1999; Burns 1978; Duckrich et al. 1990). As we will discuss later, public sector ethics training, education, and discourse often focuses on normative ethics in dichotomous conditions of right/wrong and good/bad, value/ethics, and cost/benefit flowing from consequential ethics. In discussing ethical leadership, different dimensions become valuable in better understanding moral leadership.

EARLY LEADERSHIP THEORIES

Early leadership literature (1840–1900) argued that leaders were born not made and that great leaders emerge when there is great need. Much of the literature focused on the biographies of "great" leaders. As new and better research techniques in the behavioral sciences emerged, the investigation of what makes a great leader moved toward an examination of specific "traits" common to all "great" leaders. The assumption was that all people are born with inherited traits. Some traits are particularly suited to leadership and people with the right combination of traits make good leaders (McCall and Lombardo 1983; Stogdill 1974). Exhibit 9.2 summarizes the so-called great man and trait theories of leadership.

We now have a plethora of leadership theories and measures including typologies of leadership styles (Lewin, Lippit, and White 1939; Likert 1967), behavioral theories (Merton 1957; Pfeffer and Salancik 1975), situational leadership theory (Hersey, Blanchard, and Johnson 1972, Hersey and Blanchard 1999, Hersey and Johnson 2007; Maier 1963; Tannenbaum and Schmitt 1958;

Exhibit 9.1. Case Study: Subordinates Do Emulate Their Leaders

BBC News reported an exchange between their reporter Wouter Zwart with Pete Hoekstra, who President Trump appointed as the new Ambassador to Holland only two weeks before the interview. What follows is a portion of that exchange:

Dutch Reporter: Speaking of threat, at one point you mentioned in a debate that there are no-go zones in the Netherlands and that cars and politicians are being set on fire.

Ambassador Hockstra: I didn't say that. That is actually an incorrect statement. Yeah, we would call it fake news.

Reporter: Is that fake news? Because that's what you really said.

American Ambassador: No, it's not what I said.

At this point, the reporter played a video recording of the ambassador talking.

On the played video of the Ambassador: The Islamic movement has now got to the point where they have put Europe into chaos. Chaos in the Netherlands, there are cars being burned, there are politicians that are being burned. And yes, there are no-go zones in the Netherlands.

Reporter: No?

American Ambassador: No. I don't think I did.

Source: "Trump's Ambassador to the Netherlands in 'Fake News' Blunder," *BBC News*, December 22, 2017. http://www.bbc.com/news/world-europe-42460055.

Yukl 1989), path-goal theory (House 1971; House and Mitchell 1974), leader-member exchange theory (Dansereau, Green, and Haga 1975; Graen and Cashman 1975), and contingency theory (Fiedler 1986; Fiedler and Garcia 1987; Hickson et al. 1971) to name a few.

All are worth investigating but this chapter focuses on just three cumulative theories of leadership: transactional, transformational, and servant. While each is distinct and has its own theory and literature, they are interrelated in many ways. We refer to them as cumulative because transformational includes transactional and servant leadership includes both transactional and transformational.

By necessity, the analysis of moral leadership involves both agents and actions and questions of legitimacy of authority, the consent of the followers, conscience, freedom to act, intentions, means and consequences. Analysis of a moral leader's actions depends on three characteristics: (1) the moral character of the leader, (2) the legitimacy of the values in the leader's vision, and (3) the morality of the processes, choices, and actions that leaders and followers collectively engage in (Bass and Steidlmeier 1999).

Exhibit 9.2. Great Man and Trait Theories

Great Man Theory
This theory was popularized in the mid-1800s by historian Thomas Carlyle to explain the great men and heroes in history. It was believed that people were born with God-given (now perhaps DNA) personal traits of charisma, intelligence, and wisdom that made them natural leaders.

Trait Theory
Similar to the great man theory, the trait theory of leadership assumes leaders are born with specific behavioral characteristics, and those who possess those traits in sufficient quantity are destined to be great leaders. Although considered outdated now in leadership research, trait theory is still a very active approach to studying the human personality in psychology.

Sources: Carlyle 1840; Stogdill 1974; McCall and Lombardo 1983.

---

1. Moral character addresses the leader as a moral agent. Bass and Steidlmeier (1999) explain that the leader, as a moral agent, is assessed praise or blame based on three criteria: (a) level of conscience, (b) degree of freedom to act, and (c) goodness of their intention. Any act, regardless of the agent, is judged right or wrong by three criteria: the ends sought, the means employed, and the consequences.

2. Legitimacy of values focuses on the standards and criteria of ethical behavior. Setting cultural values aside for a moment, many argue that the foundations of moral discourse are found in the unity-of-opposites found in the moral intention of egoism versus altruism and in moral consequences of benefits and costs to self and others (Bass and Steidlmeier 1999; Kanungo and Mendonca 1996). A critical issue for legitimacy of values is the worldview and beliefs they are grounded in to form a set of moral values and criteria (Bass and Steidlmeier 1999).

3. Morality of processes "reflects the legitimacy of both influence on the part of leaders and empowerment processes on the part of followers" (Bass and Steidlmeier 1999, 183). Modern Western cultures are focused on the moral democratic processes and actions of individuals in the society. Recurring themes are "liberty, utility, and distributive justice in an attempt to specify what individuals owe each other, what individuals owe the group, and what the group owes to individuals" (Bass and Steidlmeier 1999, 183).

TRANSACTIONAL LEADERSHIP

Reminiscent of Kohlberg's stages one and two of moral development, in transactional leadership followers are motivated by the leader's promises, praise, and rewards or they are sanctioned by discipline, reprimands or threats. Leaders and followers engage in implicit or explicit agreements on what is to be done in exchange for a desired allocation of resources. Leaders react to followers with contingent reinforcement based on how well the followers carry out what they have "transacted" to do. Although transactional leadership is grounded in the paradigm of self-interest, if the leader is more "other" centered, they monitor their followers' performance and offer corrective advice and encouragement. Followers are more likely to respond positively to the leader's comments and view them as educational. These leaders are engaged in active management-by-exception and the followers can grow into their fullest potential.

If the leader is more "ego" centered and waits silently for followers to make mistakes so that they can exert authority over their followers and subject them to negative reprimands, they engage in passive management-by-exception. In this case, followers are more likely to resent the comments and see them as interference (Bass and Steidlmeier 1999). This style of leadership assumes that followers are stage two Kohlberg thinkers and that a free contract exists between the leader and the follower. Further, both leader and followers believe the contract is reciprocal and each has rationally pursued his or her own best interests in that contract (Donaldson and Dunfee 1994).

The main limitation of this style of leadership is the assumption that all parties are "rationally," able to mentally weigh all the options, and are motivated by money and simple rewards, hence their behavior is predictable. In practice, there is sufficient evidence in human behavior to sustain transactional approaches, however it is limited. It is especially reinforced by the supply-and-demand situation of much employment, coupled with the effects of deeper needs, as in Maslow's hierarchy. But, when the demand for a skill outstrips the supply, transactional leadership is often insufficient, and other approaches are more effective.

Following our three-part analysis of the moral leader's actions:

1. The moral character of the transactional leader is required to tell the truth and keep promises (Bass and Steidlmeier 1999).

2. The ethical legitimacy of transactional leaders depends on their ability to grant the same liberties and opportunities to others that they claim for themselves, to distribute to all what is due them, and to use proper incentives or punishments.

3. The moral processes must respect pluralism of values and the diversity of motivations (Bass and Steidlmeier 1999; Rawls 1971).

TRANSFORMATIONAL LEADERSHIP

Long thought of as the founder of modern leadership research, James MacGregor Burns's book *Leadership* (1978) moved the focus of research in the field of leadership from the traits and actions of great men to the types of interactions between the leader and the led. For Burns, the effects of leadership had to be transforming for both the leader and the follower. To be transformational, the leader had to be morally virtuous. Both the leader and the follower needed to be inspired and ultimately transformed in performance and in outlook. This, in turn, would raise each to higher levels of motivation and morality. Transformational leaders often have charismatic qualifies that attract followers.

Researchers found that, "followers identify with the charismatic leaders' aspirations and want to emulate the leaders" (Bass and Steidlmeier 1999, 184). However, research also found that transformational leadership has a dark side. As Conger and Kanunago (1988) reported, charismatic leaders can also be narcissistic, authoritarian, and Machiavellian. They may also have a flawed vision and a need for power, lack inhibitions, and internalize values and beliefs (Bass and Steidlmeier 1999). For some time, it was thought that transformational leaders came in two flavors, villains or heroes, depending on their values and worldview (Bass 1990).

Other researchers (Howell and Avolio 1992) felt that only altruistic leaders, who are concerned with the greater common good, could be thought of as truly transformational and anything less than that had to fall into a different category of leadership. More recent research appears to be trending toward a separate designation for the white hats and the black hats in transformational leaders. To be fair, to succeed, all leaders manipulate or direct their followers, but there is enough differentiation on the four components identified in the transformational leadership literature to warrant two distinct categories within the definition of transformational: authentic-transformational and pseudo-transformational (Bass and Steidlmeier 1999).

Research in human behavior over several decades has identified four components contained in the notion of transformational leadership: (1) idealized influence (charisma), (2) inspirational motivation, (3) intellectual stimulation, and (4) individualized consideration (Bass 1985, 1998; Bass and Avolio 1993; Conger and Kanungo 1988, 1998; Kouzes and Posner 1993).

IDEALIZED INFLUENCE (CHARISMA)

This component is the vision and confidence of the leader that sets the standard for the followers to emulate. It has a spiritual as well as moral dimension (Fairholm 1998; Kanungo and Mendonca 1996). Exhibit 9.3 presents the two dimensions in terms of charisma.

INSPIRATIONAL MOTIVATION

This component of transformational leadership provides the followers with meaningful challenges to engage in shared goals and tasks in the organization. Kanungo and Mendonca (1996) link this to an empowerment process that broadens the followers' scope through participation. Bass and Steidlmeier (1999, 188) say "it is motivational and enabling, highlighting a new realization and transformation of the person." Exhibit 9.4 presents the two dimensions in terms of inspirational motivation.

INTELLECTUAL STIMULATION

This component of transformational leadership creates an architectural structure for processes, evaluation, and vision formulation and implementation (Bass and Steidlmeier 1999). Exhibit 9.5 presents the two dimensions in terms of inspirational stimulation.

Exhibit 9.3. Two Dimensions of Charisma

Authentic-Transformational	**Pseudo-Transformational**
- Universal brotherhood,	- Create fictitious we/they
- Values are morally uplifting	differences
- Committed to a clearly stated	- Deceive themselves about their
and continually enforced code	own competence
of ethics	- Behavior is inconsistent and
- Promote ethical policies, processes,	unreliable
and procedures	- Have grandiose visions
- Seek power and position at the	
expense of others	

Source: Bass and Steildlmeier, p. 187.

Exhibit 9.4. Two Dimensions of Inspirational Motivation

Authentic-Transformational	**Pseudo-Transformational**
- Focus on the best in people	- Focus on the worst in people
- Harmony, charity, good works	- Unreal dangers, plots, and
- Concern for the good that can	conspiracies
be achieved by the individual,	- Mislead and deceive
group, organization, or society for	- Talk about empowerment but
which they feel responsible	continue to seek control
- Promote ethical policies, processes,	- Concerned for the good that
and procedures	can be achieved for themselves

Source: Bass and Steidlmeier, 1999, p. 188.

INDIVIDUALIZED CONSIDERATION

The individualized consideration component of transformational leadership focuses on the basic nature of the leader: egocentric, which fosters authoritarian control, or altruistic, which empowers individuals to grow into their fullest potential (Bass and Steidlmeier 1999; Kanungo and Mendonca 1996). Exhibit 9.6 presents the two dimensions in terms of individualized consideration.

Following our earlier three-part analysis of the moral leader's actions:

1. The moral character of the authentic-transformational leader is required to be altruistic and other-focused. This type of leader channels power in socially constructive ways to serve others (Bass and Steidlmeier 1999).

Exhibit 9.5. Two Dimensions of Inspirational Stimulation

Authentic-Transformational	Pseudo-Transformational
- Focus on openness and transparency - Help followers question assumptions - Seek creative solutions to problems - Persuade others on the merits of the issue - Change follower's values by the merit and relevance of the leader's ideas and vision for the follower's benefit	- Promotes false assumptions - Emphasize authority, stifle reason - Take credit for other's ideas - Find scapegoats for failure - Substitute anecdotes for hard evidence - Secretly fail to do the right thing if it conflicts with their own narcissistic interests - Intolerant of differences in opinion - Substitute emotional argument for rational discourse - Feed on the ignorance of followers so that they will accept inconsistencies

Source: Bass and Steildlmeier, 1999, pp. 188–189.

Exhibit 9.6. Two Dimensions of Individualized Consideration

Authentic-Transformational	Pseudo-Transformational
- Treats each follower as an individual - Provide coaching, mentoring, and growth opportunities - Promote attainable shared goals - Help followers become more competent - Provide successful succession within organization - Channel power in socially constructive ways to serve others	- Maintain dependence of followers - Expect blind obedience - Enhance their status by creating distance - Manipulate arguments - Foment favoritism and competition - Use power for self-aggrandizement

Source: Bass and Steildlmeier, 1999, p. 189.

2. The ethical legitimacy of authentic-transformational leaders depends on their ability to promote and support a sense of universal brotherhood, harmony, and charity in the workplace, values that are morally uplifting and persuade others on the merits of their vision.

3. The moral processes depend on the authentic-transformational leader's ability to treat each follower as an individual, promote ethical policies, processes, and procedures, and focus on openness and transparency (Bass and Steidlmeier 1999).

THE LEADERSHIP CHALLENGE

From the results of a twenty-year study of leadership involving more than a million people, James Kouzes and Barry Posner asked the interviewees to describe the best leader they had ever had. They developed a survey (Leadership Practices Inventory) that asked people to draw on their experiences of being led by others and identify the seven top things they looked for, admired, or would willingly follow from a list of common characteristics of leaders. The results of the study showed that people preferred the following characteristics, in order:

- Honest

- Forward-looking

- Competent

- Inspiring

- Intelligent

- Fair-minded

- Broad-minded

- Supportive

- Straightforward

- Dependable

- Cooperative

- Determined

- Imaginative

- Ambitious

- Courageous

- Caring

- Mature

- Loyal

- Self-controlled

- Independent

The five actions that Kouzes and Posner identify as key for successful leadership are as follows:

1. Model the way. Modeling means going first, living the behaviors you want others to adopt. This is leading from the front. People will believe not what they hear leaders say but what they see leaders consistently do.

2. Inspire a shared vision. People are motivated not by fear or reward, but by ideas that capture their imaginations. Note that this is not about having a vision, but communicating it so effectively that others take it as their own.

3. Challenge the process. Leaders thrive on and learn from adversity and difficult situations. They are early adopters of innovation.

4. Enable others to act. Encouragement and exhortation is not enough. People must feel they are able to act and then must have the ability to put their ideas into action.

5. Encourage the heart. People act best of all when they are passionate about what they are doing. Leaders unleash the enthusiasm of their followers with stories and passions of their own.

Ignoring the combined views of over a million subjects and placing honesty first is difficult. It stresses the importance of leaders telling the truth to those they would lead. The overall process identified is clearly transformational in style, which again has a strong focus on followers.

SERVANT LEADERSHIP

Servant leadership is a practical philosophy that supports people who choose to serve first and then lead as a way to expand their service to individuals and institutions. Servant-leaders may or may not hold formal leadership positions. Servant leadership encourages collaboration, trust, foresight, listening, and the ethical use of power and empowerment. These attributes expand the notion of Burns's original idea, that the effect of leadership has to be transforming for both the leader and the follower.

Robert K. Greenleaf, founder of the Center for Applied Ethics (now known as the Robert K. Greenleaf Center for Servant Leadership) first coined the term "servant-leader" in a 1970 essay, "Servant as Leader." The servant-leader is servant first . . . "It begins with the natural feeling that one wants to serve, to serve first. Then conscious choice brings one to aspire to lead. He or she is sharply different from the person who is leader first, perhaps because of the need to assuage an unusual power drive or to acquire material possessions. For such it will be a later choice to serve—

after leadership is established. The leader-first and the servant-first are two extreme types. Between them there are shadings and blends that are part of the infinite variety of human nature" (18–19).

The difference manifests itself in the care taken by the servant-first to make sure that other people's highest priority needs are being served. The best test, which is difficult to administer, is to ask the following questions: Do those served grow as persons? Do they, while being served, become healthier, wiser, freer, more autonomous, more likely themselves to become servants? And what is the effect on the least privileged in society? Will they benefit, or, at least, will they not be further deprived?

Leadership authors, such as Warren Bennis and Jim Kouzes, management authorities like Peter Drucker, and popular inspirational writers like Scott Peck and Steven Covey, explicitly or implicitly discuss the principles of servant leadership in their writings. The ideas of Robert K. Greenleaf make up the center of the current literature on servant leadership. Larry Spears, the chief executive officer of the Greenleaf Center, describes servant leadership in *Reflections on Leadership*:

> we are beginning to see that traditional autocratic and hierarchical modes of leadership are slowly yielding to a newer model—one that attempts to simultaneously enhance the personal growth of workers and improve the quality and caring of our many institutions through a combination of teamwork and community, personal involvement in decision making, and ethical and caring behavior. This emerging approach to leadership and service is called *servant-leadership*.

The ten principles of servant leadership (adapted from Larry Spears, *Insights on Leadership* 1998, 3–6) are as follows:

1. **Listening.** Traditionally, leaders have been valued for their communication and decision-making skills. Servant leaders reinforce these important skills by making a deep commitment to listening intently to others. Servant leaders seek to identify and clarify the will of a group. They seek to listen receptively to what is being said and not said. Listening also encompasses getting in touch with one's inner voice and seeking to understand what one's body, spirit, and mind are communicating.

2. **Empathy.** Servant-leaders strive to understand and empathize with others. People need to be accepted and recognized for their special and unique spirit. One must assume the good intentions of coworkers and not reject them as people, even when forced to reject their behavior or performance.

3. **Healing.** Learning to heal is a powerful force for transformation and integration. One of the great strengths of servant leadership is the potential for healing oneself and others. In The Servant as Leader, Greenleaf writes, "There is something subtle communicated to one who is being served and led if, implicit in the compact between the servant-leader and led is the understanding that the search for wholeness is something that they have."

4. **Awareness.** General awareness, and especially self-awareness, strengthens the servant-leader. Making a commitment to foster awareness can be scary—one never knows what one may discover! As Greenleaf observed, "Awareness is not a giver of solace—it's just the opposite.

It is a disturber and an awakener. They are not seekers of solace. They have their own inner security."

5. **Persuasion.** Servant-leaders rely on persuasion, rather than positional authority, in making decisions. Servant-leaders seek to convince others, rather than coerce compliance. This particular element offers one of the clearest distinctions between the traditional authoritarian model and that of servant leadership. The servant-leader is effective at building consensus within groups.

6. **Conceptualization.** Servant-leaders seek to nurture their abilities to "dream great dreams." The ability to look at a problem (or an organization) from a conceptualizing perspective means that one must think beyond day-to-day realities. Servant-leaders must seek a delicate balance between conceptualization and day-to-day focus.

7. **Foresight.** Foresight is a characteristic that enables servant-leaders to understand lessons from the past, the realities of the present, and the likely consequence of a decision in the future. It is deeply rooted in the intuitive mind.

8. **Stewardship.** Robert Greenleaf's view of all institutions was one in which CEOs, staff, directors, and trustees all play significant roles in holding their institutions in trust for the great good of society.

9. **Commitment.** Servant-leaders believe that people have an intrinsic value beyond their tangible contributions as workers. As such, servant-leaders are deeply committed to the personal, professional, and spiritual growth of each and every individual within the organization.

10. **Building Community.** Servant-leaders are aware that the shift from local communities to large institutions as the primary shaper of human lives has changed our perceptions and caused a sense of loss. Servant-leaders seek to identify a means for building community among those who work within a given institution.

Following is a three-part analysis of the moral servant leader's actions:

1. The moral character of the servant-leader is altruistic and other-focused. They empathize with others and listen deeply (Spears 1995).

2. The ethical legitimacy of a servant-leader depends on their ability to promote awareness, and especially self-awareness, and their commitment to healing as a powerful force for transformation and integration.

3. The moral processes depend on the servant-leader's ability to seek to identify a means for building community among those who work within a given institution and effectively builds consensus within groups (Spears 1995).

WISDOM, COURAGE, AND MORAL MUTENESS

Stephen K. Bailey reminded us that "the higher a person goes on the rungs of power and authority, the more wobbly (*sic*) the ethical ladder" (Bailey 1965, 290) and "the heat in the ethical kitchen grows greater with each level of power, no public servant is immune from some heat" (Bailey 1965, 291). No matter which leadership style the public administrator employs, wisdom and courage are critical. Bailey's four essential wisdoms are:

1. There is no way of avoiding personal and private interest in the calculus of public decision making.

2. We are often as much a rationalizer as we are a rational being.

3. Successful public discourse requires an effort to transcend, sublimate, and transform narrow vested interest (i.e., dialogical discourse) but this capacity is time-consuming and is exercised imperfectly and intermittently.

4. No public decision should be a total victory for one party and a total defeat for the other.

This wisdom points to the complexity of working in the public sector. Public administration exists in a larger society that embraces both private sector values and the public interest values, but they are not always compatible. Private sector values are about profit margins for private groups and profit margins can be increased by harming the environment or using public property for less than market value. Public sector values are about the public good, which needs protection from misuse of public lands or allowing public goods to be privately used without fair compensation to the public.

When the two values sets are not compatible, public employees get caught in the conflict and the result can lead to an immoral action on the part of the public employee. Public servants can rationalize that accommodating private interests is merely a part of any democratic process but such accommodations can diminish the publics' interest through corruption or public decency through abuse of human rights. Leaders typically use discourse to help them fully understand, transcend, sublimate, and transform the narrow private interest to the public good. However, such discourse is typically not only time-consuming but is done imperfectly and inconstantly. When a successfully public decision occurs, there is no total victory for any one party but also not a total defeat for any other party.

Success almost always requires courage on the part of the public servant. Courage is difficult because, as we discussed earlier, public life is one of ambiguity and paradox. The uncertainty of the territory creates timidity and withdrawal. Thus, in order to lead, the public official must come to the workplace with an inner courage that overwhelms the organizational inertia but without arrogance. Given the conflicting pressures upon public leaders and the seeming safety of withdrawing to making no decision, Bailey tells us that possibly the most important act of courage for a public servant is ultimately the courage to decide.

According to ethics researchers Frederick Bird and James Waters (1989, 73):

Many managers exhibit a reluctance to describe their actions in moral terms even when they are acting for moral reasons. They talk as if their actions were guided exclusively by organizational interests, practicality, and economic good sense even when in practice they honor morally defined standards codified in law, professional conventions and social mores.

Their research revealed that managers often felt that openly discussing moral or ethical issues would ultimately threaten organizational harmony, efficiency, and their own reputation for power and effectiveness as leaders (Bird and Waters 1989, 76). But without moral courage as articulated by Bailey, too many public leaders ignore the consequences of their non-actions. For example, they see sexual harassment in their work space and say nothing or merely laugh it off as something silly. Or they may accept a gift or some favor from a private associate as a sign of respect or a friendly gesture of a work associate. Moral muteness is often the first step toward much more serious ethical problems that can and often do spread throughout the organization once the leader succumbs to his or her lack of courage to confront the ethical problem at its genesis. Moral muteness must be met with a full awareness of the need for inner courage to address their actions in moral terms, even though they may wish to avoid the requirements of moral courage (Bird and Waters 1989, 73).

CONCLUSION

Leon's comment certainly captures a deep negative feeling toward organizations and his hopelessness that nothing can or will get better. Leon is not alone in lamenting poor organizational leadership, but clearly a great deal of thought has gone into what is necessary to have quality leadership in our private and public organizations. Some government organizations have wonderful leadership, but consistently excellent leadership throughout government has not been achieved. Like all human activity, some public organizations have better moral leadership than others. However, the bottom line is that public employees around the world perform important service to their nations, and without strong ethical leadership in place, government service is diminished in the eyes of the public we claim to serve—sometimes with horrible repercussions. Because elected, appointed, and civil servants serve the public, they are correctly held to a high standard. Therefore, public leaders must constantly improve ethics within government and nonprofit organizations.

Ideally, a servant leadership as suggested by Greenleaf serves to create an ideal ethical context for public service. Pyramid like hierarchies, with their traditional command and control organization, make less sense in the twenty-first century and increasingly horizontal and dispersed organizations are more common. In particular, the latter type of organization greatly benefits from a servant leadership. The virtues implicit in servant leadership create ethical organizations. Nevertheless, such organizations would be wise to also apply some aspects of rule-based and consequential ethics plus administrative procedures. The proper mix depends upon the nature of the organization and the environment in which it exists.

REVIEW QUESTIONS

1. In the case study at the beginning of the chapter, how was the new ambassador mirroring his boss?

2. What was inadequate about the so-called great man and trait theories of leadership?

3. Transformational leadership involves (1) idealized influence (charisma), (2) inspirational motivation, (3) intellectual stimulation, and (4) individualized consideration. Compare and contrast each of them.

4. Compare and contrast the various styles of leadership. Do so in terms of moral character, ethical legitimacy, and moral processes.

5. What are the insights offered to us by Kouzes and Posner?

6. How can an organization create servant leadership among its executives and management?

7. Explain the linkage between virtue ethics and servant leadership.

8. How can servant leadership be applied in public organizations?

9. Explain how wisdom helps in the attainment of moral courage.

10. What is moral muteness and why is it an ethical problem?

REFERENCES

Bailey, Stephen K. 1965. "Ethics and the Public Service." In *Public Administration and Democracy: Essays Honoring Paul H. Appleby*, edited by Roscoe C. Martin, 283–298. Syracuse, NY: Syracuse University Press.

Bass, B. M. 1985. *Leadership and Performance Beyond Expectation*. New York: Free Press.

Bass, B. M. 1990. "From Transactional to Transformational Leadership: Learning to Share the Vision." *Organizational Dynamics* 18, no. 319–331.

Bass B. M. 1998. "The Ethics of Transformational Leadership." In *Ethics, the Heart of Leadership*, edited by J. Ciulla, 169–192. Westport, CT: Praeger.

Bass, B. M., and B. J. Avolio. 1993. "Transformational Leadership: A Response to Critiques." In *Leadership Theory and Research: Perspectives and Directions*, edited by M. M. Chemers and R. Ayman, 49–80. New York: Free Press.

Bass, B. M., and P. Steidlmeier. 1999. "Ethics, Character and Authentic Transformational Leadership." *Leadership Quarterly* 10, no. 2: 181–217.

Bird, Frederick B. and James A. Waters. 1989. "The Moral Muteness of Managers." *California Management Review*, 31, no. 1: 73–88.

Burns, J. M. 1978. *Leadership*. New York: Harper and Row.

Carlyle, Thomas. 1840. "The Hero as Divinity." In *Heroes and Hero Worship*.

Conger, J., and R. N. Kanungo, eds. 1988. *Charismatic Leadership: The Elusive Factor in Organizational Effectiveness*. San Francisco: Jossey-Bass.

Conger, J., and R. N. Kanungo. 1998. *Charismatic Leadership in Organization*. Thousand Oaks, CA: Sage.

Dansereau, F., Jr., G. Graen, and W. J. Haga. 1975. "A Vertical Dyad Linkage Approach to Leadership within Formal Organizations: A Longitudinal Investigation of the Role Making Process." *Organizational Behavior and Human Performance* 13: 46–78.

Donaldson, T., and T. W. Dunfee. 1994. "Toward a Unified Conception of Business Ethics: Integrative Social Contracts Theory." *Academy of Management Review* 19: 252–284.

Duckrich, J. M., M. L. Nichols, D. R. Elm, and D. A. Vollrath. 1990. "Moral Reasoning in Groups: Leaders Make a Difference." *Human Relations* 43: 473–493.

Fairholm, G.W. 1998. *Perspectives on Leadership: From the Science of Management to It Spiritual Heart*. Westport, CT: Quorum Books.

Fiedler, F. E. 1986. "The Contribution of Cognitive Resources of Leadership Performance." In *Advances in Experimental Social Psychology*, edited by L. Berkowitz. New York: Academic Press.

Fiedler, F. E., and J. E. Garcia. 1987. *New Approaches to Leadership: Cognitive Resources and Organizational Performance*. New York: Wiley.

Graen, G., and J. F. Cashman. 1975. "A Role Making Model of Leadership in Formal Organizations: A Developmental Approach." In *Leadership Frontiers*, edited by J. G. Hunt and L. L. Larson. Kent, OH: Kent State University Press.

Hersey, P., and K. H. Blanchard. 1999. *Leadership and the One Minute Manager*. New York: William Morrow.

Hersey, P., K. H. Blanchard, and D. E. Johnson. 2007. *Management of Organizational Behavior: Leading Human Resources*. New York: Prentice Hall.

Hickson, D. J., C. R. Hinigs, C. A. Lee., R. S. Schneck, and J. M. Pennings. 1971. "A Strategic Contingencies Theory of Intra-Organizational Power." *Administrative Science Quarterly* 16: 216–229.

Howell, J. M., and B. J. Avolio. 1992. "The Ethics of Charismatic Leadership: Submission or Liberation?" *Academy of Management Executive* 6, no. 2: 43–54.

House, R. J. 1971. "A Path-Goal Theory of Leader Effectiveness." *Administrative Science Quarterly* 16: 321–339.

House, R. J., and T. R. Mitchell. 1974. "Path-Goal Theory of Leadership." *Contemporary Business* 3 (Fall): 81–98.

Kanungo, R. N., and M. Mendonca. 1996. *Ethical Dimensions in Leadership*. Beverly Hills, CA: Sage.

Kouzes, J. M., and B. Z. Posner. 1993. *Credibility: How Leaders Gain and Lose It and Why People Demand It*. San Francisco, CA: Jossey-Bass.

Kouzes, J. M., and B. Z. Posner. 2002. *The Leadership Challenge*. San Francisco, CA: Jossey-Bass.

Lewin, K., R. Lippit, and R. K. White. 1939. "Patterns of Aggressive Behavior in Experimentally Created Social Climates." *Journal of Social Psychology* 10: 271–301.

Likert, R. 1967. *The Human Organization: Its Management and Value*. New York: McGraw-Hill.

Maier, N.R.F. 1963. *Problem-Solving Discussions and Conferences: Leadership Methods and Skills*. New York: McGraw-Hill.

McCall, M.W., Jr., and M. M. Lombardo. 1983. *Off the Track: Why and How Successful Executives Get Derailed*. Greensboro, NC: Center for Creative Leadership.

Merton, R. K. 1957. *Social Theory and Social Structure*, New York: Free Press.

Pfeffer, J., and G. R. Salancik. 1975. "Determinants of Supervisory Behavior: A Role Set Analysis." *Human Relations* 28: 139–153.

Rawls, John. 1971. *A Theory of Justice*. Cambridge, MA: Harvard University Press.

Spears, Larry. 1995. *Reflections on Leadership*. San Francisco, CA. Wiley.

Spears, Larry. 1998. *Insights on Leadership*. San Francisco, CA. Wiley.

Stogdill, R. M. 1974. *Handbook of Leadership: A Survey of the Literature*. New York: Free Press.

Tannenbaum, A. S., and W. H. Schmitt. 1958. "How to Choose a Leadership Pattern." *Harvard Business Review* 36 (March/April): 95–101.

Yukl, G. A. 1989. *Leadership in Organizations*. Englewood Cliffs, NJ: Prentice Hall.

10 Values and the Professional Context

PROFESSOR: *Yes, Leon. You have another question?*

LEON: *Yes, I have two questions. Is ethics really another way of saying values? How can any intelligent person call public administration a profession? Lawyers and medical doctors are professionals but not a bunch of paper pushers.*

VALUES AND ETHICS

VALUES DEFINED

What are values and how do they relate to ethics? A good point of departure to answer this question is to examine the dictionary definition. The *Oxford English Dictionary* defines "value" in part as worth, desirability, utility, qualities on which these depend, worth as estimated, valuation, in exchange, purchasing power. Merriam-Webster defines it in part as follows:

- a fair return or equivalent in goods, services or money for something exchanged;

- the monetary worth of something;

- relative worth, utility, or importance meaning degree of excellence;

- something intrinsically valuable or desirable;

- to estimate or assign the monetary worth of; and

- to rate or scale in usefulness, importance or general worth.

This chapter compares the definition of value to the definition of ethics used in chapter 2. The word "value" is not about good or bad behavior, nor is it about the "good life," as defined by Aristotle. In the preface to Montgomery Van Wart's book, *Changing Public Sector Values* (1998),

Nicholas Henry notes that the Chinese have a saying, "that to understand something, first we must name things correctly." The terms "value" and "ethics" are not the same, but are often used interchangeably. Personal history, cultural background, age, race, circumstances, and many other personal specific factors create values. Thus, a value depends on the perspective of the person or even a large set of people, such as a nation. Values become shared (intersubjective) when two or more individuals place the same sense of worth on something. As the definitions of "value" imply, we often translate that sense of worth into monetary terms using concepts associated with hedonistic calculus.

Values can be associated with either egocentric or altruistic thinking. For example, a person can assume that as rational people we are all trying to maximize pleasure in our lives. Alternatively, an altruistic person can use the same term but create quite a different set of values. For example, an altruistic person can value compassion and contributing to the larger society over material desires. Values are mostly associated with rational thought but they can also be useful to an intuitionist. For example, an intuitionist describes what worth he or she places on something as well as the intersubjective worth that several people might assign to something. In addition, particular values or sets of values can motivate someone to make a particular decision about right or wrong behavior or can motivate them in terms of how they define living a self-actualized life. Another consideration is that a set of values need not always be the same and occasionally the values, which they claim to hold, may not be logically consistent.

However, values sometimes have a relationship ethics; that is, placing a value on something can be a motivation for both ethical and unethical choices. For example, a person might value a poem that speaks to a favorite memory that has nothing to do with ethics. However, a person might value honesty that speaks to a virtue that has everything to do with virtue ethics. Values do not always involve ethics but ethics always involves values.

Some authors, such as C. L. Stevenson (Sahakian and Sahakian 1993), have argued that values are the foundation of ethical systems because they define what is acceptable or unacceptable or right and wrong. Alasdair MacIntyre, in *After Virtue* (1984), argued that values are merely preferences that can be strong or weak motivators when making choices, including ethical choices. Person X prefers and assigns greater worth to red and person Y prefers blue but assigns little worth to that color. Red and blue are neither right or wrong. They are just preferences. To say that preferences are the foundation of ethical systems is to advocate emotivism, meaning moral relativism with all the logical problems it creates.

Alasdair MacIntyre argued that emotivism fails for three reasons: First, it requires us to cite the essential expression or attitudes in question. However, any such expression is circular reasoning. For example, I like something, therefore it is good. It is good therefore I like it. Second, by definition, emotivism uses and needs an equivalent to express meaning. Some words derive their meaning from contrasts and expressing the difference from other near-parallel or even opposite words. Thus, to say you prefer something automatically provokes the question "in contrast to what?" Unfortunately, those who use emotivism do not answer that question. Thus, using emotivism is merely engaging in word games that confuse and confound the listener rather than engaging in critical thinking that should be the cornerstone of ethical thinking.

Third, although emotivism purports to be a theory about the meaning of sentences, it is merely an expression isolated to a particular occasion and carries no generic sense. An angry teacher can shout at a small boy that "Seven times seven equals forty-nine!" The anger and shouting carry no weight in terms of the correctness of his statement, which might be right or wrong depending on the technical assumption of the base number used by the person making the statement. The teacher's feelings have nothing to do whatsoever with the meaning of the statement. To equate the two is a logical fallacy. From the perspective of logic and critical thinking, emotivism and equating of values to ethics fails the test of critical thinking.

Ethical systems are normative guides that can and should help individuals and groups make wiser decisions involving right and wrong behavior and how to achieve the good life or, as Aristotle put it, "the life worthy of being lived." Such systems of logic are built on a few assumptions that ideally are logically consistent. Those key assumptions can be values as illustrated in chapter 4 by the American philosopher Josiah Royce, who built his ethical normative system on the value of loyalty. Of concern is that key value assumptions in a normative theory can be built on assumed but not necessarily *be* an actual facts. An excellent example is the Aristotle's ethical system, which is built on the assumption of self-realization as the telos, or the end goal of the human condition. Perhaps not everyone values or wants to reach self-realization. Therefore, that value cannot apply to everyone.

Values can be individual preferences and in the aggregate they remain preferences. However, as the society's values, they significantly impact public policies and people's behavior. A variety of factors influence a society's values, such as generational differences, marketing, art, and the media. For example, smoking in public places was once common, but after a strong anti-tobacco campaign in the United States and elsewhere, smoking in public spaces is rare and even whole institutions are smoke free now. In the past, social values changed slowly but in our era of instant news and social media, social values can and do change rapidly. For example, sexual harassment was common in the recent past decades but social media and news stories against it quickly shifted social values. Although there is still much to be done on this issue, initial significant progress has been made against that practice.

Sources of Values

Montgomery Van Wort argued that there are five major sources of values important to public administration: individual, professional, organizational, legal, and public interest. For him, individual values essentially means virtue ethics. Van Wort stresses that good government needs elected, appointed, and career employees who have integrity. Merriam-Webster defines integrity as the state of being complete, unbroken, and whole. Thus, people with integrity have complete lives that are in harmony with all aspects of their life, beliefs, and actions. They have consistency between what they say they believe and their actions. In the vernacular, we could say: "They walk the talk." In a democracy that has civil integrity, there exists a respect for established political-legal systems and a willingness to make necessary system changes through the process of law. However, orderly dissent, including critical speech and civil disobedience, can and do exist if the majority or those in power listen to the opposition and accept the possibility that the opposition may be correct in part or in whole.

Professional and organization values reflect group self-awareness. Professional values typically reflect a reasonably developed theory and knowledge corpus. Typically, they share a social ideal with a formal organization, exist to promote its interests, and celebrate its leading persons. Organization values almost always seek to be dynamic and healthy. Thus, organizational values often include efficiency and effectiveness but they also include preferences of organizational design, work ethics, policies toward due process, and leadership styles.

Given that public administrators are often the enforcers of the law, legal values are important. Public administrators typically have a high regard for the U.S. Constitution as well as laws at all levels, including rules, regulations, and judicial rulings. They value due process and political rights such as freedom of speech. However, some public administrators practice what critics call an excessive use of legal values, normally expressed as "legalism." Patrick Dobel (1990) cites five limitations of legalism:

- promotes timid, reactive, and rule-bound public officials,

- undermines initiative and dissent,

- invites an excessive narrowing of concern,

- ignores the inescapable discretion that public officials must exercise,

- overly represents the interests of wealthy and well-organized groups.

Elliott Richardson (1992), an eminent, well respected, former public official, made the Machiavellian observation that "in recent years, the federal government has placed increasing reliance on specific laws, regulations, and rules to guide behavior of its officers and employees . . . Their primary purpose, however, is not to promote high ethical standards, but to dispel the suspicion of unethical behavior. Moreover, some current restrictions go too far" (38).

In chapter 2, the discussion of democratic morality addressed public interest value. However, the discussion of public values goes beyond mere compliance with often vague, conflicting, or silent politically determined public policy, as it must involve fairness, justice, and equality. This special value in public administration directly opposes private interest values unless they are consistent with the larger public good. Thus, this value can lead an administrator to sometimes agree with some private interests and disagree with the same private interests under other conditions. Another hallmark of the public interest value is often an unusual degree of disagreement in particular cases as to what is or is not in the public interest. Nevertheless, there are many situations in which most public officials with public interest values can and do agree on the importance and implication of them.

BASIC ASSUMPTIONS THAT DETERMINE VALUES

NATURE OF THE UNIVERSE OF ASSUMPTIONS

Social groups can and do define what they consider to be their universal (even if not universal to others) values or at least values that are appropriate for their social group. A widespread and accepted assumption based on a faith tradition can significantly determine a set of values for a larger segment of society. For example, people in a faith community can believe in God as explained to them in a book that they consider to be divine revelations. Faith communities prescribe and expect their members to follow the values that are set forth in their religious scriptures as interpreted by their leaders. Other social groups, like fraternal orders, define values that they expect members of their group to follow. Professional groups also define values for their members. Even street gangs have values that members must recognize and obey.

Social group assumptions do influence what group members consider to be fact (even if they are not considered factual by others) as well as what values they must follow. For example, a faith community's statements can influence their members to be creationists, observe strict dietary requirements, or only wear certain "correct" clothing. Often religious beliefs influence concepts of right and wrong. In a similar manner, a government can also adopt similar values as a religion on matters of diet such as promoting organic or non-GMO products, dress such as in regulating dress codes, personnel relations, and so on. Commonly, there is an overlap with both religious and social viewpoints defining what a person's values should be. Of significance, social group values do change over time even among orthodox and conservative groups.

Nature of Human Assumptions

There are three ideal constructs of the nature of humanity: (1) humanity is essentially weak and tends to wickedness without firm guidance; (2) humanity is essentially good if properly socialized; and (3) humanity is a mix of good and bad. Noted philosophers have used these three assumptions in constructing their philosophies. For example, as previously mentioned, Hobbes assumed the first ideal construct: viewing humanity as essentially mean, nasty, and brutish. Other philosophers, such as Locke, assumed the second ideal construct, whereas James Madison, a lay philosopher, assumed the third ideal construct as his key assumption in the U.S. Constitution.

Each view results in a different set of reforms and ethical positions to resolve social problems. Those of the first set (humanity is weak) typically advocate strong leadership. They seek an enforcing system with authority, strong bureaucratic controls, a large police force, and so on. Kantian ethics is typically important to them. Those of the second set (humanity is good) typically adopt a communitarian view with weak leadership. They want weak economic controls and weak leaders as well as diffused political power using federalism, frequent elections, term limits, and citizen political empowering reforms such as referenda and recall. Virtue and consequential ethics are important to them. The second view assumes that the good sense of the public will eventually arrive at consensus and prevail to change public values needs to be done slowly. To them, a leader, who removes or lessens their individual choice, dominates their concern. For the second group, there is wisdom in limiting the leader's powers by means of institutional democratic barriers such as protecting freedom of speech and a free press, requiring two chambers to pass identical legislation, and allowing a presidential veto.

Those who adopt the third view (humanity is a mix of good and bad) advocate reforms that vary depending on history and other contextual variables that inform their understanding of the workability of the current situation. For example, after the 9/11 act of terrorism in New York City, many saw poor security at airports as a national problem and argued for federal government employees to provide that essential service rather than poorly trained and paid private guards. Another situation occurred in California, when its citizens in 2003 were not pleased with the performance of their state governor and recalled the recently elected governor and required another election. In other words, for this group solutions are normally pragmatic choices. In ethics, those who assume the middle and often pragmatic view tend to embrace critical thinking in making their choices and use a mixed approach to ethics.

THE IMPORTANCE OF VALUES

CONCEPT OF VALUES

Values sometime create enduring beliefs that influence the ethical choices of policy makers, including managers. More sophisticated approaches to ethics are normative thought systems and values that are merely statements of preference, often without logical implications. Kenneth Kernaghan (2003) separates the total field of values as applied to public administration into ethical, democratic, professional, and people values. Furthermore, his topology subdivides professional values into traditional values, such as efficiency, and new values, such as innovation. However, Kernaghan points out that his divisions do not fall into hard and fast categories, as some values fall into more than one category. For example, accountability is both an ethical and a democratic value. Value conflicts do exist among divisions, as noted in Exhibit 10.1.

Policy makers and public managers can integrate values into the structures, processes, policies, and systems of public administration practices that reflect a logical consistent system and influences social ethics. Such integration logically flows from a more fundamental set of values, which is the central component of a values regime. Such value statements of a local, regional, state, national, or international government capture the essence of public service and the concept of the public interest. To be effective, leaders must serve as models of values based on servant leadership (see chapter 9, on moral leadership) and be skilled practitioners of the art of values management in order to provide the foundation for integrating critically considered and consciously chosen values into the public service.

Exhibit 10.1. Categories of Public Service Values

Ethical	Democratic	Professional	People
Integrity	Rule of Law	Effectiveness	Caring
Fairness	Neutrality	Efficiency	Fairness
Accountability	Accountability	Service	Tolerance
Loyalty	Loyalty	Leadership	Decency
Excellence	Openness	Excellence	Compassion
Respect	Responsiveness	Innovation	Courage
Honest	Representativeness	Quality	Benevolence
Probity	Legality	Creativity	Humanity

Source: Kenneth Kernaghan, "Integrating Values into Public Service: The Values Statement as Centerpiece," *Public Administration Review* 63, no. 6: 712.

DEFINING REGIME VALUES

Australia, New Zealand, the United Kingdom, and Canada have particularly stressed the importance of setting out regime values to guide their public service. In 1993 and later in 1999, the Australian government declared their public service values first in a report and then in law. They articulate them in fifteen provisions. Some of the key provisions of the Australian Public Service (APS) are that "the APS delivers services fairly, effectively, impartially and courteously . . . and is sensitive to the diversity of the Australian public . . . the APS is apolitical, performing its functions in an impartial and professional manner" (Australian Government 1999).

The APS code of conduct follows the APS values statement. The code states that an APS employee must uphold APS values. The code contains various ethical values such as integrity, honesty, and respect, and ethical rules on confidentiality and conflict of interest. Further details are described in the APS *Guidelines on Official Conduct of Commonwealth Public Servants*, which is a one-hundred-page document that covers a wide range of values and ethics issues in legislation, regulation, and guidelines.

Stating values and implementing them are not the same. In 1998, Australia's Public Service Commission began submitting to Parliament an annual report that assessed the extent to which each agency incorporated the APS values and complied with the code of conduct. Public leaders and managers are expected to embed those values into their agency's organizational culture. The law requires agencies to establish procedures for determining if employees breach the code.

The first step in accomplishing that end was the annual report. The report explains the meaning of each value, provides a checklist of agencies and public employees to use in applying the values in their organizational context, and sets out indicators for agencies to use in evaluating the application of the values. The measures to implement the APS values include information sessions, intranet listings, use of the values in recruitment practices, inclusion in performance agreements, and training.

Exhibit 10.2 presents a portion of the APS values using the format established in Exhibit 10.1. In general, articulating the values as statements of values or principles is not important, but the statements should be concise and contain only the most fundamental values. Thus, the challenge is to limit the number of statements of values to the most fundamental. For example, the Australian government was able to limit the set to only twenty-five values.

IMPORTANT CONSIDERATIONS

Common to most governments is a built-up set of policies and statements that accumulate over the years that are often unclear, not integrated with the larger set of policies within the whole government, and occasionally contradictory. Ideally, the government needs concise interlinked statements of core values that extend to department and agency rules. Such a practice focuses attention on primary values and facilitates a better understanding of those values. Ideally, it should be a two-tiered system consisting of foundational core public service values that underpin the second level of rules. For example, the second level explains the importance, gives examples, and cites details of regulations, guidelines, and statutes on such matters as conflicts of interest as they relate to integrity and fairness.

Policy makers can articulate public service values in statutes, regulations, guidelines, or some

Exhibit 10.2. Australia's Value Statement Excerpt

Ethical	Democratic	Professional	People
High ethical standards	Apolitical	Professional	Free from discrimination
Honest	Accountability	Merit Based	Sensitive to diversity
Fair	Impartial	Effective	Courteous
	Responsible to government with frank, comprehensive, accurate, and timely advice	Work place communication, consultation, and cooperation High quality leadership Fair, flexible, safe regarding workspace Results focused Performance focused Career based Cohesive	Fair and equitable

Source: Kenneth Kernaghan, "Integrating Values into Public Service: The Values Statement as Centerpiece," Public Administration Review 63, no. 6: 716.

combination of these instruments. However, the statutory approach has the advantage of symbolizing strong government support for the values. The statutes promote public, legislative, and media discussion of the values. The statutes also inform the public in a manner that enhances public appreciation of the public service, which many politicians and media personalities commonly criticize for purposes of their own agendas. If done with bipartisan support for the values, statutes create a positive government consensus in favor of good government policies. The two major arguments for regulations and guidelines instead of the statute approach are that it avoids making values a partisan issue and updating and amending is easier for regulations and guidelines.

Values statements are quite useful but they are not sufficient for achieving integration and consistency of values in the public service. Effective values management is also essential and management does that by answering four questions:

- Where are we now?

- Where do we want to be?

- How do we get there?

- How do we make it happen?

An assessment of current practices, problems, and possible improvements is one way to answer the first question. Other approaches are customer and citizen assessments, employee assessments, performance assessments, benchmarking, and quality assessments. Management answers the second question by adopting measures that infuse respect for the core values into all aspects of the organization. Management answers the third question by using no one set approach. Clearly, there is much room for innovation. The key to the fourth and last question is leadership. Leaders must lead by example in which they fashion a new and better organization that embodies the desired enduring values. Lord Michael Patrick Nolan, who was the first chair of the Australian Committee on Standards in Public Life in 1995, is known for his seven principles of public life: leadership, selflessness, integrity, objectivity, accountability, openness, and honesty.

THE ETHICAL SPIRIT OF PUBLIC ADMINISTRATION

BENEVOLENCE

H. George Fredrickson's book *The Spirit of Public Administration* describes the spirit of public administration as "dependent on a moral base of benevolence to all citizens" (1997, 234).Here, the word "citizen" implies all the people in a nation and possibly the world. Fredrickson also said that, "Without benevolence, public administration is merely governmental work. With benevolence, our field has a meaning and purpose beyond just doing a good job; the work we do becomes noble—a kind of civic virtue" (ibid.).

"Benevolence toward all" is the ethical spirit of public affairs and administration, the focus of which is the public interest. The civic virtue of public administration is a caring altruism, which is the opposite of a hedonistic egocentric mind-set. When the practice of government slips into the latter mind-set, it no longer is public administration as its moral foundation dimension ceases to exists. Public affairs and administration is much more than government administration. The latter term is only about management for the sake of management. Public administration includes and is deeply associated with the state because the state should and must care for all of the people and the people's assets including its natural environment. However, the scope of public affairs and administration is not limited to the state as it includes all other forms of administration and collective public activity that have a moral base of benevolence toward all. For example, the scope of public administration includes nonprofit and international organizations, such as the United Nations and area hospitals.

CIVIC VIRTUE

Public affairs and administration concerns fostering efficiency, effectiveness, and equitable organizations because of its civic virtue. Why? Public resources at any moment are finite, and public-spirited organizations need to marshal those resources wisely to maximize the benefits for all. Thus, wasting resources by being uneconomic or inefficient is antithetical to the spirit of public administration. In addition, the equitable use of resources is central. Not developing all the skills and talents of the people is tantamount to not caring for all in society. For example, racism, sexism, and other forms of bias are antithetical to the spirit of the field. Public affairs and administration is about caring for everyone rather than small subsets or groups regardless of how policy makers rationalize those divisions.

Although the scope of public administration is to provide recommendations to elected and appointed policy makers and then implement the public policy the elected policy makers decide, it is not completely neutral. Instead, it is a firm advocate of nonpartisan conduct in both presenting recommendations and implementing the final policy in the public's interest to the best of its ability. Typically, public administrators support regime values for all citizens if those values are consistent with the administration's ethical spirit. If there is no consistency between the two, public administrators must *internally*, within the government institutions, advocate for benevolence toward all. Failing in that attempt, public administrators may find that they have to resign their public employment to become *external* advocates for justice and fairness. The implementation of public policy is more than a means, it also is the end purpose of civility and caring for all. Clearly, differences of approach to serve that end can and do exist. Public administrators must remain neutral on the public policy approach taken as long as they do not abandon their profession's critical ethical spirit.

That spirit includes enhancing the prospect of positive change, public responsiveness, and citizen involvement in the management of public organizations and institutions. This assumes that those changes are responsive, and enhanced citizen involvement fosters benevolence to all. Broadening the range of administrative discretion and citizen choice, trying to build organizational cultures that encourage creativity and risk taking, and developing systems for the diffusion of innovation are typically very supportive of the public administration ethical spirit. Moral agency includes weighing and balancing constitutional and legal issues with political issues within the democratic context. The ultimate responsibility is always to the constitution and the people. The ethical rudder is responsibility to the public interest.

Responsibility to the public interest ennobles the public administrator. It is not a responsibility to a particular set of citizens, but rather a commitment to be fair, just, and equitable to all. Certainly, in the context of market capitalism, the spirit of public affairs and administration must dominate in order to help mitigate the worst consequences of capitalism and complement its most positive consequences. For example, public administrators in both government and nonprofit organizations need to manage the social safety net so that each person can realize their opportunities for self-actualization. Such a role in society brings dignity and nobility to the public service beyond money and fame.

Before the election of the forty-fifth president, Frederickson argued that the Reagan administration was one of the most corrupt in recent memory. He said the most likely reason for that corruption was differences in standards for ethics between government and business. The Reagan administration subscribed to the notion that government should be run like a business and therefore relied on business leaders for key public service positions in the national government. Those hired did not embody the required ethical spirit of public administration. They defined success as putting in place the private interests of their former business associates. To such people, the notion of "public interest" translated into the point of view of "their group's" interest. They rationalized their decisions by asserting they were on the winning side of the election and therefore had a mandate for action. In the American system, accepting bribes is considered both unethical and illegal, but for political operatives intervening on behalf of a political contributor it is not only "legal" it is smart "political administration." Nevertheless, it *is* also unethical and inconsistent with the spirit of public administration.

THE PROFESSIONAL CONTEXT OF PUBLIC ADMINISTRATION

ETHICS AND RATIONALITY

The normative ethics of Kant and Aristotle differ in terms of the importance of intelligence. For Kant, one can be both good and stupid. In contrast, Aristotle maintained that a stupidity of a certain kind, which we call the absence of good (common) sense, precludes goodness. Some people with good sense may do poorly in school and some geniuses have very limited good sense. Good sense does not necessarily correlate with IQ. However, genuine practical intelligence or good sense reflects an awareness of the human telos. In Aristotle's view, the virtue ethics practitioner must be able to exert self-control, and the organization ethicists or the individuals that create a set of virtues must be able to think critically. Thus, for public affairs, virtue ethics promotes a flexible self-enforcing accountability that adapts to the situation at hand.

Judgment and a community context are essential qualities for the virtuous public administrator and are not as necessary for the Kantian law-abiding administrator. As previously mentioned, the golden mean in virtue ethics implies that for each virtue there is a corresponding vice representing the extreme on both sides of the mean. The mean or middle ground is found in wisdom and self-control to know when to stand and fight and when not to. This continuum of each desirable virtue explains why a fixed criterion to judge goodness, as in Kant's logic, does not make sense to the person applying virtue ethics.

In virtue ethics, the social good assumes wide community agreement on what the good is, which creates the *polis* bond among the members of the community. In virtue ethics, the community can be a nation, state, region, or city, but, as we have discussed earlier, it can also be a profession or an organization. (The latter is the focus of chapter 11, on creating a personal ethics, and the former is the focus of chapter 12, on creating public organizational ethics.) This polis perspective embodies a shared recognition of and pursuit of a public good.

In the Kantian and utilitarian contemporary world views, a profession, such as public administration, is simply a social arena in which each individual in the profession pursues his or her own self-interests and self-chosen concept of the good life. In those world views, political institutions exist to provide order and context to promote the public welfare. In contrast, the virtue ethics world view not only requires the exercise of virtues but it also encourages the development of moral and ethical judgment in its members. Each profession must look to its professional community to help define the professional telos. In this view, political institutions exist to help each professional public servant and citizen self-actualize toward their "internal good."

THE PRACTICE

In the American context, public administration concerns advancing and protecting the public interest as stated in the Constitution's preamble. To illustrate, public employees teach a child to read, protect a neighborhood from crime, treat a patient for an illness, and rescue lives from a blazing building. By its very nature, public affairs implicitly involves higher values that transform a society into a civilization. Public administration is focused on internal goods because achievement in the profession itself is a "good" for the public employees and because they realize that they are doing something meaningful to help others. If the institution of government hires the correct employees and trains them well for their jobs, then the work of government is performed at a higher level of competency and proficiency. For example, if public servants manage the budget correctly, then resources are allocated to provide the public with needed services that maximize the social and economic outcome for the betterment of the whole community.

In public affairs, every subpractice has its own set of virtues that fit the practice and the telos that it serves. This is important to public administration, as every subpractice requires a certain kind of relationship among those who participate in it. As public administrators perform their practice, they engage in a shared purpose and shared sense of their standards of excellence. Both influence their professional context. As a practice, public administration is a community of past, present, and future professionals that share a common telos and viewpoint. In chapter 2, Appleby and Bailey helped the reader to understand that an important part of the common viewpoint in public administration is the notion of the public interest. In this chapter, George Frederickson helps us to appreciate the importance of benevolence in terms of how public administration must understand the public interest.

In our modernist and postmodernist contemporary world, one can easily ignore, assume, or say that the telos of public administration does not exist and maybe even that it should not exist. In addition, egocentric thinkers argue that public service is just a job, with great benefits that merely advances a person's power and fortune. In contrast, authors such as Appleby, Bailey, Frederickson, Van Wart and Kernaghan disagree and believe that public affairs has a special value beyond businesses that operates for their private interest. This is not to argue that private sector jobs are unimportant. They are the nation's and world's economic engine that gives society its standard of living. By its very nature, public administration implicitly involves values that transform a community into a society and a society into a civilization. Public administration is a demonstration of MacIntyre's internal goods as achievements in the profession are a good for everyone in society.

THE PROFESSIONAL CONTEXT

Public affairs and administration always exist (1) in the context of a society and (2) if people, with an egocentric consciousness, permit and even encourage corruption or other immoral behavior. It is wise to use a mix of ethical theories and administrative procedures to keep corruption and other immoral behavior at a minimum. An important part of that mix is the retention and enhancement of integrity directed at sustaining but also improving institutions. Unfortunately, politics, motivated by private interest groups, too often foster and even encourage the erosion of virtues within public affairs and administration. Thus, political and managerial reformers must reinforce the development of virtues within public service by addressing both the individuals and the institutions.

In the application of ethics in public affairs, the reality is that conflict in society will exist. In a materialistic culture, individuals and groups place extreme value on achieving wealth, fame, and power. In such an environment, virtues such as justice within public administration can hinder achieving external goods for many private interest groups. In such circumstance, political leaders and others punish public administrators for acting for the public good rather than for influential private interests. However, because virtue ethics have internal goods even in those conflicts, public servants have their internal rewards and no political leader can diminish the professional public administrator who acts with integrity.

Virtue ethics in particular requires a practice context that has a telos or quest. For public administration, that telos or quest is the benevolent pursuit of the public's interest. The quest provides the profession of public administration with an understanding of what is the "good." It gives focus and purpose to the practice but it also gives focus to what virtues are most important in any given circumstance. It enables professionals to order other goods and extend individual and collective understanding of the purpose and context of the virtues. It permits a conception of the good that enables professionals to understand the place of integrity and constancy in life. Internal rewards are not only recompensing in themselves, they also build character with ever-expanding self-knowledge of what is truly important in life.

CONCLUSION

To answer Leon's questions, values and ethics are significantly different. Although both are normative, with ethics there is a logical system of thought to guide one in making decisions about right and wrong behavior. An ethical theory can guide someone and even a society to make better moral decisions as well as define what is a "good life" and how to achieve it. With values, there is merely a raw wanting or preference without a logical system of thought. With ethics, one can argue that a person or a set of people is acting rationally and correctly. With values, one can only observe that a person is acting consistently or inconsistently with their espoused values, but there is no way to say one is correct and the other incorrect. With ethics, we are free to choose based on our rational thoughts and no longer be slaves to our history, genes, prejudices, and so on. With values, we just function with that which we like and love. Without ethics, logic is of little help to resolve civil disputes as one person's values are just as good or bad as another person's. With ethics, we create a civil society by using logic to discuss, argue, debate, and arrive at a consensus as to what is best for all.

Public administration is more than pushing papers. It is a *practice*. Medical doctors have a telos in the practice of helping people to stay healthy. Lawyers have a telos in the practice of helping people successfully live in a nation of laws. Public administrators have a telos in the practice of facilitating the public interest rather than the private good, and in that effort they put the civil into a society. In chapter 2, we learned that ethics for public administrators is remarkably significant in a democracy. Authors like Aristotle argue that ethics are important and we need to apply them in the context of a professional community such as public administration. For example, Democratic Morality helps to maintain a democratic form of government because civil servants and other public officials are a part of the democratic process that mills selfish private interests into a democracy's public interest for benevolent purposes. Thus, there is a unique and important social ethics that does apply to public administrators that is essential for those who believe in a democracy of the people rather than government dominated by its influential private interest groups.

Every professional group, such as the American Society for Public Administration and the

International City Managers Association, has developed standards of excellence and the professional's fundamental values to clarify the internal good of public service in the various functions of public affairs. Fortunately, that work has been on going for decades. Given the scope of this task, international, federal, state, and local governments can contract with these and other non-profit professional associations to develop the standards of excellence and distribute them to the appropriate elected officials, politically appointed persons, and career public employees. The hope is that these standards will eventually be enacted as binding resolutions in governments.

For public affairs and administration, telos is the benevolent pursuit of the public interest as explained by Frederickson. The quest provides the profession of public administration with an understanding of what is the "good." It gives focus and purpose to the practice, but it also gives attention to what virtues are most important in any given circumstance. The quest enables professionals to prioritize other goods and extend its individual and collective understanding of the purpose and context of the virtues and permits a conception of the good that enables professionals to understand the place of integrity and constancy in life.

REVIEW QUESTIONS

1. Explain the difference between values and ethics.

2. In what ways does the assumption made about the nature of humanity influence our approach to government and the role of ethics in government?

3. Explain the Australian approach to values statements and its usefulness to society.

4. Why is Fredrickson's association of benevolence with the spirit of public administration important in terms of the social ethics of public administration as a profession?

5. Why is linking virtue ethics to a practice important? What is a practice and what does it have to do with a profession?

6. How can contemporary society move beyond Kant in terms of ethics? Should it do so, and if so, why?

7. How is the distinction between external and internal goods useful in the context of social ethics?

8. Make the case that public administration is a profession.

REFERENCES

Aristotle. 1980. *The Nicomachean Ethics*. Oxford,: Oxford University Press.
Australian Government. 1993. *Building a Better Public Service*. Canberra, Australia: Management Advisory Board.
Australian Government. 1995. *Guidelines on Official Conduct of Commonwealth Public Servants*. Canberra, Australia: Public Service Commission. Accessed July 5, 2002 but it is no longer available and has been updated to:

Australian Government Commission for Public Sector Employment, Code of Ethics (2014). https://publicsector. sa.gov.au/policies-standards/code-of-ethics/. Accessed July 14, 2014.

Australian Government. 1999. *Public Service Act 1999, No. 147*. https://www.legislation.gov.au/Details/.../443a274c-db38-4eed-a7eb-765c9ecd8f69, and *Public Service Bill 1999. Explanatory Memorandum*. http://classic.austlii. edu.au/au/legis/cth/bill_em/psb1999162/. Accessed July 14, 2018.

Committee on Standards on Public Life. 1995. *The Seven Principles of Public Life*. Accessed May 28, 2018. https://www .gov.uk/government/publications/the-7-principles-of-public-life/the-7-principles-of-public-life—2.

Devetere, Raymond J. 2002. *Introduction to Virtue Ethics: Insights of the Ancient Greeks*. Washington, DC: George-town University Press.

Dobel, J. Patrick. 1990. "Integrity in the Public Service." *Public Administration Review* 50, no. 3: 356–366.

Frederickson, H. George, ed. 1993. *Ethics and Public Administration*. Armonk, NY: M. E. Sharpe.

Frederickson, H. George. 1997. *The Spirit of Public Administration*. San Francisco: Jossey-Bass Publishers.

Griffin, James. 1996. *Value Judgments: Improving Our Ethical Beliefs*. Oxford: Oxford University Press.

Kernaghan, Kenneth. 2003. "Integrating Values into Public "Service: The Values Statement as Centerpiece." *Public Administration Review* 63, no. 6: 711–19.

MacIntyre, Alasdair. 1984. *After Virtue*. Notre Dame, IN: University of Notre Dame Press.

Oakley, Justin, and Dean Cocking. 2001. *Virtue Ethics and Professional Roles*. Cambridge, UK: Cambridge University Press.

Richardson, Elliott, and the Council of Excellence in Government. 1992. "Ethical Principles for Public Servants." *Public Manager* 4 (Winter).

Sahakian, William S., and Mabel Lewis Sahakian. 1993. *Ideas of the Great Philosophers*. New York: Barnes and Noble.

Van Wart, Montgomery. 1998. *Changing Public Sector Values*. New York: Garland Publishing.

Windt, Peter Y., Peter C. Appleby, Margaret P. Battin, Leslie P. Francis, and Bruce M. Landesman. 1989. *Ethical Issues in the Professions*. Englewood Cliffs, NJ: Prentice Hall.

Woodbridge, Frederick J. E. 1958. *Hobbes Selections*. New York: Scribner.

11 Creating a Personal Ethics

PROFESSOR: *Yes, Leon?*

LEON: *Let me get this right. You're saying that adults can be taught and should be taught ethics. But isn't that some sort of programming or mind control?*

Leon is essentially correct. Each person should be responsible for creating his or her own personal ethics but this does not mean that some assistance in doing that isn't important. Like any other type of learning, education can help the individual develop into the type of person he or she wants to be. Creating a personal ethics ideally should occur over a lifetime and should involve more aspects of their life than a person's professional career. Unfortunately, in Western culture, the influence of modernism, postmodernism, and the desire to be secular has moved many public administration professionals away from a serious consideration of consciously and deliberately developing a personal ethics (Lynch and Lynch 1997).

This chapter offers specific normative advice on personal ethics in public administration at the individual level and also explains how individuals can create their own personal ethics. We are not suggesting that this plan is the one for all public administrators in all situations at all times. Each person must make his or her choices in terms of personal professional ethics and as time and situations change, we strongly suggest that personal ethics be updated to adjust to new situations.

This chapter assumes that educators and trainers should teach ethics but not prescribe any specific set of ethics, with the exception of the following nine basic concepts: (1) receptivity personal growth, (2) renunciation of egocentrism, (3) truthfulness, (4) optimism, (5) courage, (6) fairness, (7) context awareness, (8) democracy, and (9) oneness of the public interest. The choice of a personal ethical theory is the ultimate choice of every human being and the authors of this textbook believe it must remain an individual choice. However, most people do not give any time or thought to their personal ethics or how to or why they make the choices or decisions they make. Most also do not appreciate that non-decisions in most situations are real de facto decisions. Unconscious choices are subject to the full range of ethical consequences. Better decisions result from deliberate and conscious reflection and consideration. The suggested professional public administrator ethics suggested here is merely a model for developing a thoughtful personal ethic that can help practitioners make good, well-reasoned ethical choices.

Whether we have given it much thought or not, we all have a default process for assessing truth and assigning worth to our thoughts and actions. For some, truth is found in one or more authorities in our lives that tells us what is true, good, just, or right. An authority can be a beloved family member such as a parent or grandparent, a legal institution, a religious organization, a boss, a workplace policy, or even a trusted media outlets. Our "authority" can be simply our gut feelings about goodness, right, and wrong, or we may be sufficiently rational to seek evidence that convinces us of the veracity or goodness of an action or decision. Whatever our current default setting is, we should rationally seek evidence to assess truth and assigning worth to our thoughts and actions. That evidence and your rationale for supporting it should stand up to the scrutiny of others in your workplace.

THE BEGINNING: THREE PRINCIPLES FOR PUBLIC ADMINISTRATORS

Codes of ethics for public administrators are generally rule-based rather than virtue-oriented in design. In other words, they set a floor for the minimum on what we should do in certain situations rather than suggest an aspirational higher order action we could to take.

In Brian Fry's (1998) *Mastering Public Administration*, he quotes Luther Gulick, who was one of the founders of public administration as an academic and professional discipline: "Gulick came to believe that the essence of spiritual life is not in the formal elements of religion but in the basic values of 'fundamental honesty, individual human dignity, justice and human rights, the opportunity for creative fulfillment, social responsibility, *charity* as defined by St. Paul, selfless devotion to noble causes, and deep emotional participation in the Universe'" (280). The first three principles reflect Gulick's thoughts.

RECEPTIVE TO GROWTH

This principle is about being receptive to our own continuing ethical growth and an awareness of its larger significance over a lifetime. As new situations develop, our physical and ethical circumstances change. This first principle encourages each person to be receptive to professional ethical growth. Without growth, the ethical development of the person is arrested and the benefits from it are not attained.

The first principle requires a receptive mind that remains open to other alternatives and other explanations but also considers doubt as a friend. In other words, it means a passionate mind that seeks deep learning that permits and stimulates intellectual and internal growth. A mind should never be closed but be always open to ethical growth. Ethics is something we can and should continue to perfect.

Abandon Egocentric Materialism

The second principle for a public administrator is to seek their satisfaction from advances to the public good rather than from personal material success. In contemporary social thought, "success" is defined in terms of personal wealth, fame, beauty, and power, which are often inculcated into us through media manipulation. Unfortunately, in the workplace, superiors define "success" through awarding promotions, salary increase, or meritorious recognition. Although positive gestures, such actions miss the point that the ultimate duty of the public servant is to the public interest and not to their own or others' materialistic goals. In the United States, the oath of office is to the U.S. Constitution and not to a person, office, or any materialistic goal. Ideally, individuals in public service look for the middle path between living a selfless life and seeking materialistic life goals for themselves.

Truthfulness

The third principle is sincere truthfulness to oneself and others. Most people realize that trust is important in public affairs and administration. Being less than truthful cripples and even destroys public faith in the programs and services of the administrators as well as the elected and appointed officials. Eventually, it can even destroy faith in the government. Professionals in public service need to earn and maintain the trust of their colleagues, their elected bosses, and the people they ultimately serve. Thus, this principle, which is also a virtue, is central to building and maintaining a viable public service.

THE LAST SIX PRINCIPLES

Bailey's Three Principles

In "Ethics and the Public Service," Stephen K. Bailey (1964) described the following three additional principles:
- Having an optimism that affirms the worth of taking risks for the public good and that sees the infinite possibilities for good in the uncertain, the ambiguous, and the inscrutable.

- Having an inner courage to overcome self-arrogance, being loyal to the oath to the constitution, and being willing to face down others who do not advance the larger public interest, including those who do not respect the minority rights of everyone.

- Exhibiting fairness tempered with charity, reflecting an ineffable standard of justice and public weal motivated by equal love and respect for all.

Three More Principles from Bailey and Appleby

Public administrators must be aware of the contextual forces in their environment and act accordingly. As noted previously, how a public administrator recognizes or sees the world is central to virtue ethics. For example, recognizing the moral ambiguity of all humans and all public policies is important as it provides an essential operative perspective for enlightened professionals who do not live in an idealized vacuum. There are contextual forces that condition public service moral priorities. A moral administrator cannot turn a blind eye to those forces, but instead must always grasp their importance to weigh all options for the correct course of action.

To illustrate this principle, the ethical public administrator must appreciate the paradoxes of procedure. An essential tool for public administration is a set of standard operating procedures (SOPs). However, this tools can be the right choice in one situation or the wrong choice in another situation. Therefore, a moral administrator may at times need to use good judgment to override or subordinate specific SOPs, but such judgments must be based on thoughtful reflection and respect for the importance of organizational procedure in the running of an ethical organization (Bailey 1964).

Public servants must embody the morality of democracy . Paul H. Appleby helps us realize that an American moral conduct must also exist in the context of democratic public institutions that continually strive to achieve what he called "Democratic Morality." Public administrators in democratic countries must always consider ethics in the context of hierarchy, politics and especially their country's constitution and laws. Public servants are called upon to turn the mill that grinds the various private and special interests so that eventually the democratic "public will" is produced. With that understanding, Appleby explains that moral public administrators are essential to the production of that very important "product" called democracy. Public administrators are part of the bulwark of democratic society and therefore must always ensure the mill produces the public will or the publics' interest rather than a particular private or special will or interest.

Finally, the Golden Rule must be considered in the context of public administration. Some form of the Golden Rule—Do unto others as you would have them do unto you—exists in most cultures. This universal wisdom speaks to valuing the public interest. With a little editing for purposes of public affairs and administration, this final principle reads: "Do unto the public all that is their right and is properly their due."

SUMMARY OF THE NINE PRINCIPLES

The nine principles noted here lay the groundwork for individual public administrators. If public administrators were to maintain open, receptive, and inquiring minds, shun passions, wealth, fame, and power, and manifest complete and sincere truthfulness in their daily activities, then society would have a remarkable public service. The first three principles —Receptivity, Renunciation, and Manifestation—are easy enough to remember, as would a more elaborate statement for each key word in the code. The second three principles—Optimism, Courage, and Fairness—are also easy to recall. The third trilogy of principles—Context, Democracy, and Oneness—are a little harder to recall but are equally important. If public administrators maintain optimism, exhibit courage, are always tempered by fairness and charity, are flexible to their context, respect democratic morality, and value the public good, then significantly each public administrator would have the inner satisfaction of knowing they have acted in the public interest.

CREATING INDIVIDUAL ETHICS

Ethics should be mindfully considered throughout a person's life, but increasingly Western culture dismisses ethics as unimportant. Ideally, formal ethical education and training would greatly help a public administrator consider the previously mentioned nine principles. To fully comprehend these principles while using the suggested training, one needs a caring heart to guide an ever-growing intellect in order to maximize both the intuitive and rational aspects of the mind.

STARTING POINT

The first task in preparing the groundwork for the goal of creating a personal ethics is to decide which principles and virtues you wish to have as you move through your moral life development stages. One useful technique in setting the stage for ethical training is to take something like the James Rest and Darcia Naverez's Defining Issues Test (DIT), to determine where you fall in the Moral Development stages. As mentioned in chapter 4, the DIT is a modernized and adapted version of Kohlberg's original moral development test (Rest et al. 1999). You can compare your score to those in similar work situations in order to understand how you compared to others in their vast data base. Remember that this assessment only addresses how you make decisions as it does not assign a value to any decision you actually take. There is no particular value for being at the highest moral development level because such an expectation is unreasonable and possibly misleading. A healthy mix of mostly altruism and some egoism is the most functional for situations in the life of a public administrator.

If you decide you might be egocentric, it is important to focus on becoming more altruistic. Moral development is about realizing that development is not a matter of moving up a scale but rather understanding how to properly mix the two types of consciousness levels (egocentric and altruistic) in various life situations. In other words, try to acquire the wisdom needed to properly deal with life situations through the use of a mix of egoism and altruism. Creating a small discussion group of trusted friends and colleagues can help advance the individual and group moral development process. Those discussions usually include anonymous examples of conflicting moral situations and a discussion about how individuals in the group might handle them.

DEVELOPING MORALLY

The key to more functional moral development is primarily through the heart and not the mind. First, you, as an individual, focus on gaining a strong sense of self-worth that is grounded in the middle path between insecurity and narcissism. Then, you imagine extending your compassion. For example, if you have only compassion for yourself, try to extend your self-love and compassion to those immediately around you. Next, try to even more expand your circle of compassion, eventually embracing the society you serve. Ideally, you can from a small group where other like-minded individuals can talk about extending compassion with a group facilitator keeping the group focused on maintaining civility within the group and guiding the discussion with the goal of each person learning to expand their compassion to the larger society.

The compassion or love discussed here is not a physical love or a dependence on another.

Rather, it is what the ancient Greeks referred to as "agape" or selfless love focused on caring for the well-being of others. This compassion should not be about making excuses for others but appreciating others for themselves as sentient beings. And if need be, compassion can be in the form of "tough love." For example, compassion can be demonstrated while still denying requests for support for dysfunctional habits. As you become more compassionate, try to expand your compassion to your immediate family, group, society, and, finally, to the larger world including the environment.

Once understood that you can expand compassion, you can ask: "How will this change how I see and interact with my various relationships? Movies and literature provide wonderful examples of egocentric transformation. They help us understand that that our more advanced conscious awareness guides us into better addressing ethical situations. In addition, group discussions help us experience our discovery in how consciousness influences ethical decision making rather than others telling us the "right" answer. The time needed for these ideas to process is a function of the people in the group and the depth of the conversation. Achieving greater moral development occurs when previously held egocentric consciousness is changed to the point where one can understand and apply altruism in situations that require it or would benefit from that ethical behavior.

Moral Lessons: Finding Their Own Lessons

Life experiences combined with moral reflection provide important lessons for moral and ethical development. Therefore, we need to regularly reflect on what we consider are important life situations as they likely contain one or more ethical lessons for us. Eventually, we begin to realize that our life events are important because, with reflection, we can become aware of our life stories and the ethical lessons they teach us.

To do so, think past your obvious personal awareness to probe the more sophisticated mindfulness that is the generic life lesson. For example, you may have experienced a situation in which a friend or colleague borrowed some money from you and is unwilling to pay back loan. The situation then evolves as lack of repayment is now effecting your relationship. What is the heart of that lesson? Is it not paying you back is a form of breaking a trust? It is that you feel taken advantage of? Or perhaps it is you value your friend and you feel you may lose that friendship. Keep probing first for the surface lesson and continue probing for a more sophisticated life guiding wisdom that you can apply to other life situations. When you dig deeper you may find your friend fell on very hard times and he did not have the capacity to repay you and he was too embarrassed to tell you.

Because moral development is cognitive, each person can learn from their own life experiences, especially from their negative experiences, as noted by Schopenhauer in chapter 4. The trick is to begin to recognize the more mindful lessons in your life. Those lessons can also be acquired from a book, movie, or even a poem, you will therefore never run out of lesson to learn. The goal is to continually discover wisdom that will help you grow ethically and morally. The magical "ah ha" moment of awareness occurs when you grasp, appreciate, and recognize that the reflection on your individual life lessons allows you to apply it to larger issues and grow continually. As inferred from

Schopenhauer, we need to realize that we are in control of creating our own normative ethical theory and we can alter it at will.

This way we can appreciate that just living life each day mindfully gives us a steady stream of wisdom lessons that we can use to improve our personal ethics. As Nelson Mandela reminded us, "No one is born hating another person because of the color of his skin, or is background, or is religion. People must learn to hate, and if they can learn to hate, they can be taught to love, for love comes more naturally to the human heart than its opposite" (1994).

A person's life experiences constitute a learning laboratory for their ethical and ultimately their moral growth. For example, life's negative lessons flow from ego, body, and mind. However, life's positive lessons flow from oneness, compassion, and heart. All anyone needs is some time to reflect internally or in a small group of fellow seekers of life's lessons. Negatives turn into positives when we view life experiences as learning opportunities. For example, when we see and realize that most individuals or groups act solely for their own benefit, we begin to understand the ego and how it controls lives, including our own. Part of the learning opportunity is seeing the unfortunate consequences that flow from the "my, me, mine" attitude, which is commonly referred to as "self-ishness" or being "egocentric."

MORAL LESSONS: LEARNING FROM THE COMPASSIONATE HEART

Egocentric self-awareness is commonly blind and deaf to wisdom but those handicaps can be overcome. We develop self-awareness through a compassionate heart, often resulting from a hurt caused by our own or another person's ego driven actions. The compassionate heart teaches us self-awareness as we realize the pain we feel from others often flows from the pain we caused by our own actions. Unfortunately, those who are blind and deaf to self-awareness do not see themselves acting selfishly. Direct heart felt conversations are, at best, difficult. We can best learn our lessons by observing and considering egocentric behavior in popular films, literature, and case studies. After watching the films, reading the literature, or reading the case studies, we can analyze and discuss the impact of egos on various characters in the film, story, or case study. We can consider the emotional reactions of that material on ourselves, the other characters, and the situation in general. What wisdom lessons can we use to improve our own personal ethical theory? Increased self-awareness is always something that must be discovered and making that discovery is a priority in the development of our personal ethics but it takes a prolonged deliberate commitment to action.

As internal/external learning opportunity occurs, a person or group is seen as just being human instead of being identified by physical characteristics (e.g., race, gender, age, physical make-up, sexual orientation, religion, and nationality). This allows oneness to move forward without confrontation. Egocentric people identify others in terms of their physical attributes and they use these distinctions to separate themselves from others and the larger oneness. As mentioned in chapters 1 and 8, when we see others as separate identities or groups rather than as the richness and depth of the whole, our brain tells us to "protect our own" and "defend" against the other. The goal of moving toward being more altruistic is achieved by thinking more in terms of oneness and appreciating the advantages of thinking in that manner.

In the age of the "selfies," society may put value on extreme egoism, but in the public service we realize that we do not have to think that way. The mind has remarkable powers to redirected egocentric thoughts into selfless ones. This happens when the public servant grasps that the conscious awareness is the ultimate positive guide for the mind. We think with our minds, but "know" with our hearts. Moral positive lessons begin to flow when individuals begin to identify themselves with oneness. When the individual bases their policy or implementation decisions on how others think and feel and try to understand their situation, then a sense of oneness guides their ethical decision making. Like many other unities of opposites, mind and heart must act in harmony; however, the heart must be the lead partner in the relationship because the compassionate heart is by far the more important of the two. An expanded consciousness directs the administrator's strengths and mitigates their weaknesses in directions that always improve the person.

The more important moral lessons occur when we see or better yet experience an emotionally profound inspiring experience. In such situations, we experience an uplifting feeling that (1) moves us to new levels, (2) makes the creative possible, and (3) permits continual growth. The feeling captures us by first allowing personal growth and second opening us up to unlimited possibilities. We learn from those experiences but also from the impact that they have on us. When such a feeling occurs, we can incorporate the feeling and its positive impact on us as we continue to develop our personal virtue ethics.

MORAL LESSONS: IMPORTANCE OF A FACILITATOR AND SMALL GROUP DISCUSSIONS

Thus far, we have discussed developing our personal ethics as an individual endeavor. As we have previously discussed, we, as individuals, are the moral actors and we are uniquely responsible for our own personal growth and development, but the effort made is infinitely easier if there is a dedicated small group of like-minded professionals seeking to expand their conscious self-awareness guided by a trained facilitator or organizational ethicist. A challenge for an excellent facilitator is helping trainees discover oneness. It occurs when the individual (1) sees him- or herself as having some altruistic feelings, (2) identifies him- or herself as is a part of the larger oneness that is everything, and (3) values what was previously considered separate as being parts of the one or whole.

For most people, the positive learning opportunity of oneness is difficult to describe, but they know it when they feel it. In addition, most people admire it when they see it in the actions of others. That fact can be helpful to the trainer. For example, a trainer can show a film of George Washington, Abraham Lincoln, Mahatma Gandhi, or Martin Luther King, Jr., and most trainees will appreciate the sense of oneness they see in those moral leaders. To maximize the learning experience, the post film discussion can focus not only on having the trainees identify the ways the exemplar acted in terms of the oneness but also how the trainees can act in a manner similar to the exemplars in their lives.

The key to moral lessons training is the use of small interactive groups with a skilled group facilitator. Typically, the group meets once a week for at least an hour. The number of sessions can be as few as ten or as many as the group wishes. An organizational ethicist (trainer) moderates the group without participating in the sharing of group member experiences. A training goal is to encourage each group member to participate in active sharing.

The facilitator explains the moral learning opportunities to the group, including the importance of learning from negative and positive experiences. Ideally, the facilitator gets each group member to present at least one example of each type of learning opportunity and the group member explains the impact it had on their personal ethical theory. The facilitator encourages the group members to react and discuss each presentation in terms of the moral lessons learned. At appropriate times in the process, the facilitator should summarize the moral lessons acquired from each session.

META GROWTH

Once there is apparent progress in moral development of members within the group, then the trainer can move the trainees to the meta stage. With better communication between heart and mind, the trainees can develop their own composite images of what they hope to change or transform in their life. In other words, each trainee needs to develop their personal ethical theory framed in terms of the virtues they think they want to exhibit in their lives. Clearly, this is an ongoing lifetime process; the trainer needs to stress that the trainee's theory will evolve as they grow with their continuing learned experiences in their lives. The trainer can help by providing samples of virtues from the middle path from other sources. Each trainee needs to self-discover the negative realities of extreme hedonism and their need to develop their own inner-self mind-set.

Ideally, the trainer helps the trainees understand the wisdom of creating an updated individual ethical mental image of the kind of person they want to be. The trainer needs to understand that very few if any of the trainees will come close to a full moral self-actualization. Therefore, the goal of the trainer is to help those trainees who wish to reprogram their inner gyroscope to define their desired moral behavior to find manageable steps to accomplish those goals and then live those ethical principles and virtues in the future. Whatever progress they make is sufficient, as, by definition, it is their own self-defined path. Some will be satisfied with small steps and others will set higher expectations.

As a final step, to convert the wisdom learned into a tangible lifestyle change, the organizational ethicist asks each trainee to identify the positive principles and virtues he or she wants to acquire. Each trainee prioritizes their desired virtues based on their personal ethical theory using an awareness of Aristotle and MacIntyre. Ideally, each trainee will share their list with the group and get input from the others. The trainees then associate positive habits that can be developed, and negative habits that need to be mitigated. The goal is for each trainee to decide what his or her current positive habits are in the context of their personal ethics. In addition, the trainees identify their current negative habits they think are detrimental and what additional positive habits they wish to develop. Finally, at the end of this training, the trainees will have a workable plan to transform themselves within some reasonable and realistic time frame.

LIFELONG LEARNING

Lifelong learning through training is key to continual growth and updating moral improvement plans. Individuals live their principles and virtues through habits they create and then make their moral choices based on a personally developed ethical theory that fits their needs. Those positive habits will reflect the virtues of a conscious awareness that cares and extends out to others with compassion. Essentially, in this process, a person is trying to keep their existing good habits, lose their bad habits, and create new habits that reflect the virtues that they think are important for them.

Creating new good habits is easy to say but often difficult to do. Therefore, once the initial training is completed, trainees will benefit from being assigned a mentor to discuss their progress in establishing their virtue habits as they continue to attend the same discussion group meetings, but less frequently. This allows the trainees to continue to share their experiences as they progress in establishing their desired habits. Realistically, establishing those habits requires a daily regime of practice and dedication, much like the diligent practices of athletes in developing their athletic skills. If the person is not pleased with their progress in reaching their goals, or if the goals were too unrealistic, then he or she might wish to rethink their targets again within the context of their discussion group.

CONCLUSION

Leon is correct in his worry about mind control. If an ethics instructor tells the students or participants what to believe and what not to believe, then it is mind control. Ethics training is about controlling the mind, but the individual must control their own mind and create the habits they wish to have. This does not mean that the trainer, such as the organizational ethicist, is passive and does not guide the group, but the ultimate decider of the individual's needs for ethics training is the individual. Especially in virtue ethics, education and training is about the trainer acting only as a facilitator to help the person have inner directed consciousness growth through self-discovery. Thus, each person is responsible for their own mind, soul, and destiny. The role of public organizations in personal ethics training is merely to support each person's ethical growth. The ethical training recommended in this chapter takes patience and, most of all, perseverance. It is life long learning experience that requires the full commitment of both the organization and the individuals participating.

REVIEW QUESTIONS

1. What are the nine virtues for public administration cited in this chapter? Explain why each is functional in creating a better ethical public administrator.

2. How can public administrators create a viable ethics within themselves?

3. Why is the meta stage critical in creating ethics within a public administrator? What must happen in the life stage?

4. In what way do Appleby's and Bailey's thoughts help us frame a personal code of ethics in the public sector?

REFERENCES

Appleby, Paul H. 1952. *Morality and Administration in Democratic Government*. Baton Rouge, LA: Louisiana State University.

Appleby, Paul. H. 1965. "Public Administration and Democracy." In *Public Administration and Democracy*, edited by Roscoe C. Martin. Syracuse, NY: Syracuse University Press.

Aristotle. 1925. *The Nicomachean Ethics*. Translated by David Ross. New York: Oxford University Press.

Bailey, Stephen K. 1964. "Ethics and the Public Service." *Public Administration Review* 24, no. 4: 234–243.

Bode, Carl, and Malcolm Cowley, eds. 1981. *The Portable Emerson*. New York: Penguin Books.

Chandler, Ralph Clark. 1997. "Plato and the Invention of Political Science." In *Handbook of Organization Theory and Management: The Philosophical Approach*, edited by Thomas D. Lynch and Todd J Dicker, 17–56. New York: Marcel Dekker.

Cruise, Peter. 1998. "Of Proverbs and Positivism: The Logical Herbert Simon." In *Handbook of Organization Theory and Management*, edited by Thomas D. Lynch and Todd J. Dicker, 273–287. New York: Marcel Dekker.

Farmer, David John. 1997. "Adam Smith's Legacy." In *Handbook of Organization Theory and Management: The Philosophical Approach*, edited by Thomas D. Lynch and Todd J. Dicker, 141–164. New York: Marcel Dekker.

Felder, Leonard. 2017. "The Ten Challenges (The Second Challenge)." leviafayette.com. Accessed June 30, 2017.

Fox, Charles J., and Hugh T. Miller. 1997. "Postmodern Philosophy, Postmodernity, and Public Administration." In *Handbook of Organization Theory and Management: The Philosophical Approach*, edited by Thomas D. Lynch and Todd J. Dicker, 415–437. New York: Marcel Dekker.

Fry, Brian R. 1998. *Mastering Public Administration: From Max Weber to Dwight Waldo*. New York: Chatham House.

Griffith, Mark E. 1997. "John Locke's Influence on American Government and Public Administration." In *Handbook of Organization Theory and Management: The Philosophical Approach*, edited by Thomas D. Lynch and Todd J. Dicker, 125–140. New York: Marcel Dekker.

Joyce, Douglas James, and Linda deLeon. 1999. "Ethics in the Information Age." *International Journal of Organization Theory and Behavior* 2 (3/4): 349–381.

Kung, Hans. 1996. *Global Responsibility: In Search of a New World Ethic*. New York: Continuum.

Lynch, Thomas D., and Cynthia E. Lynch. 1997. "God and Public Administration: Are They Compatible?" Paper presented at the American Society for Public Administration Conference, Philadelphia, PA, July 1997.

Lynch, Thomas D., and Todd J. Dicker, eds. 1997. *Handbook of Organization Theory and Management: The Philosophical Approach*. New York: Marcel Dekker.

Lynch, Thomas D., and Cynthia E. Lynch. 1998. "An Alternative Approach to Ethics." Paper presented at the Twenty-Fourth International Congress of Administrative Science, Paris, France, September 1998.

Lynch, Thomas D., and Cynthia E. Lynch. 1998. "Applying Spiritual Wisdom to the Practice of Public Administration." Paper presented at the Public Theory Network, Colorado Springs, CO, March 1998.

Lynch, Thomas D., and Cynthia E. Lynch. 1998. "Twenty-First Century Philosophy and Public Administration." In *Handbook of Organization Theory and Management: The Philosophical Approach*, edited by Thomas D. Lynch and Todd J. Dicker, 463–478. New York: Marcel Dekker.

Lynch, Thomas D., and Cynthia E. Lynch. 1998. *The Word of the Light*. Seattle, WA: Hara Publishing.

Mandela, Nelson. 1994. *Long Walk to Freedom*. http://www.beliefnet.com/inspiration/2009/07/nelson-mandela.aspx?p=3#mlgIUwio84oWYjXL.99. Accessed July 27, 2018.

Martin, Lawrence L. 1997. "Jeremy Bentham: Utilitarianism, Public Policy, and the Administrative State." In *Handbook of Organization Theory and Management: The Philosophical Approach*, edited by Thomas D. Lynch and Todd J. Dicker, 111–123. New York: Marcel Dekker.

Paquda, Bahya Ben Joseph ibn. (1909) 1974. *Duties of the Heart*. Translated by Edwin Collins. Reprint, New York: Dutton.

Rest, James, Darcia Narvaez, Muriel J. Bebeau, and Stephen J. Thoma. 1999. *Postconventional Moral Thinking: A Neo-Kohlbergian Approach.* Mahwah, NJ: Lawrence Erlbaum.

Whitney, W. D., trans. 1890. *Translation of the Katha-Upanishad.* Baltimore: John Hopkins University Press. http://www.jstor.org/stable/2935810.

Willa, Bruce, and Edward F. Plocha. 1999. "Reflections on Maintaining a Spirituality in the Government Workplace: What It Means and How to Do It." *International Journal of Organization Theory and Behavior* 2 (3/4): 325–347.

Windt, Peter V., Peter C. Appleby, Margaret P. Battin, Leslie P. Francis, and Bruce M. Landesman. 1989. *Ethical Issues in the Profession.* Englewood Cliffs, NJ: Prentice Hall.

12 Creating Public Organizational Ethics

PROFESSOR: *Yes, Leon.*

LEON: *I can understand you believe that creating organization ethics is a good idea. However, given its dismal record of success, is it not a lost cause?*

Creating public organizational ethics is more than an aspiration. There is a systematic way to develop organizations that are ethically superior. However, a systemic professional organizational intervention of quality takes time, money, and top-level organizational support. This chapter lays out a strategy for how to best achieve a desired moral behavior within a public organization. The approach described here assumes there is a mix of selfish and selfless employees within any organization. This chapter also assumes that the particular mix of types of employees influences the workability of the various normative theories as they are applied to public organizations. By knowing the influence of the mix, the organization's ethicist can rationally develop an organizational intervention strategy. The familiar term "special relativity" is appropriate to describe the theory of this chapter because this approach focuses on a primary independent variable—the various normative ethical theories and complementary procedures.

In this theory, the range of employee's consciousness level is the secondary independent variable. It influences which normative ethics theories is appropriate for the primary independent variable. That in turn influences the expected organization's ethical and moral outcomes or the dependent variable. In this proposed approach to organizational ethical theory, the critical secondary independent variable is the degree to which the organization's employees are selfish or selfless. This approach is relative because it is used situationally. Thus, this approach is not a one-size-fits-all or cookie-cutter tactic. Once that is known, the organization's ethicist can rationally determine the appropriate mix of normative ethical theories to best achieve the desired ethical and moral outcomes for their particular organization.

As in many of the preceding chapters, there are some important truths in Leon's questioning. In general, varying degrees of immorality exist within public organizations, as noted in chapter

213

3. However, the record suggests that a robust and proactive approach to organizational ethics can result in achieving desired ethical goals. Many of the greatest Western philosophers of the last century concluded that ethics is merely emotive, both theoretically and practically. It is also clear that the use of ethics can be an effective organizational tool to create ethical workplaces and even inspire ethical behavior in the greater society.

Nevertheless, Leon is correct that the current record to date is dismal. This book, and especially this chapter, proposes a fresh new approach to organizational ethics that—if applied—could change the record from dismal to successful. Charles Beard, one of the founders of modern public administration, said: "I am convinced that the world is not a mere bog in which men and women trample themselves . . . and die. Something magnificent is taking place here amid the cruelties and tragedies, and the supreme challenge to intelligence is that of making the noblest and best in our curious heritage prevail" (cited in Morris 1997, 85). The use of organizational ethics can be successful once organizational leaders comprehend how to efficiently use ethics and exercise their will to do so.

THEORETICAL ASSUMPTIONS

CONCEPTUAL RELATIONSHIPS

Whether announced or not, all authors base their theories on hypothetical assumptions. The conceptual relationship assumption used in this approach to ethics is that certain determined factors (the secondary independent variable) will influence the workability of another determined set of factors (the primary independent variables) and that in turn will influence another set of factors (the dependent variables). Exhibit 12.1 illustrates these interrelationships.

The secondary independent variable in this special relativity theory is a mix of selfish and selfless consciousness of the organization's employees concerning how each person identifies their "self." For example, ego-centered, hedonistic people identify themselves as individuated body and mind. Alternatively, altruistic people identify themselves as being an integral part of the everything or at least of humankind. Thus, for them, harm to anyone is considered harm to them. Most people are not exclusively one type or another but rather a mix of both selfishness and selflessness. For example, a person might be predominately altruistic in her belief that harming anyone harms her, but she might be somewhat ego-centered when it comes to her family, in that, caring for family is more important than work for helping others.

This combination of egoism and altruism in an organization defines the employee's "self" *and that* influences the workability of the primary independent variable, which is a mix of organizational procedures, management practices, and normative ethical theories in the workplace. The various normative ethical theories are the motivators of that primary independent mix. As discussed previously, the most significant normative theory is the rule-based ethics associated with the philosopher Immanuel Kant. The least significant is consequential ethics associated with the philosophers Jeremy Bentham and John Stuart Mill. Virtue ethics, associated with the philosophers Aristotle and most recently Alasdair MacIntyre, was influential for centuries but lost its influence in the twentieth century. It is now regaining influence.

The dependent variable—the desired moral behavior—is the same conceptually but in practice

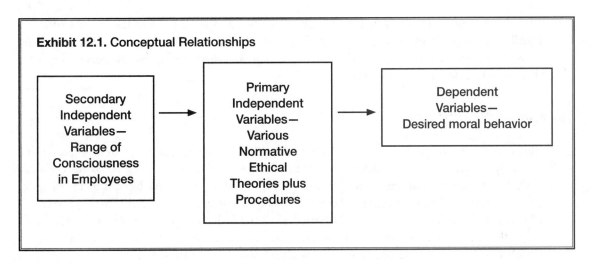

Exhibit 12.1. Conceptual Relationships

Secondary Independent Variables— Range of Consciousness in Employees → Primary Independent Variables— Various Normative Ethical Theories plus Procedures → Dependent Variables— Desired moral behavior

may vary depending on the contextual situation. Some of the common ethical outcomes for most public organizations in the United States include wanting a safe and hospitable work environment with no corruption, no racism, and no sexism. Contextual situations vary because organization missions vary and therefore the context in which organization exist are not the same. For example, a police department might be concerned about the common ethical outcomes but might also be particularly concerned about creating a strong "police-to-community relationship." To achieve that end, the behavior of the police toward a minority community might be especially important in establishing that positive relationship.

UNITY OF OPPOSITES

The secondary independent variable—selfish-selfless mix—appears to be linear. Some might interpret it as a continuum from extreme egoism to extreme altruism or simply two discrete attributes. However, it can and should be understood as a unity of opposites, as explained in chapter 1. This variable depends on a person's conscious awareness, which consists of three moral ideal types: egocentric thinkers, altruistic thinkers, and mixed thinkers. It appears to be a continuum because, in the understanding of an expanded "self," it is easy to organize individuals from being egocentric to being completely caring and compassionate for everyone and everything. Between the first and last points on a scale, the ever-increasing degree of caring and compassion is easily understood as a continuum. However, the relationship of selfish to selfless is better thought of as a unity of opposites because, as in any such relationship, the key polar concepts of selfish and selfless help define each other. The advantage of viewing the relationship as a unity of opposites is that two views normally exist in persons at the same time despite the fact they conflict. The mix depends on the varying values of the individual. For example, a man can have a strong allegiance to his country while at the same time having stronger feelings about his home and family. A woman can be egocentric about herself in every way except her child where she is very altruistic.

There are several assessment tools available for determining where employees fall in the selfish to selfless unity of opposites. For example, the "Personal Values Card Sort" developed by W. R.

Miller et al. (2001) reveals the values that define the person we want to be. The "Narcissistic Personally Inventory" (NPI-16), developed by Danial R. Ames et al. (2006) is a measure of narcissism. Anyone or combination of several should provide a good snapshot of where the person fits in the unity of opposites on a variety of issues.

THE THEORY'S PRACTICALITY

This approach to ethical theory can help organizational leaders realize that they can mandate desired ethical values and their organization ethicists can achieve organizational moral behavior consistent with the organization's desired ethical values. The organization's top leadership can define their desired organizational ethical values; and ethicists, within the organization, can design the correct mix of normative theories, procedures, and practices to establish the desired moral behavior. This theory helps the ethicists understand what employee consciousness characteristics will inhibit or enhance the effectiveness of specific normative theories, procedures, and practices. Knowing this, ethicists can create the desired ethical climates within an organization. By its nature, descriptive theory cannot tell a person how they ought to make good or bad moral decisions but it can help organizational ethicists decide what specific normative theories, procedures, and practices would be the most successful in guiding and directing employees toward the desire moral behavior. In addition, descriptive theory can assist in the development of performance indicators to inform the top policy makers and ethicists if the mandated ethical outcomes are working as they wished.

If the ethicists' expected moral outcomes are not achieved as intended, there can be three reasons: (1) the implementation of the ethicists' intervention was done poorly, (2) unanticipated outside factors affected the moral behavior in an unexpected manner, and (3) the descriptive / normative theories used were not valid. To determine which reason or combination of reasons prevents a successful outcome, a set of reporting practices need to exist. Exhibit 12.2 explains the key reporting feedback loops. Each of the three reasons are addressed to identify the problem because together they determine whether the theory and its application are producing the desired moral behavior within the organization.

Progress reporting is needed to see if the primary independent variables—organization procedures, practices, and normative ethics—are in place and working as expected. Evaluation of the ethical outcomes is needed to see if the outcomes are the desired ethical outcomes of the organization's leadership. Monitoring the influence of outside factors tells us if outside factors are possibly influencing the dependent variables. If the evaluation reporting systems indicate that the desired ethical outcomes are not being achieved but the primary independent variables such as organization procedures, practices, and normative ethics are working as planned, then either outside factors are preventing success in achieving the desired moral behavior (dependent variables) or the theory itself is wrong. The outside factors can normally be eliminated as a reason for not achieving the desired moral behavior (dependent variables) by monitoring them and determining if they are negatively influencing the organization procedures, practices, and normative ethics (the primary dependent variables). Empirical investigation can determine if the theory is positively assisting in the use the organization procedures, practices, and normative ethics (primary independent variables) to help organizations create the desired moral behavior within the targeted organizations. Once the theory is subsequently affirmed, the organizational ethicists have a new and useful tool.

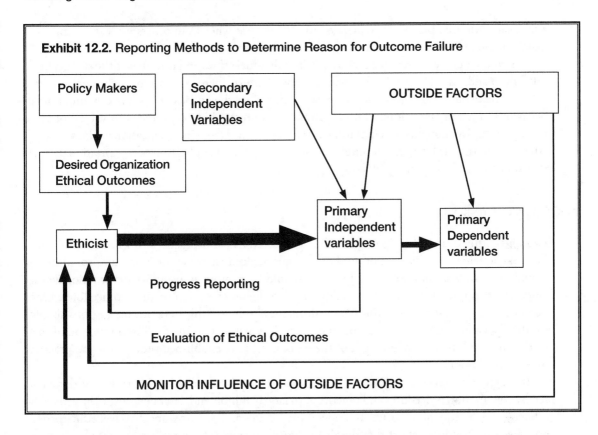

Exhibit 12.2. Reporting Methods to Determine Reason for Outcome Failure

This approach can be quantified. Ethicists can create and employ computer modeling that comes very close to predicting which combination of normative theory, procedures, and practices will most likely create a set of desired moral outcomes in given situations. Computer modeling will lower the costs of implementing ethical interventions because costly trial and error methods of ethical interventions will not be needed. The applications of computer modeling can create increased predictive approaches to using normative ethics, procedures, and practices to achieve desired ethical behavior within organizations in varying organizational contextual situations.

DEFINING THE DEPENDENT VARIABLES

ORGANIZATIONAL RIGHT CONDUCT

When the subject of ethics is raised, the unit of analysis is normally the individual. However, in this chapter, the focus of ethics is for the organization to achieve desired ethical behavior within itself. *Ethics* concerns right and wrong human behavior, but that behavior can be in the context of an individual or an organization. The ancient Greeks focused on the desired individual outcome of ethics and reached two different conclusions. For example, Aristippus and Epicurus were hedonists whereas Plato and Aristotle were rationalists. To some, living the *good life* meant living a life that optimized pleasure and avoided unpleasantness whereas to others it meant living a life *worthy* of being lived as a contributing citizen to the community.

This conflict of views creates a dichotomy in individual ethics and thus makes the subject more difficult to address. However, in an organizational context, there need not be dichotomous views because the organization's top leadership can define what they consider right and wrong human behavior in their organizational context. Thus, the conflicting ideology, religious values, or some untested intuitive thoughts need not influence fundamental values in organizational ethics. Instead, ethicists can base the likely ethical intervention on a consistent application of organizational values that apply scientifically obtained facts.

EGOCENTRIC THINKERS

Egocentric thinkers tend to ignore or sabotage procedures and practices to gain material benefits from activities such as corruption. For example, egocentric persons can impair procedures by arguing that they should not apply to them, should be eliminated using whatever rationale that works for them, or bribe officials to allow them to be an exception to those procedures. Once hedonists are successful in negating a procedure, they often will fully take advantage of its absence for their personal gain. The success of an egocentric person's resistance will be a function of their intelligence and the level of strength of the weakness of the established procedures and practices of the organization.

This type of behavior is highly predictable and ethicists can normally identify it. If done correctly, organization procedures and practices can largely inhibit and deter hedonistic thinkers, who sabotage organizational activities. To know if procedures and practices are effective, ethicists need an active organizational effort that monitors the effectiveness of their intervention. If procedures and practices are unsuccessful or have limited success, organizational leaders and ethicists should be in a position to remedy the problem.

Consequential ethics can motivate egocentric thinkers to act morally. Because this type of thinker is self-interested (a hedonist), motivating them is a matter of appealing to what they believe is pleasure and helping them avoid what they believe is pain. A good example of this is classical capitalism developed by Adam Smith. In that economic theory, individuals and corporations are in business to make a profit but the presence of competition curbs the success of profit seeking while encouraging the business to produce useful goods and services for society. However, if there is insufficient competition, businesses can overcharge for their goods and services, which makes the business very wealth while the members of society pay unnecessary higher prices. This becomes a transfer of wealth from the lower and middle class to the upper economic class. For consequential ethics to be successful, the egocentric thinker must believe that being ethical is in their own best interest and is a means to reap some sort of material gain. Thus, if successful, consequential ethics manipulates egocentric thinkers by taking advantage of their greed.

Using consequential ethics in an organizational setting can involve removing the opportunity for personal or corrupt gain from employees and moving those gains to the organization. Susan Rose Ackerman (1999) suggests that this is often done by letting employees or customers pay an extra fee to the organization in order to get special treatment that would otherwise be rendered through bribes paid to lower-level employees. The purpose of the bribe—to get special treatment—still exists but the money goes to the organization rather than to the corrupt employee. This simple practice avoids various low-level types of bribery in an organization. An example of this is premium parking slots in an organization's parking lot. A low-level employee in "human resources" gives premier parking spots to those employees who give the employee a bribe. A consequential ethics remedy is to have the organization offer their employees the opportunity to pay a little extra for a premier parking slots. This eliminates the low-level corruption and the organization gains an additional revenue stream.

Rule-based ethics cannot motivate egocentric thinkers to be ethical unless there is some punishment or reward associated with a rule. In fact, rules usually do not motivate this type of thinker. The rewards and punishments are motivational as they incentivize the individual to move toward the desired moral behavior within the organization. However, those rewards and punishments must be sufficiently valuable or harmful to the person to establish the desired behavior.

Businesses and sometimes public organizations reward productive employees with a bonus. This motivator is really another name for a legal bribe but it is an inducement that society and government consider ethical. Interestingly, when bonuses are used in the public sector, they often do not motivate better productivity. Instead, they motivate misreporting organizational performance. Alternatively, organizations can use punishments as motivators. For example, an organization may wish to eliminate sexual harassment in their workplace. Merely saying sexual harassment is ethically wrong rarely motivates a change in behavior, but using serious penalties to get the employee's attention does motivate proper moral behavior.

Virtue ethics can also motivate egocentric thinkers to be ethical. However, it is a time-consuming and costly process. First, ethicists must do an employee assessment of their "self" worldview (selfish or selfless) because the approach of training egocentric and altruistic employees is significantly different. Next, an ethics training program for egocentric thinkers is developed and conducted, the effectiveness of the training is assessed, and the virtue training is updated based on what was learned in the training evaluation. The purpose of the training is for the trainees to lose bad moral habits and acquire good habitual behavior. If the trainees preform correctly, they will need some type of reward such as a bonus and a certificate for successfully completing the training. If they perform poorly, they will need some sort of punishment or negative consequence such as having to repeat the training.

Follow-through is important in virtue ethics training. An active evaluation effort is important to assess whether the training is achieving its objective of changing moral behavior. If it is not and the ethicists believe the training was not done correctly, then they must improve the training by reconsidering the normative theory at its core or the implementation of the training. In addition, employees must maintain the instilled good virtues. If bad behavior reappears and good behavior is no longer present, repeat training is necessary. The ethicist trainers need to understand the complexities of virtue ethics and consider how they can use scenarios to motivate egocentric thinkers.

Virtue ethics requires highly educated and trained ethicists who can identify likely scenarios of misbehavior, create the necessary training so that proper behavior is instinctive, and evaluate ongoing behavior within the organization. If successful, even the most egocentric trainees will be able to develop good ethical habits. Good training can direct hedonists toward caring and compassionate behavior while blocking their focus on self-gratification.

ALTRUISTIC THINKERS

Procedures and practices are something an altruistic person can accept but also easily reject. Selfless thinkers must believe the procedures and practices are not only consistent with their *values* but that the procedures and practices actually promote what they believe is important. If they think otherwise, organizational leaders must not place them in situations that require them to follow those procedures or practices. Even when the procedures are consistent with altruistic thinkers' values, they are very likely to use their intellect to try to improve the existing procedures or practices to maximize their personal altruistic values.

Altruistic thinkers approach consequential and rule-based ethics differently than egocentric thinkers do. A selfless person rejects the fundamental assumption of the greatest good for the greatest number because from their point of view it marginalizes the minority. Anything less than the whole is antithetical to altruistic thinkers. Rule-based ethics will only motivate selfless thinkers to be ethical if they rationally agree with the values that created the rules and they believe them to be fair. Thus, if they deem the rules will benefit society as defined by their *values*, they will often enthusiastically embrace those rules. However, if they think the rules are dysfunctional from the perspective of caring and compassion, altruists will resist those rules. Thus, these thinkers can be the leading supporters or the primary rebels of any given set of rules.

Leaders in organizations need to appeal to the altruists' rational minds and their caring and compassionate hearts. If that rational element is not present in their preparation, the training will probably not be successful. Thus, ethicists should consider them to be truly important educational and leadership challenges. Altruistic thinkers tend to be reformers related to liberal but sometimes conservative causes. Because "internal goods" motivate them, ethicists need to determine what their internal goods are and speak to them accordingly.

Altruistic thinkers approach virtue ethics rationally in terms of their values just as they do in rule-based ethics. Ethicists need to determine if the altruistic person shares the organization's *values*. If they do, the ethicists need to rationally stress that consistency and create tutoring programs that reinforce that fact. After the ethicists identify the desired virtues for the altruistic thinker, they, with the assistance of the trainers, decide on what virtues to aim for that are consistent with enhancing the employees values. The effort to establish virtues for selfless thinkers can take more time than for hedonists. Both involve acquiring desirable habits and losing undesirable habits through a training regimen. The challenge rests with the trainee's acceptance of the organization's telos. If that proves impossible or even very difficult in either case, that trainee really is not a good fit for the organization.

MIXED THINKERS

Mixed selfish and selfless thinkers reason using a unity of opposites that depends on the context of the situation. In other words, mixed thinkers are going to be selfish in some circumstances and selfless in others. However, a note of caution is necessary. A selfish person can appear selfless in terms of family but on more careful consideration what appears to be selfless family caring is merely thinking of the family members as being an extension of themselves. To be truly selfless, the family members need to be thought in terms of their individual worth to the family. For example, a selfless person would consider and accept a family member that chooses to go their own way on an important family issue but a selfish person is not so accepting.

Thinking about ethical choices in practical living situations is more easily understood because of the unity of opposites concept. Mixed thinkers believe that sometimes it is appropriate to be selfish but other times to be selfless. Life choices happen in a situational context and circumstances influence the decision in what appears to be selfish or selfless behavior. Thus, this apparent mixing may seem inconsistent unless one realizes the mixing occurs due to a unity of opposites context that exists in the mind of the person. For example, a man with remarkable musical talent practices a great deal to bring out and sharpen his potential artistic abilities and in that process neglects others. Thus, his practicing seems self-centered but he knows his contribution to the joy of others depends on mastering his musical skill through practice. Is the budding musical genius selfish or selfless? If he only wishes to improve musically for himself or for a higher paid contract, he is selfish. However, if he wishes to share the consequence of his developed genius with others or improve the art form, then he is selfless. Often, a selfless versus selfish determination is not a function of what occurs but rather the actor's intention.

WORKING WITH MIXED THINKERS

Two factors need to be identified when working with mixed thinkers in order to create a desired ethical environment in an organization. What conditions or situations bring out their selflessness and their selfishness? For example, a woman can be remarkably selfless about sharing the workload in the office and meeting office goals until she is asked to work on a weekend, which would interfere with her family responsibilities. In an organizational setting, ethicists must at times appeal to the selfless altruistic conditions and at other times use a hedonistic approach to ethics in egocentric conditions. If the conditions tend to demand a mixed use of self-identity consciousness after analyzing the circumstances, the ethicists must decide on an approach that will most likely produce the best ethical outcomes. For example, acceptance that asking employees to work overtime on the weekends should be avoided. But, what situations could override the employee's selflessness or selfishness to agree to work? If family and work emergencies occur at the same time, what factors must exist for the employee to decide to go to the work emergency that will not harm her family? Or, can the agency somehow take care of her family in a work emergency.

These factors determine the extent and character of a person's selflessness and selfishness. The context of selfless and selfish can be narrow or broad in various situations. For the ethicist, knowing the degree of narrowness and broadness as well as the trigger for the contextual situations is an important insight in developing an organizational ethical intervention plan. Another related challenge for the ethicist is realizing that a selfish person can use selfless arguments and rhetoric to influence organizations to bend to their desires. For example, an ego-centered employee can appear supportive of top management goals in order to get more upper management support for their particular materialistic interests within the organization. The challenge for the ethicists is to recognize such individuals and develop the proper ethical training to address such behavior if that is appropriate in the context of the organization.

All ethical interventions need to recognize that all the types of thinkers—selfish, selfless, and mixed—do exist. Being aware of that and the varying degrees within each group is the starting point in designing the primary independent variables (organization procedures and practices as well as normative ethical theories). Also realizing that not all employees are likely to have the same impact on organizational ethical behavior is important. Thus, the task of the ethicist in considering the primary independent variables is truly a professional challenge.

PRIMARY INDEPENDENT VARIABLES

USING PROCEDURES AND PRACTICES

Procedures and practices influence employees to behave morally and therefore they are important tools. For example, double entry accounting is detailed and time-consuming but it is an excellent procedure in helping to minimize corruption because it makes faking the accounting records much more difficult and thus lowers the likelihood of financial corruption. Requiring a practice of having two separate people cross-check every count of cash helps avoid human error in counting but it also makes an illegal act less likely as by definition two individuals would need to be involved. Another useful practice is to require periodic audits and special audits when there are personnel changes that involve the handling of money. Using cameras to see what employees and others are doing in the workplace is also a useful practice, especially when involving money handling, inventory control, and sensitive behavior dealing with the public are involved.

The list of possible useful procedures and practices is long and beyond the scope of this chapter, but a few generic considerations are important. First, procedures and practices are useful but they can also be dysfunctional as they can be quite intrusive, expensive, and frustrating, and may lower employee morale or create a distrusting work environment. Ethicists typically are not aware of the usefulness of various procedures and practices and administrative experts need to work with them to develop appropriate ethical intervention plans. Second, technology is evolving fast and procedures and practices need to be reevaluated regularly to assess their relevance in terms of their effectiveness. Third, the correct amount of procedures and practices is conditional and those conditions that do change, thus procedures and practices need to be updated periodically to reflect the changing social values within the larger society.

USING NORMATIVE ETHICAL THEORY

In an organizational approach to creating a desired organization ethical behavior, three normative theories (rule-based ethics, consequential ethics, and virtue ethics) can be used in combination with organizational procedures and practices. Ethicists use all of these normative theories in developing an organizational intervention plan to create the desired organizational ethical outcomes. That plan should be a combination of the three normative theories that are adjusted based upon the secondary independent variables (types of consciousness). What follows is a brief description of the three normative ethical theories and how ethicists can use them to achieve desired moral behavior.

RULE-BASED ETHICS

Rule-based ethics focuses on people's intentions and consequential ethics focuses on the expected outcome of their actions. That dissimilarity is important as rules must motivate human intentions but not all people are motivated by them. As has been mentioned many times, ego-centered people are motivated by the expected material outcome of their actions for themselves directly or indirectly. Thus, this type of employee must be aware of the penalties and rewards associated with following the rule or breaking it and those penalties and rewards must be sufficiently motivational to achieve the desired moral behavior within the organization. For altruistic thinkers, rules can be meaningful without rewards and punishment if they are consistent with their own telos values. Ethicists need to appreciate those realities when they use rules to achieve desired moral behavior.

Additionally, rules might require a complex rational reasoning process on the part of employees that is not realistic in some organization settings. A related problem is that both emotional and logical fallacies can easily creep into the application of rules that can easily produce unintended unethical behavior. Rule-based ethics often demand strong willpower beyond what can be expected in consequential ethics. To deal with that reality, organizations create ethics boards to respond to confused employees' questions about the rules. Certainly, the use of an ethics board is often helpful in many situations but may not be practical in all organizational situations. For example, if a policeman is in a violent arresting situation that requires instant decision making, getting a timely answer to an inquiry on an action from an ethics board is obviously impossible. If a review is done in an after action report and the officer is found to have breached an ethics rule, that report can have a devastating effect on his or her career.

CONSEQUENTIAL ETHICS

In the past few decades, the second most used normative ethics has been consequential / utilitarianism ethics. It is remarkably influential on a personal level in determining what is good and bad but also in economic thought as proper economic interventions to achieve a desired social and economic outcome. For example, utilitarianism very much influences the use of the economic analytical technique of cost-benefit analysis when employed to determine the "best" project to fund.

Consequential ethics is hedonistic, but less so than the Ancient Greece version. Thus, consequential ethics works with hedonists but it does not work not as well for altruistic employees. This ethical theory defines "good" not in terms of the "good life" or as "a life worth living" but rather in terms of what will achieve the most pleasure and avoid pain for the greatest number. It is often used in organizational decision making for deciding if the goods (benefits) are greater than the costs (punishments or other negative outcomes). To apply consequential ethics in an organizational setting, ethicists often need to know complex mathematics (e.g., statistics). To use this normative ethics theory, an ethicist sometimes creates a contextual situation for employees to encourage them to make ethical decisions that fit the organization leaders' values.

An example of its application is when an ethicist is called upon to discourage city fire marshals from taking bribes. If the low paid fire marshals are hedonists and are aware that they would be dismissed if they are caught taking a bribe, the ethicist could reason that those negative consequences could be strengthened to discourage taking bribes. Another consequential intervention is to increase the salary of fire marshals to make them value their jobs more. Yet another intervention could be to make the criminal penalties much more severe. This dual approach of reward and punishment might prove successful unless the bribes are very large or the employees are not hedonists and thus not influenced by such interventions.

VIRTUE ETHICS

Virtue ethics requires a high degree of rationality and the ability to turn that rationality into habitual practices. Individual employees can rationally decide what virtues they wish to have and not have. They establish for themselves new positive habits that reflect the organization's values and lose negative habits that are inconsistent with those values. For most, such a task is remarkably difficult to accomplish without support. Alternatively, the organization can employee ethicists who are trained in virtue ethics and how to avoid logical fallacies discussed in chapter 8. Organizational leaders can define values that create the kind of moral climate that they wish for their organization. The ethicists are tasked to take those values and define the virtues and training necessary to achieve the desired moral behavior.

Ethicists establish virtues in employees through training that creates positive habitual behavior and loses negative habitual behavior. Virtue ethics is a two-step process. First, either the employee or organizational ethicists decide what virtues are desired given the organizations values. The employee or ethicist then rationally decide what training is appropriate to create the desired virtues and lose the negative ones and design that helps the employee create a new positive habit training. In almost all circumstances, organizational ethicists are better educated and skilled to select the needed virtues and do the necessary training. In creating the habitual behavior based on desired virtues, ethicists must be sensitive to the notion that almost all virtues have extremes—from minimum to maximum—and the zone of the *mean* between the two extremes is most likely the ideal virtue needed for most situations. For example, the ideal virtue of courage is in the mean between cowardice and recklessness. Although that can fluctuate depending on the circumstances of the situation. The virtue of wisdom to assess a situation correctly is always paramount. Ethicists training should include wisdom exercises to help employees understand how to evaluate what is the most appropriate mean in various circumstances.

Organizational ethicists can work with employees who are egocentric, altruistic, and mixed. They can take the wanted ethical outcomes as defined by the organization's leadership and create virtue ethics training to instill the desired habitual responses that create the expected moral behavior within the organization. Altruistic employees tend to be more challenging trainees because they are capable of only accepting training that is in harmony with their fundamental values. When altruistic employees find the organization values are in conflict with their higher values, they feel lost, frustrated, disappointed, and despondent. Such feelings often are manifested as illness, acting out in the workplace, or just quitting. Given that altruistic employees can be remarkable contributors to the organization, leaders should be open to reconsidering the organization's values occasionally.

CONCLUSION

Leon is correct. Organizations have a dismal record of effectively using ethics. Too often an organization's use of ethics is feeble and ineffectual. For example, codes of ethics are posted on walls but few bother to read them. A very small percentage of employees is influenced by them. Calls to act with integrity are ignored or met with confusion as to how that can be accomplished. Rules grow in complexity and eventually are beyond being useful in the workplace. Ethics officers are often assigned to senior staff "as other duties as assigned" and have little if any formal ethics training. A one-size-fits-all approach is often used to achieve the desired employee moral behavior. Realistically, one ethical intervention strategy is not appropriate for all employees because various employees react differently to normative ethics, procedures, and standards. With the failure of organizational ethical intervention, bad moral behavior increases and even formerly good employees ignore behaviors through their moral muteness (Bird and Waters 1989, 73). Over time that immorality can spread like a cancer throughout the whole organization.

Why are policy makers and ethicists unsuccessful in achieving good ethical practices within their organizations? Today, most ethicists are trained exclusively in Kantian ethics and ignore other procedurals and practices that can be useful. They fail to apply a holistic ethical intervention and often exclude the use of virtue ethics that includes wisdom training. At the federal level most employee training for ethics is an annual one-hour session covering changes in ethics-related laws or a required computer exercise that is designed for all employees regardless of their level of self-consciousness. Without sensitivity to the individual's needs for ethics education, organization policy leaders somehow think that they can decree ethical problems away. Policy leaders and ethicists fail to accept that ethics within organizations is an ongoing process that must always be about trying to achieve wanted moral outcomes and their ethical interventions must be continuously be adapting to changing circumstances within and outside the organization.

However, Leon's pessimism is wrong. Organization ethics is not a lost cause. It just requires deeper and more nuanced thinking and a full throated commitment to training. The recommended changes to organizational ethics require a huge institutional commitment of time and effort. However, the benefits to organizations are also enormous in such matters as reducing corruption, ending sexual harassment in the workplace, and bringing an end to racism and sexism within organizations. This recommended approach to organizational ethics will permit ethicists to effectively plan to achieve policy makers' desired ethical outcomes as they evolve, including adjusting training to address any shortcomings in achieving desired ethical outcomes. Creating ethical organizations is an ongoing process that can create remarkably positive work environments in even the most challenging workplace.

REVIEW QUESTIONS

1. This chapter uses both descriptive and normative ethics. What part is descriptive? What part is normative? Do they complement each other while not violating the "is" and "ought" difference?

2. Describe the challenge presented by Charles Beard in this chapter? What is it?

3. This chapter builds on a key conceptual relationship. What is it?

4. In what way does the secondary independent variable drive the dependent variable?

5. This chapter discusses continuum and unity of opposites. Compare and contrast the two. Why is the difference conceptually important?

6. In what way is the presented special relativity theory for organizational ethics practical? In what way is this theory special? In what way is this relative?

7. There are three feedback loops in this theory. How are they of practical use?

8. The two units of analysis in ethics are the individual and the organization. Why is this distinction important in terms of creating a practical and useful ethics theory?

9. Compare and contrast the egocentric and altruistic thinkers.

10. In what way is the mixed thinker more complex than either the egocentric or altruistic thinker?

11. Explain why procedures and practices should be considered as elements of an organizational ethics theory.

12. Why do organizations often have a dismal record of ethical effectiveness?

13. Why should organizational ethics not be considered a lost cause?

REFERENCES

Ackerman, Susan Rose. 1999. *Corruption and Government: Causes, Consequences, and Reform.* Cambridge, UK: Cambridge University Press.

Ames, Danial R. Paul Rose and Cameron P, Anderson. 2006. "The NPI-16 as a Short Measure of Narcissism." *Journal of Research in Personality,* 40, no.4: 440–450.

Aristotle. 1980. *The Nicomachean Ethics.* Oxford: Oxford University Press.

Bird, Frederick B., and James A. Waters. 1989. "The Moral Muteness of Managers." *California Management Review* (Fall): 73–88.

Cooper, Terry. 1987. "Hierarchy, Virtue, and the Practice of Public Administration." *Public Administration Review*" 47, no. 4: 320–328.

Government Accounting Office. 1994. Now the Government Accountability Office. https://www.gao.gov/about /index.html.

Government Accounting Standards Board. 1994. https://www.gasb.org/jsp/GASB/Page/GASB LandingPage &cid=1176160042327. Accessed July 18, 2018.

Louisiana Board of Ethics. n.d. http://www.ncsl.org/portals/1/documents/ethics/louisiana.pdf. Accessed on July 18, 2018.

Miller, W. R., J.C'de Baca, D. B. Matthews, and P. L. Wilbourne, 2001. "*Personal Values Card Sort.*" Albuquerque: University of New Mexico. www.motivationalinterviewing.org/sites/default/files/valuescardsort_0.pdf. Accessed July 23, 2018.

Morris, Tom. 1997. *If Aristotle Ran General Motors: The New Soul of Business.* New York: Henry Holt.

Appendix

U.S. Constitution and Amendments

Written in 1787, ratified in 1788, and in effect since 1789, the U.S. Constitution is the world's longest surviving written charter of government. It has remained in force for over two centuries and successfully separates and balances governmental powers in a way that (a) safeguards majority rule while protecting minority rights, (b) preserves individual liberty and equality, and (c) sets the boundaries for federal versus state powers. More a concise statement of national principles than a detailed plan of operation, interpretation of the Constitution continually evolves to meet the changing needs of a society profoundly different from the eighteenth-century world of its creation. The Constitution has been amended twenty-seven times, most recently in 1992. The first ten amendments are called the Bill of Rights.

Preamble

We the People of the United States, in Order to form a more perfect Union, establish Justice, insure domestic Tranquility, provide for the common defence, promote the general Welfare, and secure the Blessings of Liberty to ourselves and our Posterity, do ordain and establish this Constitution for the United States of America.

Article I

Section 1

All legislative Powers herein granted shall be vested in a Congress of the United States, which shall consist of a Senate and House of Representatives.

Section 2

The House of Representatives shall be composed of Members chosen every second Year by the People of the several States, and the Electors in each State shall have the Qualifications requisite for Electors of the most numerous Branch of the State Legislature.

No Person shall be a Representative who shall not have attained to the Age of twenty five Years, and been seven Years a Citizen of the United States, and who shall not, when elected, be an Inhabitant of that State in which he shall be chosen.

Representatives and direct Taxes shall be apportioned among the several States which may be included within this Union, according to their respective Numbers, which shall be determined by adding to the whole Number of free Persons, including those bound to Service for a Term of Years, and excluding Indians not taxed, three fifths of all other Persons. The actual Enumeration shall be made within three Years after the first Meeting of the Congress of the United States, and within every subsequent Term of ten Years, in such Manner as they shall by Law direct. The Number of Representatives shall not exceed one for every thirty Thousand, but each State shall have at Least one Representative; and until such enumeration shall be made, the State of New Hampshire shall be entitled to chuse three, Massachusetts eight, Rhode-Island and Providence Plantations one, Connecticut five, New York six, New Jersey four, Pennsylvania eight, Delaware one, Maryland six, Virginia ten, North Carolina five, South Carolina five, and Georgia three.

When vacancies happen in the Representation from any State, the Executive Authority thereof shall issue Writs of Election to fill such Vacancies.

The House of Representatives shall chuse their Speaker and other Officers; and shall have the sole Power of Impeachment.

Section 3

The Senate of the United States shall be composed of two Senators from each State, chosen by the Legislature thereof, for six Years; and each Senator shall have one Vote.

Immediately after they shall be assembled in Consequence of the first Election, they shall be divided as equally as may be into three Classes. The Seats of the Senators of the first Class shall be vacated at the Expiration of the second Year, of the second Class at the Expiration of the fourth Year, and of the third Class at the Expiration of the sixth Year, so that one third may be chosen every second Year; and if Vacancies happen by Resignation, or otherwise, during the Recess of the Legislature of any State, the Executive thereof may make temporary Appointments until the next Meeting of the Legislature, which shall then fill such Vacancies.

No Person shall be a Senator who shall not have attained to the Age of thirty Years, and been nine Years a Citizen of the United States, and who shall not, when elected, be an Inhabitant of that State for which he shall be chosen.

The Vice President of the United States shall be President of the Senate, but shall have no Vote, unless they be equally divided.

The Senate shall chuse their other Officers, and also a President pro tempore, in the Absence of the Vice President, or when he shall exercise the Office of President of the United States.

The Senate shall have the sole Power to try all Impeachments. When sitting for that Purpose, they shall be on Oath or Affirmation. When the President of the United States is tried, the Chief Justice shall preside: And no Person shall be convicted without the Concurrence of two thirds of the Members present.

Judgment in Cases of Impeachment shall not extend further than to removal from Office, and disqualification to hold and enjoy any Office of honor, Trust or Profit under the United States: but the Party convicted shall nevertheless be liable and subject to Indictment, Trial, Judgment and Punishment, according to Law.

SECTION 4

The Times, Places and Manner of holding Elections for Senators and Representatives, shall be prescribed in each State by the Legislature thereof; but the Congress may at any time by Law make or alter such Regulations, except as to the Places of chusing Senators.

The Congress shall assemble at least once in every Year, and such Meeting shall be on the first Monday in December, unless they shall by Law appoint a different Day.

SECTION 5

Each House shall be the Judge of the Elections, Returns and Qualifications of its own Members, and a Majority of each shall constitute a Quorum to do Business; but a smaller Number may adjourn from day to day, and may be authorized to compel the Attendance of absent Members, in such Manner, and under such Penalties as each House may provide.

Each House may determine the Rules of its Proceedings, punish its Members for disorderly Behaviour, and, with the Concurrence of two thirds, expel a Member.

Each House shall keep a Journal of its Proceedings, and from time to time publish the same, excepting such Parts as may in their Judgment require Secrecy; and the Yeas and Nays of the Members of either House on any question shall, at the Desire of one fifth of those Present, be entered on the Journal.

Neither House, during the Session of Congress, shall, without the Consent of the other, adjourn for more than three days, nor to any other Place than that in which the two Houses shall be sitting.

SECTION 6

The Senators and Representatives shall receive a Compensation for their Services, to be ascertained by Law, and paid out of the Treasury of the United States. They shall in all Cases, except Treason, Felony and Breach of the Peace, be privileged from Arrest during their Attendance at the Session of their respective Houses, and in going to and returning from the same; and for any Speech or Debate in either House, they shall not be questioned in any other Place.

No Senator or Representative shall, during the Time for which he was elected, be appointed to any civil Office under the Authority of the United States, which shall have been created, or the Emoluments whereof shall have been encreased during such time; and no Person holding any Office under the United States, shall be a Member of either House during his Continuance in Office.

Section 7

All Bills for raising Revenue shall originate in the House of Representatives; but the Senate may propose or concur with Amendments as on other Bills.

Every Bill which shall have passed the House of Representatives and the Senate, shall, before it become a Law, be presented to the President of the United States: If he approve he shall sign it, but if not he shall return it, with his Objections to that House in which it shall have originated, who shall enter the Objections at large on their Journal, and proceed to reconsider it. If after such Reconsideration two thirds of that House shall agree to pass the Bill, it shall be sent, together with the Objections, to the other House, by which it shall likewise be reconsidered, and if approved by two thirds of that House, it shall become a Law. But in all such Cases the Votes of both Houses shall be determined by Yeas and Nays, and the Names of the Persons voting for and against the Bill shall be entered on the Journal of each House respectively. If any Bill shall not be returned by the President within ten Days (Sundays excepted) after it shall have been presented to him, the Same shall be a Law, in like Manner as if he had signed it, unless the Congress by their Adjournment prevent its Return, in which Case it shall not be a Law.

Every Order, Resolution, or Vote to which the Concurrence of the Senate and House of Representatives may be necessary (except on a question of Adjournment) shall be presented to the President of the United States; and before the Same shall take Effect, shall be approved by him, or being disapproved by him, shall be repassed by two thirds of the Senate and House of Representatives, according to the Rules and Limitations prescribed in the Case of a Bill.

Section 8

The Congress shall have Power To lay and collect Taxes, Duties, Imposts and Excises, to pay the Debts and provide for the common Defence and general Welfare of the United States; but all Duties, Imposts and Excises shall be uniform throughout the United States;

To borrow Money on the credit of the United States;

To regulate Commerce with foreign Nations, and among the several States, and with the Indian Tribes;

To establish an uniform Rule of Naturalization, and uniform Laws on the subject of Bankruptcies throughout the United States;

To coin Money, regulate the Value thereof, and of foreign Coin, and fix the Standard of Weights and Measures;

To provide for the Punishment of counterfeiting the Securities and current Coin of the United States;

To establish Post Offices and post Roads;

To promote the Progress of Science and useful Arts, by securing for limited Times to Authors and Inventors the exclusive Right to their respective Writings and Discoveries;

To constitute Tribunals inferior to the supreme Court;

To define and punish Piracies and Felonies committed on the high Seas, and Offences against the Law of Nations;

To declare War, grant Letters of Marque and Reprisal, and make Rules concerning Captures on Land and Water;

To raise and support Armies, but no Appropriation of Money to that Use shall be for a longer Term than two Years;

To provide and maintain a Navy;

To make Rules for the Government and Regulation of the land and naval Forces;

To provide for calling forth the Militia to execute the Laws of the Union, suppress Insurrections and repel Invasions;

To provide for organizing, arming, and disciplining, the Militia, and for governing such Part of them as may be employed in the Service of the United States, reserving to the States respectively, the Appointment of the Officers, and the Authority of training the Militia according to the discipline prescribed by Congress;

To exercise exclusive Legislation in all Cases whatsoever, over such District (not exceeding ten Miles square) as may, by Cession of particular States, and the Acceptance of Congress, become the Seat of the Government of the United States, and to exercise like Authority over all Places purchased by the Consent of the Legislature of the State in which the Same shall be, for the Erection of Forts, Magazines, Arsenals, dock-Yards, and other needful Buildings;—And

To make all Laws which shall be necessary and proper for carrying into Execution the foregoing Powers, and all other Powers vested by this Constitution in the Government of the United States, or in any Department or Officer thereof.

SECTION 9

The Migration or Importation of such Persons as any of the States now existing shall think proper to admit, shall not be prohibited by the Congress prior to the Year one thousand eight hundred and eight, but a Tax or duty may be imposed on such Importation, not exceeding ten dollars for each Person.

The Privilege of the Writ of Habeas Corpus shall not be suspended, unless when in Cases of Rebellion or Invasion the public Safety may require it.

No Bill of Attainder or ex post facto Law shall be passed.

No Capitation, or other direct, Tax shall be laid, unless in Proportion to the Census or enumeration herein before directed to be taken.

No Tax or Duty shall be laid on Articles exported from any State.

No Preference shall be given by any Regulation of Commerce or Revenue to the Ports of one State over those of another; nor shall Vessels bound to, or from, one State, be obliged to enter, clear, or pay Duties in another.

No Money shall be drawn from the Treasury, but in Consequence of Appropriations made by Law; and a regular Statement and Account of the Receipts and Expenditures of all public Money shall be published from time to time.

No Title of Nobility shall be granted by the United States: And no Person holding any Office of Profit or Trust under them, shall, without the Consent of the Congress, accept of any present, Emolument, Office, or Title, of any kind whatever, from any King, Prince, or foreign State.

Section 10

No State shall enter into any Treaty, Alliance, or Confederation; grant Letters of Marque and Reprisal; coin Money; emit Bills of Credit; make any Thing but gold and silver Coin a Tender in Payment of Debts; pass any Bill of Attainder, ex post facto Law, or Law impairing the Obligation of Contracts, or grant any Title of Nobility.

No State shall, without the Consent of the Congress, lay any Imposts or Duties on Imports or Exports, except what may be absolutely necessary for executing its inspection Laws: and the net Produce of all Duties and Imposts, laid by any State on Imports or Exports, shall be for the Use of the Treasury of the United States; and all such Laws shall be subject to the Revision and Control of the Congress.

No State shall, without the Consent of Congress, lay any Duty of Tonnage, keep Troops, or Ships of War in time of Peace, enter into any Agreement or Compact with another State, or with a foreign Power, or engage in War, unless actually invaded, or in such imminent Danger as will not admit of delay.

Article II

Section 1

The executive Power shall be vested in a President of the United States of America. He shall hold his Office during the Term of four Years, and, together with the Vice President, chosen for the same Term, be elected, as follows:

Each State shall appoint, in such Manner as the Legislature thereof may direct, a Number of Electors, equal to the whole Number of Senators and Representatives to which the State may be entitled in the Congress: but no Senator or Representative, or Person holding an Office of Trust or Profit under the United States, shall be appointed an Elector.

The Electors shall meet in their respective States, and vote by Ballot for two Persons, of whom one at least shall not be an Inhabitant of the same State with themselves. And they shall make a List of all the Persons voted for, and of the Number of Votes for each; which List they shall sign and certify, and transmit sealed to the Seat of the Government of the United States, directed to the President of the Senate. The President of the Senate shall, in the Presence of the Senate and House of Representatives, open all the Certificates, and the Votes shall then be counted. The Person having the greatest Number of Votes shall be the President, if such Number be a Majority of the whole Number of Electors appointed; and if there be more than one who have such Majority, and have an equal Number of Votes, then the House of Representatives shall immediately chuse by Ballot one of them for President; and if no Person have a Majority, then from the five highest on the List the said House shall in like Manner chuse the President. But in chusing the President, the Votes shall be taken by States, the Representatives from each State having one Vote; a quorum for this Purpose shall consist of a Member or Members from two thirds of the States, and a Majority of all the States shall be necessary to a Choice. In every Case, after the Choice of the President, the Person having the greatest Number of Votes of the Electors shall be the Vice President. But if there should remain two or more who have equal Votes, the Senate shall chuse from them by Ballot the Vice-President.

The Congress may determine the Time of chusing the Electors, and the Day on which they shall give their Votes; which Day shall be the same throughout the United States.

No Person except a natural born Citizen, or a Citizen of the United States, at the time of the Adoption of this Constitution, shall be eligible to the Office of President; neither shall any person be eligible to that Office who shall not have attained to the Age of thirty five Years, and been fourteen Years a Resident within the United States.

In Case of the Removal of the President from Office, or of his Death, Resignation, or Inability to discharge the Powers and Duties of the said Office, the Same shall devolve on the Vice President, and the Congress may by Law provide for the Case of Removal, Death, Resignation or Inability, both of the President and Vice President, declaring what Officer shall then act as President, and such Officer shall act accordingly, until the Disability be removed, or a President shall be elected.

The President shall, at stated Times, receive for his Services, a Compensation, which shall neither be encreased nor diminished during the Period for which he shall have been elected, and he shall not receive within that Period any other Emolument from the United States, or any of them.

Before he enter on the Execution of his Office, he shall take the following Oath or Affirmation:—"I do solemnly swear (or affirm) that I will faithfully execute the Office of President of the United States, and will to the best of my Ability, preserve, protect and defend the Constitution of the United States."

Section 2

The President shall be Commander in Chief of the Army and Navy of the United States, and of the Militia of the several States, when called into the actual Service of the United States; he may require the Opinion, in writing, of the principal Officer in each of the executive Departments, upon any Subject relating to the Duties of their respective Offices, and he shall have Power to Grant Reprieves and Pardons for Offences against the United States, except in Cases of Impeachment.

He shall have Power, by and with the Advice and Consent of the Senate, to make Treaties, provided two thirds of the Senators present concur; and he shall nominate, and by and with the Advice and Consent of the Senate, shall appoint Ambassadors, other public Ministers and Consuls, Judges of the supreme Court, and all other Officers of the United States, whose Appointments are not herein otherwise provided for, and which shall be established by Law: but the Congress may by Law vest the Appointment of such inferior Officers, as they think proper, in the President alone, in the Courts of Law, or in the Heads of Departments.

The President shall have Power to fill up all Vacancies that may happen during the Recess of the Senate, by granting Commissions which shall expire at the End of their next Session.

Section 3

He shall from time to time give to the Congress Information on the State of the Union, and recommend to their Consideration such Measures as he shall judge necessary and expedient; he may, on extraordinary Occasions, convene both Houses, or either of them, and in Case of Disagreement between them, with Respect to the Time of Adjournment, he may adjourn them to such Time as he shall think proper; he shall receive Ambassadors and other public Ministers; he shall take Care that the Laws be faithfully executed, and shall Commission all the Officers of the United States.

SECTION 4

The President, Vice President and all Civil Officers of the United States, shall be removed from Office on Impeachment for, and Conviction of, Treason, Bribery, or other high Crimes and Misdemeanors.

ARTICLE III

SECTION 1

The judicial Power of the United States, shall be vested in one supreme Court, and in such inferior Courts as the Congress may from time to time ordain and establish. The Judges, both of the supreme and inferior Courts, shall hold their Offices during good Behaviour, and shall, at stated Times, receive for their Services, a Compensation, which shall not be diminished during their Continuance in Office.

SECTION 2

The judicial Power shall extend to all Cases, in Law and Equity, arising under this Constitution, the Laws of the United States, and Treaties made, or which shall be made, under their Authority;— to all Cases affecting Ambassadors, other public ministers and Consuls;—to all Cases of admiralty and maritime Jurisdiction;—to Controversies to which the United States shall be a Party;—to Controversies between two or more States;—between a State and Citizens of another State;— between Citizens of different States;—between Citizens of the same State claiming Lands under Grants of different States, and between a State, or the Citizens thereof, and foreign States, Citizens or Subjects.

In all Cases affecting Ambassadors, other public Ministers and Consuls, and those in which a State shall be Party, the supreme Court shall have original Jurisdiction. In all the other Cases before mentioned, the supreme Court shall have appellate Jurisdiction, both as to Law and Fact, with such Exceptions, and under such Regulations as the Congress shall make.

The Trial of all Crimes, except in Cases of Impeachment, shall be by Jury; and such Trial shall be held in the State where the said Crimes shall have been committed; but when not committed within any State, the Trial shall be at such Place or Places as the Congress may by Law have directed.

SECTION 3

Treason against the United States, shall consist only in levying War against them, or in adhering to their Enemies, giving them Aid and Comfort. No Person shall be convicted of

Treason unless on the Testimony of two Witnesses to the same overt Act, or on Confession in open Court.

The Congress shall have Power to declare the Punishment of Treason, but no Attainder of Treason shall work Corruption of Blood, or Forfeiture except during the Life of the Person attainted.

ARTICLE IV

SECTION 1

Full Faith and Credit shall be given in each State to the public Acts, Records, and judicial Proceedings of every other State. And the Congress may by general Laws prescribe the Manner in which such Acts, Records and Proceedings shall be proved, and the Effect thereof.

SECTION 2

The Citizens of each State shall be entitled to all Privileges and Immunities of Citizens in the several States.

A Person charged in any State with Treason, Felony, or other Crime, who shall flee from Justice, and be found in another State, shall on Demand of the executive Authority of the State from which he fled, be delivered up, to be removed to the State having Jurisdiction of the Crime.

No Person held to Service or Labour in one State, under the Laws thereof, escaping into another, shall, in Consequence of any Law or Regulation therein, be discharged from such Service or Labour, but shall be delivered up on Claim of the Party to whom such Service or Labour may be due.

SECTION 3

New States may be admitted by the Congress into this Union; but no new State shall be formed or erected within the Jurisdiction of any other State; nor any State be formed by the Junction of two or more States, or Parts of States, without the Consent of the Legislatures of the States concerned as well as of the Congress.

The Congress shall have Power to dispose of and make all needful Rules and Regulations respecting the Territory or other Property belonging to the United States; and nothing in this Constitution shall be so construed as to Prejudice any Claims of the United States, or of any particular State.

SECTION 4

The United States shall guarantee to every State in this Union a Republican Form of Government, and shall protect each of them against Invasion; and on Application of the Legislature, or of the Executive (when the Legislature cannot be convened) against domestic Violence.

ARTICLE V

The Congress, whenever two thirds of both Houses shall deem it necessary, shall propose Amendments to this Constitution, or, on the Application of the Legislatures of two thirds of the several States, shall call a Convention for proposing Amendments, which, in either Case, shall be valid to all Intents and Purposes, as Part of this Constitution, when ratified by the Legislatures of three fourths of the several States, or by Conventions in three fourths thereof, as the one or the other Mode of Ratification may be proposed by the Congress; Provided that no Amendment which may be made prior to the Year One thousand eight hundred and eight shall in any Manner affect the first and fourth Clauses in the Ninth Section of the first Article; and that no State, without its Consent, shall be deprived of its equal Suffrage in the Senate.

ARTICLE VI

All Debts contracted and Engagements entered into, before the Adoption of this Constitution, shall be as valid against the United States under this Constitution, as under the Confederation.

This Constitution, and the Laws of the United States which shall be made in Pursuance thereof; and all Treaties made, or which shall be made, under the Authority of the United States, shall be the supreme Law of the Land; and the Judges in every State shall be bound thereby, any Thing in the Constitution or Laws of any state to the Contrary notwithstanding.

The Senators and Representatives before mentioned, and the Members of the several State Legislatures, and all executive and judicial Officers, both of the United States and of the several States, shall be bound by Oath or Affirmation, to support this Constitution; but no religious Test shall ever be required as a Qualification to any Office or public Trust under the United States.

ARTICLE VII

The Ratification of the Conventions of nine States, shall be sufficient for the Establishment of this Constitution between the States so ratifying the Same.

Done in Convention by the Unanimous Consent of the States present the Seventeenth Day of September in the Year of our Lord one thousand seven hundred and Eighty seven and of the Independence of the United States of America the Twelfth In Witness whereof We have hereunto subscribed our Names,

G. Washington, Presidt and deputy from Virginia

[signors]

AMENDMENT I (1791)

Congress shall make no law respecting an establishment of religion, or prohibiting the free exercise thereof; or abridging the freedom of speech, or of the press; or the right of the people peaceably to assemble, and to petition the Government for a redress of grievances.

AMENDMENT II (1791)

A well regulated Militia, being necessary to the security of a free State, the right of the people to keep and bear Arms, shall not be infringed.

AMENDMENT III (1791)

No Soldier shall, in time of peace be quartered in any house, without the consent of the Owner, nor in time of war, but in a manner to be prescribed by law.

AMENDMENT IV (1791)

The right of the people to be secure in their persons, houses, papers, and effects, against unreasonable searches and seizures, shall not be violated, and no Warrants shall issue, but upon probable cause, supported by Oath or affirmation, and particularly describing the place to be searched, and the persons or things to be seized.

AMENDMENT V (1791)

No person shall be held to answer for a capital, or otherwise infamous crime, unless on a presentment or indictment of a Grand Jury, except in cases arising in the land or naval forces, or in the Militia, when in actual service in time of War or public danger; nor shall any person be subject for the same offence to be twice put in jeopardy of life or limb; nor shall be compelled in any criminal case to be a witness against himself, nor be deprived of life, liberty, or property, without due process of law; nor shall private property be taken for public use, without just compensation.

AMENDMENT VI (1791)

In all criminal prosecutions, the accused shall enjoy the right to a speedy and public trial, by an impartial jury of the State and district wherein the crime shall have been committed, which district shall have been previously ascertained by law, and to be informed of the nature and cause of the accusation; to be confronted with the witnesses against him; to have compulsory process for obtaining witnesses in his favor, and to have the Assistance of Counsel for his defence.

AMENDMENT VII (1791)

In Suits at common law, where the value in controversy shall exceed twenty dollars, the right of trial by jury shall be preserved, and no fact tried by a jury, shall be otherwise re-examined in any Court of the United States, than according to the rules of the common law.

AMENDMENT VIII (1791)

Excessive bail shall not be required, nor excessive fines imposed, nor cruel and unusual punishments inflicted.

AMENDMENT IX (1791)

The enumeration in the Constitution, of certain rights, shall not be construed to deny or disparage others retained by the people.

AMENDMENT X (1791)

The powers not delegated to the United States by the Constitution, nor prohibited by it to the States, are reserved to the States respectively, or to the people.

AMENDMENT XI (1795)

(note: Article III, section 2 was modified by this amendment.)

The Judicial power of the United States shall not be construed to extend to any suit in law or equity, commenced or prosecuted against one of the United States by Citizens of another State, or by Citizens or Subjects of any Foreign State.

AMENDMENT XII (1804)

(note: A portion of Article II, section 1 was superseded by this amendment).

The Electors shall meet in their respective states and vote by ballot for President and Vice-President, one of whom, at least, shall not be an inhabitant of the same state with themselves; they shall name in their ballots the person voted for as President, and in distinct ballots the person voted for as Vice-President, and they shall make distinct lists of all persons voted for as President, and of all persons voted for as Vice-President, and of the number of votes for each, which lists they shall sign and certify, and transmit sealed to the seat of the government of the United States, directed to the President of the Senate;—The President of the Senate shall, in the presence of the Senate and House of Representatives, open all the certificates and the votes shall then be counted;—The person having the greatest Number of votes for President, shall be the President, if such number be a majority of the whole number of Electors appointed; and if no person have such majority, then from the persons having the highest numbers not exceeding three on the list of those voted for as President, the House of Representatives shall choose immediately, by ballot, the President. But in choosing the President, the votes shall be taken by states, the representation from each state having one vote; a quorum for this purpose shall consist of a member or members from two-thirds of the states, and a majority of all the states shall be necessary to a choice. And if the House of Representatives shall not choose a President whenever the right of choice shall devolve upon them, before the fourth day of March next following, then the Vice-President shall act as

President, as in the case of the death or other constitutional disability of the President (note: superseded by section 3 of the 20th amendment.)—The person having the greatest number of votes as Vice-President, shall be the Vice-President, if such number be a majority of the whole number of Electors appointed, and if no person have a majority, then from the two highest numbers on the list, the Senate shall choose the Vice-President; a quorum for the purpose shall consist of two-thirds of the whole number of Senators, and a majority of the whole number shall be necessary to a choice. But no person constitutionally ineligible to the office of President shall be eligible to that of Vice-President of the United States.

Amendment XIII (1865)

(note: a portion of Article IV, section 2 was superseded by this amendment)

Section 1. Neither slavery nor involuntary servitude, except as a punishment for crime whereof the party shall have been duly convicted, shall exist within the United States, or any place subject to their jurisdiction.

Section 2. Congress shall have power to enforce this article by appropriate legislation.

Amendment XIV (1868)

(note: Article I, section 2 was modified by section 2 of this amendment)

Section 1. All persons born or naturalized in the United States and subject to the jurisdiction thereof, are citizens of the United States and of the State wherein they reside. No State shall make or enforce any law which shall abridge the privileges or immunities of citizens of the United States; nor shall any State deprive any person of life, liberty, or property, without due process of law; nor deny to any person within its jurisdiction the equal protection of the laws.

Section 2. Representatives shall be apportioned among the several States according to their respective numbers, counting the whole number of persons in each State, excluding Indians not taxed. But when the right to vote at any election for the choice of electors for President and Vice President of the United States, Representatives in Congress, the Executive and Judicial officers of a State, or the members of the Legislature thereof, is denied to any of the male inhabitants of such State, being twenty-one years of age (changed by section 1 of the 26th amendment), and citizens of the United States, or in any way abridged, except for participation in rebellion, or other crime, the basis of representation therein shall be reduced in the proportion which the number of such male citizens shall bear to the whole number of male citizens twenty-one years of age in such State.

Section 3. No person shall be a Senator or Representative in Congress, or elector of President and Vice President, or hold any office, civil or military, under the United States, or under any State, who, having previously taken an oath, as a member of Congress, or as an officer of the United States, or as a member of any State legislature, or as an executive or judicial officer of any State, to support the Constitution of the United States, shall have engaged in insurrection or rebellion against the same, or given aid or comfort to the enemies thereof. But Congress may by a vote of two-thirds of each House, remove such disability.

Section 4. The validity of the public debt of the United States, authorized by law, including debts incurred for payment of pensions and bounties for services in suppressing insurrection or rebellion, shall not be questioned. But neither the United States nor any State shall assume or pay any debt or obligation incurred in aid of insurrection or rebellion against the United States, or any claim for the loss or emancipation of any slave; but all such debts, obligations and claims shall be held illegal and void.

Section 5. The Congress shall have power to enforce, by appropriate legislation, the provisions of this article.

Amendment **XV** (1870)

Section 1. The right of citizens of the United States to vote shall not be denied or abridged by the United States or by any State on account of race, color, or previous condition of servitude.

Section 2. The Congress shall have power to enforce this article by appropriate legislation.

Amendment **XVI** (1913)

(note: Article I, section 9 was modified by this amendment)

The Congress shall have power to lay and collect taxes on incomes, from whatever source derived, without apportionment among the several States, and without regard to any census or enumeration.

Amendment **XVII** (1913)

(note: Article I, section 3 was modified by this amendment)

The Senate of the United States shall be composed of two Senators from each State, elected by the people thereof, for six years; and each Senator shall have one vote. The electors in each State shall have the qualifications requisite for electors of the most numerous branch of the State legislatures.

When vacancies happen in the representation of any State in the Senate, the executive authority of such State shall issue writs of election to fill such vacancies: Provided, That the legislature of any State may empower the executive thereof to make temporary appointments until the people fill the vacancies by election as the legislature may direct.

This amendment shall not be so construed as to affect the election or term of any Senator chosen before it becomes valid as part of the Constitution.

Amendment **XVIII** (1919)

(note: this amendment was repealed by amendment 21)

Section 1. After one year from the ratification of this article the manufacture, sale, or transportation of intoxicating liquors within, the importation thereof into, or the exportation thereof from the United States and all territory subject to the jurisdiction thereof for beverage purposes is hereby prohibited.

Section 2. The Congress and the several States shall have concurrent power to enforce this article by appropriate legislation.

Section 3. This article shall be inoperative unless it shall have been ratified as an amendment to the Constitution by the legislatures of the several States, as provided in the Constitution, within seven years from the date of the submission hereof to the States by the Congress.

Amendment XIX (1920)

The right of citizens of the United States to vote shall not be denied or abridged by the United States or by any State on account of sex.

Congress shall have power to enforce this article by appropriate legislation.

Amendment XX (1933)

(note: Article I, section 4 was modified by section 2 of this amendment)

Section 1. The terms of the President and Vice President shall end at noon on the 20th day of January, and the terms of Senators and Representatives at noon on the 3d day of January, of the years in which such terms would have ended if this article had not been ratified; and the terms of their successors shall then begin.

Section 2. The Congress shall assemble at least once in every year, and such meeting shall begin at noon on the 3d day of January, unless they shall by law appoint a different day.

Section 3. If, at the time fixed for the beginning of the term of the President, the President elect shall have died, the Vice President elect shall become President. If a President shall not have been chosen before the time fixed for the beginning of his term, or if the President elect shall have failed to qualify, then the Vice President elect shall act as President until a President shall have qualified; and the Congress may by law provide for the case wherein neither a President elect nor a Vice President elect shall have qualified, declaring who shall then act as President, or the manner in which one who is to act shall be selected, and such person shall act accordingly until a President or Vice President shall have qualified.

Section 4. The Congress may by law provide for the case of the death of any of the persons from whom the House of Representatives may choose a President whenever the right of choice shall have devolved upon them, and for the case of the death of any of the persons from whom the Senate may choose a Vice President whenever the right of choice shall have devolved upon them.

Section 5. Sections 1 and 2 shall take effect on the 15th day of October following the ratification of this article.

Section 6. This article shall be inoperative unless it shall have been ratified as an amendment to the Constitution by the legislatures of three-fourths of the several States within seven years from the date of its submission.

Amendment XXI (1933)

Section 1. The eighteenth article of amendment to the Constitution of the United States is hereby repealed.

Section 2. The transportation or importation into any State, Territory, or possession of the United States for delivery or use therein of intoxicating liquors, in violation of the laws thereof, is hereby prohibited.

Section 3. This article shall be inoperative unless it shall have been ratified as an amendment to the Constitution by conventions in the several States, as provided in the Constitution, within seven years from the date of the submission hereof to the States by the Congress.

Amendment XXII (1951)

Section 1. No person shall be elected to the office of the President more than twice, and no person who has held the office of President, or acted as President, for more than two years of a term to which some other person was elected President shall be elected to the office of the President more than once. But this Article shall not apply to any person holding the office of President, when this Article was proposed by the Congress, and shall not prevent any person who may be holding the office of President, or acting as President, during the term within which this Article becomes operative from holding the office of President or acting as President during the remainder of such term.

Section 2. This article shall be inoperative unless it shall have been ratified as an amendment to the Constitution by the legislatures of three-fourths of the several States within seven years from the date of its submission to the States by the Congress.

Amendment XXIII (1961)

Section 1. The District constituting the seat of Government of the United States shall appoint in such manner as the Congress may direct:

A number of electors of President and Vice President equal to the whole number of Senators and Representatives in Congress to which the District would be entitled if it were a State, but in no event more than the least populous State; they shall be in addition to those appointed by the States, but they shall be considered, for the purposes of the election of President and Vice President, to be electors appointed by a State; and they shall meet in the District and perform such duties as provided by the twelfth article of amendment.

Section 2. The Congress shall have power to enforce this article by appropriate legislation.

Amendment XXIV (1964)

Section 1. The right of citizens of the United States to vote in any primary or other election for President or Vice President for electors for President or Vice President, or for Senator or Representative in Congress, shall not be denied or abridged by the United States or any State by reason of failure to pay any poll tax or other tax.

Section 2. The Congress shall have power to enforce this article by appropriate legislation.

Amendment XXV (1967)

(note: Article II, section 1 was affected by this amendment)

Section 1. In case of the removal of the President from office or of his death or resignation, the Vice President shall become President.

Section 2. Whenever there is a vacancy in the office of the Vice President, the President shall nominate a Vice President who shall take office upon confirmation by a majority vote of both Houses of Congress.

Section 3. Whenever the President transmits to the President pro tempore of the Senate and the Speaker of the House of Representatives his written declaration that he is unable to discharge the powers and duties of his office, and until he transmits to them a written declaration to the contrary, such powers and duties shall be discharged by the Vice President as Acting President.

Section 4. Whenever the Vice President and a majority of either the principal officers of the executive departments or of such other body as Congress may by law provide, transmit to the President pro tempore of the Senate and the Speaker of the House of Representatives their written declaration that the President is unable to discharge the powers and duties of his office, the Vice President shall immediately assume the powers and duties of the office as Acting President.

Thereafter, when the President transmits to the President pro tempore of the Senate and the Speaker of the House of Representatives his written declaration that no inability exists, he shall resume the powers and duties of his office unless the Vice President and a majority of either the principal officers of the executive department or of such other body as Congress may by law provide, transmit within four days to the President pro tempore of the Senate and the Speaker of the House of Representatives their written declaration that the President is unable to discharge the powers and duties of his office. Thereupon Congress shall decide the issue, assembling within forty-eight hours for that purpose if not in session. If the Congress, within twenty-one days after receipt of the latter written declaration, or, if Congress is not in session, within twenty-one days after Congress is required to assemble, determines by two-thirds vote of both Houses that the President is unable to discharge the powers and duties of his office, the Vice President shall continue to discharge the same as Acting President; otherwise, the President shall resume the powers and duties of his office.

Amendment XXVI (1971)

(note: Amendment 14, section 2 was modified by section 1 of this amendment)

Section 1. The right of citizens of the United States, who are eighteen years of age or older, to vote shall not be denied or abridged by the United States or by any State on account of age.

Section 2. The Congress shall have power to enforce this article by appropriate legislation.

Amendment XXVII (1992)

No law varying the compensation for the services of the Senators and Representatives shall take effect, until an election of Representatives shall have intervened.

Index

Italic page references indicate exhibits, illustrations, and boxed text.

About the Authors

THOMAS D. LYNCH, PhD is Professor Emeritus from Louisiana State University (LSU) and an Ordained Interfaith Minister. Currently, he is teaching online courses part-time for California State University Northridge. Over the span of his more than thirty-five-year career in the Public Administration field he taught in several Master of Public Administration programs including the Maxwell School at Syracuse University, Mississippi State University, Florida International University, Florida Atlantic University, and Louisiana State University. Among other subjects, he has published extensively on ethics.

CYNTHIA E. LYNCH, PhD is an Associate Professor and has taught the Master of Public Administration programs at the University of Texas–Rio Grande Valley (formerly the University of Texas–Pan American), Southern University and A&M College, University of Hawai'i, Hawai'i Pacific University, and Walden University. She is also an Ordained Interfaith Minister. She has been teaching Public Administration Graduate Seminar foundation course, ethics, organization theory and design, and nonprofit management courses for more than a decade. She is also a consultant and advisor to nonprofit organizations in both the United States and Mexico.